Agency Theory: Methodology, Analysis

Forschungsergebnisse der Wirtschaftsuniversität Wien

Band 3

PETER LANG
Frankfurt am Main · Berlin · Bern · Bruxelles · New York · Oxford · Wien

Alexander Stremitzer

Agency Theory: Methodology, Analysis

A Structured Approach to Writing Contracts

PETER LANG
Europäischer Verlag der Wissenschaften

Bibliographic Information published by Die Deutsche Bibliothek
Die Deutsche Bibliothek lists this publication in the Deutsche Nationalbibliografie; detailed bibliographic data is available in the internet at <http://dnb.ddb.de>.

Sponsored by the Vienna University
of Economics and Business Administration.

ISSN 1613-3056
ISBN 3-631-52973-2
US-ISBN 0-8204-7354-5

www.peterlang.de

For my parents and Margret W.

Preface

Designing a contract is often more of an economic than a legal problem. A good contract protects parties against opportunistic behavior while providing motivation to cooperate. This is where economics and, especially contract theory, may prove helpful by enhancing our understanding of incentive issues. The purpose of this book is to provide specific contract tools which will help to write better contracts in real world environments.

Concentrating on moral hazard literature, I have derived a tentative checklist for drafting contracts. This work is not complete. On the theoretical side, both the important literature on Adverse Selection and on Incomplete Information could not be covered. On the empirical side, this book strongly advocates casuistic work without actually providing any comprehensive case study. I am strongly aware of these shortcomings.

Still, I think that this book makes a contribution toward filling an important gap arising from the obvious imbalance in literature between devising ever more sophisticated models and attempts to summarize and apply them. Having said this, I must acknowledge that the book is still very abstract. There are also passages which are more contrived than I would like them to be, but at the present stage I was not able to achieve more simplicity without avoiding the tricky issues.

I still hope that the practical intent of this book becomes evident. Ina way, this aim is reflected by the relative prominence of methodological discussions. While in a specialized research environment such debates may be considered superfluous as the researchers in the field implicitly share the same methodological premises, this is not the case as soon as one is interested in applications. Most often, applied research requires entering into interdisciplinary dialogue. My own experience is that, in order to get such dialogue started, explicit knowledge of methodological choices is essential.

This book is based on my dissertation at the Vienna University of Economics and Business Administration. I would like to express my thanks to my academic advisors Wilhelm Bühler and Mikulas Luptacik. I am also especially grateful to Bernulf Bruckner for our many invaluable discussions and to Genia Schönbaumsfeld for her willingness to read and criticize early drafts of the philosophical part. These discussions helped to clarify many of the thoughts contained in this book. I also wish to thank Karim Medjad and Bernard Garette who first stimulated my interest in the economic analysis of contracts during my stay at HEC-Paris. Finally, I am very grateful to Stephen Hansen for agreeing to proof-read the manuscript, and for his many (not only stylistic) comments. All remaining errors are, of course, mine.

Contents

Exhibits

I Introduction

1 The Contracting Problem

Trade will only take place if each party feels certain that the counterparty honours its obligation once it has performed its part. It can only derive this certainty from an enforceable contract. In contracting, three problems have to be dealt with: The contract parameters must be defined, observed and a mechanism for enforcement provided. For every conceivable contract parameter, problems might arise on any one of these levels. Either they cannot be solved or at least not without cost. If, however, the problem of contracting is not solved, no trade will take place, resulting in a loss of welfare. Provisions for solving the contracting problem can therefore be valuable even if they come at a cost.

Consider a principal who hires an agent to develop a marketing strategy for a certain product. One might think that what he cares for is to be able to sell more of the product at a possibly higher price. However, this is not exactly what the principal demands of the agent. If there is a boycott against the principal's products or should a highly publicized blackmailing affect consumers' preferences for the good, the principal will suffer a loss. Will he blame this loss on the agent? Probably not. Not to be mistaken, the principal's aim ultimately is to sell more at a higher price. And he knows that in order to get there, he has to take action. Some of this action, though, may require specialized know-how or just time, which the principal does not have. He also knows that even if these tasks are performed, there is still some uncertainty about how things will turn out. He may ask himself whether he is willing to take this risk, or whether he would prefer to shed some of the risk; but the two questions of delegation via an agency relationship and risk management are a priori unrelated to each other. Therefore, when hiring a "marketing specialist", the principal really wants to make sure that he exerts effort and does everything a marketing specialist can do to boost sales. But if he cannot contract on effort (or something related), no trade will occur.

When trying to contract on effort, the first problem, however, can be to **define** what this contribution expected from the agent actually comprises. This will be especially difficult if the principal does not know the **production function** or, to put it differently, if he does not know the drivers of success or failure in this area. In particular, this will be true in settings where tasks require **specialized knowledge** and are **non-routine**. In such cases, it is likely that no reliable information based on prior experience exists, neither in the principal's organization nor readily available through simple research. But, even if the principal can define total contribution expected from the agent, he may very well not be able to observe it. Maybe he can **observe** it at a cost by putting in place some kind of monitoring device. Possibly, he cannot observe it at all.

Even if the principal can observe effort, this will not be enough. In order to contract on it, an agreement must also be **enforceable**. Consider the above example, wherein the company hires the marketing specialist. The marketing specialist visits the company's premises, spends time, produces a report, but, in the end, the company feels that he did not exert effort. Perhaps the company's managers have observed that the marketing specialist and his team were working on two projects at a time. The managers cannot prove that when they entered the consultants's on-site office the consultants seemed to behave strangely, quickly switching from one computer document to another, etc. Without entering into further details, it becomes clear that there are verifiable, objective "**hard facts**" on the side of the agent, but only elusive, subjective "**soft facts**" on the part of the principal. If the parties rely on the court system for enforcement, it is clear that there will be problems of enforcement for the principal. The concept of effort is too elusive for the **court with its bias towards objectivity**. In order for a contingency to be **enforceable** in court it must be **verifiable**, and in order to be verifiable it must be **objective**. Thus, the court enforcement mechanism sets constraints on the set of contingencies that can be used as performance criteria in a contract.

This set of performance criteria can, of course, be expanded by introducing other enforcement mechanisms. First of all, the parties are free to **choose any jurisdiction** and any court in the world to settle disputes. There might be differences in quality and bias[1]. Second, parties can resort to **arbitrage**, barring the recourse to courts (where possible). Arbitrageurs usually represent a third party that is more accustomed with the subject matter of the contract than unspecialized courts. So, they will probably be able to deal with "softer" contingencies, relying on their judgement and thereby making it possible to enlarge the set of contractible contingencies.

But there is an even more radical alternative: One can try to put in place a **self-enforcing mechanism** which is able to enforce **subjective performance measures** that depend to a certain extent on the **discretion** of the parties involved. The basic problem of subjective performance measures is the following: If the decision of whether effort was exerted or not is left to one of the two parties, say, the principal, he will have the incentive to report that no effort was exerted. Thus he releases himself from his own obligations to pay the agreed-upon fee. In other

---

[1] It is said e.g. that a seller will always prefer Swiss law and a buyer German law.

words, he will have the incentive to **renege** in any event. So, any mechanism relying on subjective performance measures must adress this problem.

One such self-enforcing mechanism is the **tournament mechanism**. Here, the principal, dealing with a group of agents, makes a **verifiable pledge as to the total amount** of bonus paid out to one agent or group of agents. However, the decision on what agent or group of agents receive the bonus is left at the discretion of the principal. This allows him to introduce judgement. The argument goes that, since the principal cannot save by reneging, he will live up to his obligation. This is true if he has at least a **marginal preference for rewarding merit and keeping his promise** and there are **no side-payments**[2] from the agent to the principal[3] which will cause the **mechanism to break down**. In fact, **promotion** can be seen as some sort of tournament mechanism. This mechanism can be used when dealing with many agents, or if one wants to reward relative overperformance and punish relative underperformance.

Another self-enforcing mechanism is the **reputation mechanism**, which will be treated at length later in the analytic part of this thesis. Still, just to provide a taste of the argument: The idea is that if the principal or the agent reneges on their promises their reputation will suffer, not allowing them to do certain kinds of business in the future. This is surely the case with the **specific counterparty**, but also with **other counterparties**, if the **news is spread**. So, long-term reputation concerns may counterbalance the prospect of short-term gains on reneging.

The principal must therefore be able 1) to define total contribution, 2) to observe it and 3) to enforce it. It can be seen from the above that, on each of these levels, problems might arise. Sometimes these problems can be solved at a cost, but sometimes they cannot be solved at all. In this case, the parties can only switch to alternative measures of performance.

2 Applications

Based on relatively recent developments in microeconomic theory, such as game theory and economics of information, contract theory has a wide range of applications. The design of incentive contracts within and between companies (e.g. with suppliers or sales partners), the structuring of financial transactions, the design of market structures, pricing and guarantee arrangements and the economic

---

[2] Side payments would induce a cooperative equilibrium in game theoretical terminology.

[3] Social relations and favours can play a part.

analysis of legal and other institutions are only a few possible examples. In contrast to the usual problem of optimization *within constraints*, contract theory is concerned with the optimization *of constraints*. When stuck in a setting where the interaction of people leads to suboptimal solutions, the challenge is to design contracts which allow them to reach better outcomes.

3 Models of Contracting

There are various kinds of contracting models. Different classifications exist, but none is universally recognized. The author tends to distinguish between models of "moral hazard", "adverse selection" and "incomplete information". Moral hazard problems arise if the agent can benefit from taking advantage of information asymmetry after the contract is concluded. This can come in the form of action that he can take which cannot be observed by the principal, or by information that, at a given point of the interaction, becomes available to the agent but not to the principal. Moral hazard problems therefore come in two variants: Moral hazard with hidden action and moral hazard with hidden information. Adverse selection models refer to asymmetric information *before* the contract is concluded. Sometimes models of moral hazard with hidden information are also regarded as problems of adverse selection. Possible strategies to overcome the adverse selection problem are signaling and screening. In the case of signaling, the agent is trying to send a credible signal revealing private information. This can be done by taking some kind of action which would cause a loss to the agent if he was not telling the truth. In the case of screening, it is the principal who, by offering a menu of different contracts, tries to extract information from the agents. Signaling and screening are sometimes treated as separate types of models. Models of incomplete contracts deal with the problem that contracts are often concluded knowing that not all possible contingencies are covered by the contract, because this would be either too expensive or impossible due to bounded rationality. Incomplete contracts are therefore often considered as belonging to "transaction cost economics", while moral hazard and adverse selection are considered as belonging to "economics of information" – the difference being that the first assumes less perfect rationality than the second.

4 Obsession with Modeling Single Effects

The literature on contracting is extensive and complex. A considerable investment of time has to be made to read articles which model only a tiny effect within the broader phenomenon of, say, moral hazard with hidden action. While simultaneous modeling of many effects is not sensible, as will be argued below, modeling single effects is the right thing to do. However, little effort is given in trying to summarize the different effects and in trying to show how these can be applied to specific problems. Real-world problems usually comprise a multitude of effects. When assessing a contract between a company and its sales partners, there is usually both a moral hazard and an adverse selection problem. If the sales partners are not exclusive partners, there is the effect of many principals competing for the attention of one sales partner. Many other effects can probably be found in the specifics of a particular situation. It can, of course, be argued that some effects are more important than others which can subsequently be safely ignored; however, it would at least be good not to make a leap of faith but to carefully weigh different effects according to relevance. As will be argued later, this weighing should be done close to the specific problem.

5 Methodological Reflection

In order to apply contract theory to specific problems, it is not sufficient to summarize the different effects. The specific methodological problems of application also need to be discussed. In addition, although economic method is largely analytical and this approach is helpful, it must also be clear that there are other important sources for understanding contracts. As contracts like other institutions are the product of evolution, it is plausible to grant them the presumption of implicit wisdom. Contract theory is therefore a potentially multidisciplinary field combining the methods of economics, law, sociology, history, anthropology and psychology.

Starting with some brief remarks on philosophy of science in general and then proceeding to a discussion of orthodox microeconomic methodology, this thesis will present the methodological foundations of contract theory. It will be argued that contract theory takes a microanalytical approach but can learn from the implicit wisdom of existing institutions if and insofar as they can be interpreted as the product of evolution. A mix of analytical models and casuistic work is expected to be most fruitful.

6 A Note to the Reader

Part II can be seen as an attempt by the author to come to terms with the epistemological foundations of science. Although in some respects it sets the stage for part III, it is clearly longer than needed for an economic monograph and is not necessary in order to follow the rest of the text. Although the analysis in part IV is only concerned with moral hazard with hidden action, the methodological reflections in part III are much more general. The reason for this seeming imbalance is that this thesis is intended as both proposal and description of a research programme plus the realization of a tiny bit of it. So, the methodological discussion is meant to be an essential part of this thesis in its own right rather than just a preliminary exercise. Part V summarizes the result, provides a checklist for analysing contracts from the perspective of moral hazard and finally provides an outlook for further research.

The author tries to insert many synoptic sections in order to make the text more readable than it was in earlier drafts. Each part opens with a complete overview. In the analytical part, hypotheses which are to be derived are stated at the beginning of the Section. At the end of each Section, results are discussed verbally without taking recourse to mathematical notation. This should make it possible for the non-technical reader to browse through the material while treating the analytical parts as black boxes.

II Epistemic Problems and Philosophy of Science

1 Overview

In Chapter 2 the objectives of economics as a science will be discussed. It will be stated that economics intends to derive conditional statements which tell people how they can interfere with the course of events. Economics therefore follows the positivist programme, although it does not fully take over positivist methodology.

In Chapter 3 the fundamental question of what makes a theory scientific is raised. The traditional way of answering this question consists of calling a theory true because it is well founded. This leads to the question of the ultimate justification of science.

Chapter 4 offers a brief overview of traditional attempts to solve the problem of absolute justification. For the sake of argument, criticism is presented from a radically sceptical perspective. Section 4.1 addresses the problem of the nature of reality, its relation to human beings and their consequences for human cognition. Starting from the concept of a preestablished meaning that reveals itself to human beings through rational thinking, the argument turns to another concept focusing more on the active constitution of reality by the perceiver. Yet, pursuing this argument in the sense of radical scepticism leads to fruitless solipsism. Additional assumptions about the human faculty of cognition and its commensurability with the (outside) world are needed. Reflecting the specific sources of human cognition, the controversy between empiricism and rationalism is briefly mentioned - pointing to the difficulties of both approaches. Finally, the concept of intersubjectivity is considered mentioning the tight relationship of this concept to anthropological assumptions. It is concluded that the very possibility of cognition requires assumptions that are not beyond doubt. Section 4.2 deals with strategies to derive scientific statements. If it is accepted that the human faculty of cognition depends on both sense-perception and rationality, the question is asked whether there exists a strategy that allows one to derive statements about reality which depend on simple, readily acceptable postulates. Such statements could then be regarded as being absolutely justified and intersubjectively valid. In this sense, inductivism, pragmatism and falsificationism are briefly discussed in consecutive Sub-Sections; although finally it must be said that the project of an absolute justification has so far failed.

Chapter 5 discusses the consequences of this failure. Section 5.1 addresses the argument that the impossibility of providing absolute justification leads to scepticism. However, failure to prove the existence of an absolute justification does not prove its non-existence. Therefore, scepticism is just one possible conclusion among others which will subsequently be argued to be highly inadequate on the grounds of its absurd consequences. Yet, as is pointed out in Section 5.2, rejecting scepticism is not tantamount to embracing dogmatism, which seems to have shown itself to be equally inappropriate. This is because dogmatism can be used to immunize any arbitrarily chosen premiss or statement, and also because it is an obstacle to scientific and methodological progress. Section 5.3 proposes common sense or intuition as a basis for arguing that some statements are better than others. After all, optimism may be justified by stating that the human way of viewing the world offers man at least some of the orientation he seeks. If no mechanism is found to settle disputes, however, this approach can lead to relativism. Two parties could disagree but both would cite common sense as the basis for their statement. Section 5.4 argues that, even if the concept of absolute truth is to be abandoned, the notion of analytical truth - which guarantees truth relative to premisses - is very meaningful. It is suggested that casting scientific statements in axiomatised versions offers methodological advantages. The consequences of such an approach are to divide the scientific argument into two spheres: The sphere of analytical truth and the sphere of discussion about first principles.

Chapter 6 addresses the question of the cognitive status of such a first principle. Section 6.1 explores the consequences of relativism that follows if the decision on the first principle is made by everybody on his own, without any additional structure. It is argued that the consistency rule embodied in the axiomatised approach ensures a minimum of objectivity, but that science then loses its claim as a peaceful and impersonal arbiter if it is not possible to move beyond relativism. Overcoming relativism is therefore the objective of Section 6.2. It is argued that the notion of the validity of scientific statements is tightly associated with the idea of objectivity common to human beings. Therefore, analogous to the categorical imperative in ethics, the crucial point is that science is conducted with the intent to serve the idea of truth – although no enforceable mechanism can be devised that would overcome relativism in practice. It is argued, then, for pragmatic reasons to allow for relative anarchism in science and to only require consistency and openness for criticism as formal criteria.

Chapter 7 lays down the methodological implications of the previous discussion. It proposes to structure science into two spheres: The sphere of first principles and the sphere of analytical truth. It is argued that such an axiomatised approach facilitates communication and increases transparency.

2 The Objectives of Science

Economics, as it is understood in this thesis, ultimately has a practical purpose[4]. Its aim is neither to provide identity[5] nor to be a logical pastime[6]. "It wants to know in order to predict and to predict in order to interfere"[7]. This objective is taken from the positivist programme[8]. If nature can be harnessed for human ends, why should not the same be possible with social relations for the sake of social welfare? Theory thus serves purposeful human action[9]. In the words of *Mises,*

---

4 This is quite in line with the positivist programme which wanted to transfer the approach of the natural sciences to social sciences. It is based on the philosophy of Bacon (see e.g. Schülein, Reitze (2002), p. 61) and turned against Hegel. Also, Hobbes (Mader (1992a), p. 176) explicitly calls for a practical intention.

5 As is arguably the case for arts and humanities (see Mader (1992a), p. 53); The distinction between "sciences" on the one hand and "arts and humanities" on the other is relevant as it has methodological consequences. The method of the natural sciences is clearly positivist, empirical and ahistoric. The method of arts and humanities is the "historical method", also referred to as "Hermeneutics" or "Verstehen". Their objective is to study the different expressions of human existence as they are revealed in different situations and conditions during history. The only thing that remains more or less the same in this flow of events is the human being. So by studying history, literature and art in the past and present, human beings try to answer the eternal question of "who they are".

6 As is arguably the case for some ill-conceived economic models; see Hutchison (1994), p. 29

7 Comte (1852), p. 91, "Savoir pour prévoir afin de pourvoir", translated by the author.

8 For an introductory chapter on the philosophy of Comte, see e.g. Mader (1992b), pp. 142-151. In the Anglo-Saxon tradition the word "science" is used synonymous with "natural sciences". The term "social sciences" is also common, but only underscores social sciences′ ambition to emulate the natural sciences. Therefore the positivist programme in philosophy which advocates the transfer of the method of natural sciences to the study of social relations (hoping to bring about progress to social relations similar to the impressive progress achieved in the realm of technology) is engraved into terminology. This is different in the German tradition. The term "Wissenschaft" is used in a much wider sense: It traditionally comprises the natural sciences ("Naturwissenschaft"), arts and humanities ("Geisteswissenschaft" or "Humanwissenschaft"), mathematics and logic ("Formalwissenschaft") and the social sciences ("Sozialwissenschaft"). In the German tradition the social sciences and especially economics methodologically stand somewhere in between arts and humanities and natural sciences. This does not matter so much for the objectives of economics, which were stated to be clearly in line with the positivist programme. But especially, when it comes to the problem of controlled experiment in economics and to the discussion of methodological individualism, the method of "Verstehen" arguably plays an important role (see: part II of the text). There is a very rich discussion of this in the German tradition, and it is interesting to see how the now dominant Anglo-Saxon tradition appears a bit uneasy when addressing this question because of its terminological self-imprisonment.

9 Of course purposeful action presupposes a human being with a free will whose needs and wants are taken as an absolute given, and who thinks in categories of teleology - taken as the only possible human way of thinking. If this is too reductionist for some readers, they are

"The archetype of causality research was: Where and how must I interfere in order to divert the course of events [...] He searches for the regularity of the law, because he wants to interfere. Only later was this search more extensively interpreted by metaphysics as a search after the ultimate cause of being and existence"[10]. The argument, that such a prediction is not possible in economics[11], is not accepted but it is acknowledged that precision and margins of error are certainly higher for economic predictions than for other sciences[12]. However, "assuming that prediction [...] remains an inevitable activity in real-world economic life"[13], the question is not whether the status of economic predictions is high in an absolute sense, but rather if there is "any margin of advantage economists may or may not have over non-economists in providing less inaccurate predictions"[14]. In the view of the author there is no way economics could circumvent this challenge.

Theory, in the positivist sense, can therefore be defined as the teleological element which is necessarily part of every purposeful human action. This definition allows the casting of theories as an integral part of practical life. It also allows for deriving a formal property of theory as something ultimately concerned with predictions in the form of conditional statements[15].

3 What makes Science scientific?

If the objective of science is to support purposeful human action it seems natural to assume that a scientific theory's quality should be judged by its reliability. A theory is reliable if expectations based upon it are not frustrated. This raises the question of what distinguishes a reliable or "good" theory from an unreliable or "bad" theory. This is essentially the question about the foundation of science[16]. A good theory would be a "scientific" theory because of a set of properties that makes it distinct from a bad theory, which could be just any statement. These

---

referred to part II where it is shown that these concerns can be accommodated by adopting a wide notion of human preferences.

10 Mises (1949), p. 22 (4.ed. 1996)

11 see McCloskey (1985), p. 15 cit. Hutchison (1994), p. 29

12 see Hutchison (1994), p. 29

13 Hutchison (1994), p. 32

14 Hutchison (1994), p. 32

15 Conditionals have an "if-then structure".

16 Science is simply taken as a short-cut for: "The sum of all endeavours to create good theory."

properties are traditionally truth in the sense of correspondence with reality[17], or at least objectivity[18].

Scientific knowledge is traditionally argued to be well-founded and therefore true[19]. Well-founded knowledge is supposed to derive its truth from an underlying cause; but where does this cause derive its truth from? It can easily be seen that this approach leads to infinite regression if one does not ultimately find an absolute justification on which all further knowledge is based. This search for the absolute justification has traditionally been the task of philosophy. Once firmly established, it would ideally prescribe a method leading directly from this ultimate source of truth to scientific knowledge in any field of interest.

So, why bother about these questions in an economic monograph? Would it not be more efficient (and much easier) to stop thinking about methodology[20] and just follow the method prescribed by philosophy of science? After all, every reasonable man would be forced to agree that everything one comes up with is scientific and therefore true. Unfortunately, it is not that easy. The reason is that philosophy has proven far more successful at showing the shortcomings of different approaches to the problem of the ultimate justification than it has been at solving the problem itself. Like it or not, it simply is a brute fact that at present there is no compelling solution to the problem of absolute justification. The next Chapter will take a radically sceptical perspective in order to to drive this point home.

4 Absolute Justification

4.1 Basic Concepts of Cognition

One concept of cognition is to assume that there is a preestablished objective meaning in the world. As human beings are part of this world, they also have access to its meaning. This can be thought of as a more or less passive process. The meaning is already there. It has only to be received. Often, this meaning is assumed to have a certain structure. It could, therefore, e.g. have a rational

---

17 This is the Aristotelian definition (see Mader (1993a), p. 126). The same concept is somewhat more weakly expressed as "approximation of reality"; see Chalmers (1994), pp. 151-159

18 Although there are different shades to the notion of objectivity, the essential element is independence from the will of the perceiving subject in one way or another.

19 see Mader (1992a), p. 13

20 especially for an economist who advocates separation of labour

structure. Then, of course, human beings only have access to it, if they engage in rational thinking as opposed to believing in irrational myth. This was arguably the programme of the early days of western philosophy. These assumptions, however, now appear very speculative.

Alternatively, one could give up the notion of a preestablished meaning and argue that there will never be any meaning independent of its human perceiver. So, meaning is the product of an active act of constitution in the perceiver's mind. It follows that the world cannot be known "as such" but can only be known "for us".

But why for us? What do I know of the meaning the world has to others? Can I be sure that there *is* a world? Can I be sure that there *are* others? The last bulwark against scepticism of this kind is my own self-consciousness[21]; but impressive as this certainty may seem, it also reveals itself as being quite useless. Nothing interesting concerning how to access reality can be derived from it. Descartes e.g. proposed rational thinking and suggested that God could not be so heartless as to bestow man with such a faculty if it was not in order to help him find orientation in the world. Once again, one has to make a leap of faith. Of course, modern thinkers would probably not refer to God but rather to biological evolution to support their optimism that the human faculty of cognition actually provides some orientation in the world.

Descartes' obsession with rational thinking as the only source of the human faculty of cognition is also controversial. There is clearly another obvious candidate: sense perception. The controversy between empiricism[22] and rationalism will not be thoroughly discussed. It shall only be mentioned that both approaches encounter difficulties: The rationalist approach has difficulty explaining the **body-spirit relationship** - a problem if an outside world is assumed. The empiricist approach, on the other hand, has difficulty explaining how cognition is possible without any preestablished **notions** and ideas[23].

By saying that there is no meaning independent of the perceiver, one seems to elegantly circumvent the tricky question of whether there is an outside world.

---

[21] This is Descartes' famous cogito principle.

[22] in its extreme form also called sensualism

[23] By transgressing from perception to a statement of perception, a **notional apparatus** is needed. It could be objected that the notional apparatus itself is derived from perception. Someone could observe several objects, look for a common characteristic and give it a name; but merely the choice of different objects on the basis of a common characteristic presupposes the notion of that characteristic.

In fact, one could say that the question does not matter. For even if there was an outside world, nothing could be said about it. Still, there remains the experience that things are happening against my will. So, in the reality that my mind constructs, there is an element which I cannot control at will, which is – in a sense – objective. Whether there is an outside world or not, I must still be confident that there is a basic commensurability between my thinking and this objective element which I will call the world. This is basically an ontological assumption very close to the structural symmetry assumed above.

The world can be further differentiated thusly: There is an animated and unanimated world. The animated world is comprised of entities that I consider similar to myself and which I will call my fellow human beings. When I say that my fellow human beings are *similar* to myself, I am also saying that there is a set of relevant characteristics which make them and me human. This is, I make anthropologic assumptions. If there is a specifically human faculty of cognition, a specifically human way to think and to sense, then there is also a specifically human way to view the world. This means that, in so far as the construction I make is a specifically human construction, it is *necessary* and therefore objective in the sense of **intersubjectivity**.

In conclusion, it can be said that assumptions have to be made in order to allow for the possibility of cognition. These assumptions seem very subtle and it does not seem reasonable to oppose them. Strictly speaking, however, they are not beyond doubt. From arguably the only bulwark against scepticism, human self-consciousness, nothing interesting can be derived. The list of additional assumptions usually includes an ontological assumption which claims some degree of commensurability between human thinking and the world, and an anthropological assumption which states some specifically human faculty of cognition.

4.2 Strategies to derive scientific statements

4.2.1 Introduction

So far, fundamental concepts of cognition have been discussed, and it has been seen that the possibility of cognition cannot, strictly speaking, be taken for granted. However, even if it is assumed that such fundamental assumptions as those discussed above are met, nothing has been said about specific strategies to derive scientific statements.

If human cognition, as was suggested above, is divided into sense perception and rationality, and if the spontaneity of the intelligible "I" is such that sensual perception functions in terms of space and time and rationality in terms of causality and teleology, cognition is possible[24]. Perceptions in space and time would be initially subjective. In order for them to become objective they would have to be further structured[25]. This would happen in terms of causality and teleology as the only categories available to the human mind. Either everybody who is exposed to the same data would come up with exactly the same answer, or - regarding cognition as a reflexive activity - can at least be convinced to agree to the same answer in an ideal discourse situation[26]. Therefore, the following Subsection will explore if there exist strategies which lead to theories that every reasonable human being would be forced to accept (intersubjectivity). Once again, a radically sceptical perspective is taken when criticising the different approaches.

4.2.2 Inductivism

One approach would be to consider a statement to be scientific if it is either directly founded on observation or derived by means of deductive logic from such a statement[27]. If it is accepted that deductive logic is the epitome of human structured thinking, the question is how is it possible to derive general statements from observation. For inductivism the answer is "inductive logic". It plainly states that if it is observed that A follows B in many instances and under many different conditions, then A *always* follows B[28]. Of course, there are two key assumptions: If such a statement is to be considered objectively valid it must be assumed that both perception and "inductive logic" are objectively valid. Accordingly, objections are raised against both "inductive logic" and the status of perception.

Russell's example of the desolate fate of the **"inductivist turkey"**[29] displays the argument that inductive logic cannot be proven by deductive logic: Suppose a turkey observes that he is fed regularly at a certain time. As he is scientifically minded he does not want to jump to conclusions and observes this behaviour under many different conditions and circumstances. Still, when he recognizes that

---

24 see Mader (1992a), p. 207. This is in the spirit of Kant.

25 see Mader (1992a), p. 207

26 The requirement of honest dialogue is posed by Kant in "Was ist Aufklärung" (1784) for the "Public use of reason" and taken up by Apel, Habermas and Schnädelbach in their efforts to transform transcendental philosophy to "Universalpragmatik". See Mader (1993), p. 220-220

27 This is the methodological programme of neo-positivism of the "Wiener Kreis"; see Mader (1992b), p. 154; Chalmers (1994), p. 38

28 see Chalmers (1994), p. 19

29 see Bertrand Russell cit. Chalmers (1994), p. 20

he is fed at the same time independent of weather conditions on all days and during all seasons, he finally acknowledges this as a scientific regularity. The following day, he is slaughtered. Attempts to save the inductivist approach by taking recourse to the notion of **probability**[30] will not help. If it is acknowledged that there is an unlimited potential set of possible perceptions, this probability will always tend toward zero. If a limited set of perceptions is assumed, this is an additional assumption. A possible reason why this should be the case is that nature is assumed to be stable and structurally simple, so that as more and more observations are available, statistical inferences can be made with ever smaller marginal error.

Also the **status of perception** in inductivism is subject to criticism. On the one hand, perception is in doubt as a sure source of scientific knowledge[31]. On the other hand, perception is shown to be theory-laden[32]. Perceptions are therefore subject to the same distortions as theory. In the first case it is maintained that there are different experiences of perception, because these are the product of physical and psychological factors which can both differ among individuals. In the second case - the argument that perception is theory-laden - it is pointed out that by transgressing from perception to a statement of perception[33] a notional apparatus is used which is itself based on theory[34]. Induction does not create a direct link between perception and statement, but only a link between a statement of perception and a more general statement[35]. In addition, perceptions are always guided by theory as for the necessary choice between relevant and irrelevant[36].

Inductivism as a practical approach to conducting science depends on the assumption that perception and "inductive logic" are objectively valid. These

---

30 see Chalmers (1994), p. 24

31 see Chalmers (1994), p. 28f

32 see Chalmers (1994), p. 32f

33 see Chalmers (1994), p. 33f: Every statement presupposes to be communicated by language or by some other means.

34 see Section II4.1

35 Insofar as it is structurally close to deduction also linking different kinds of statements.

36 see Chalmers (1994), p. 36f: Observations and experiments are always guided by theory, or at least should be. Otherwise, only lists of aimless observations would be drawn up. It is, however, the objective of science to test, extend and improve theories. There is always a hypothesis that is tested. Observations which are considered to be unequivocally irrelevant will therefore be excluded. Yet in order to distinguish between relevant and irrelevant observations, a guiding theory is needed. If the theory from which the guidelines to conduct the experiment were derived is false, relevant factors could be mistakenly excluded.

assumptions are not beyond doubt. They therefore do not ensure that the construction of the world obtained by using inductivist methodology is intersubjectively valid: It is possible for reasonable people to disagree.

4.2.3 Pragmatism - Foundation by Method

Another way to justify a scientific statement is to argue that it was derived by a **successful method**. This argument could be used to support inductivism or any other method claimed to have been successful.

This argument has no problem in accepting the idea that both sensual perception and thinking are fallible; but it assumes that these errors can be corrected by observing methodological prescriptions[37]. Bacon e.g. distinguishes the following common sources of distortion of human cognition: The prejudice of subjectivity (idola specus), of language (idola fori), of tradition (idola theatri) and a certain degree of incommensurability of the human faculty of cognition and the structure of reality (idola tribus)[38]. The scientific method makes sure that sensual perception, which is the basis for induction and is thus the ultimate source of knowledge, is "supported" by controlled experiment. In addition, it provides rules to "guide" thinking. By prescribing a common method for everybody, subjectivity of cognition is reduced. Language is reformed in order to fit the necessity of exactness in science. History and tradition are explicitly excluded as an obstacle to cognition.

The quality of a scientific statement therefore depends on the method that was used to derive it, more specifically on the suitability of this method to correct the sources of distortion in thinking and perception; but why should one method be better than another in this respect? One possible justification could be that theories, derived using a specific method, are generally successful in explaining and predicting things. But can past success be used as an appraisal criterion? Essentially, it is claimed that something that was successful in many different cases will be successful in all or at least in most cases. But this is exactly what is claimed by "inductive logic".

Ultimately, foundation by method is shown to be based on "inductive logic" which can be justified neither by deductive logic[39] nor by experience[40]. Therefore, it is either circular or makes an additional assumption[41].

---

37 see Mader (1992a), p. 197

38 see Mader (1993), pp. 168-171; Schülein, Reitze (2002), pp. 60-64

39 see David Humes proof of circularity: in e.g. Chalmers (1994), S. 20

4.2.4 Falsificationism

Attempts to provide an ultimate justification for scientific statements can be credited rather for prematurely cutting off the argument by referring to some "metaphysical insight" which cannot be proven than for pushing it to a point where no further criticism is possible. Ironically, this is also true for the inductivist and pragmatic foundation of science, the very attempt that was meant to fight back metaphysics.

Even if no unassailable justification can be given for any scientific statement, however, it does not mean that all theories are equal; but why should any particular theory be better than any other, if both are not proven true? One reason why this might be the case was put forward by *Popper* who stressed the "logical asymmetry between falsification and verification"[42]. If a general statement is claimed to be universally true in space and time, while at the same time it has already failed in the past to explain and predict reality, it cannot be true. If, however, something has worked in the past, while it cannot be said that it is true, there is still a possibility for it to be true[43]. Of course, this presupposes a world functioning according to rules which are stable over time - but even if stability is admitted, only the problems of "inductivist logic" are circumvented. The problem of the status of perception remains. Therefore, falsificationism does not solve the epistemological problems, but - as will be argued below (III6.9) - rather has a different emphasis compared to verificationism as an approach to practical research.

Falsificationism as an attempt to establish an absolute criterion to distinguish between good and bad theory depends on the metaphysical assumption of stability and the objectivity of perception. Therefore, epistemological problems are not completely solved.

4.2.5 Conclusion

It has been shown that there is no possibility to absolutely justify a theory. The argument was only cursorily sketched, but seen logically, any attempt to justify a theory can be shown to reside on a metaphysical assumption, fall prey to

40 see Russell's story of the inductivist turkey, in e.g. Chalmers (1994), S. 20

41 In the case of inductivism such an additional assumption, neither based on deductive logic nor on experience, violates the very standards inductivism proclaims.

42 see Blaug (1994), p. 111

43 see Chalmers (1994), p. 41

circularity or lead to infinite regression[44]. This is an important result, because it dispels the widespread prejudice among scientists and the layman alike that science always depended on simple postulates of reason like deductive logic. Kant calls this the dialectic of reason: Reason demands a firm ground but seems unable to provide it[45].

5 Beyond Absolute Justification

5.1 Against Scepticism

It should be acknowledged here that, at present, one cannot distinguish between good and bad theory by means of simple commonly accepted postulates of reason[46]. This result is relevant in so far as it can and was indeed argued that - in the absence of absolute justification - it could not be proven that science was any more than a mere habit[47] or psychological illusion. Consequently, suspending judgement[48] would be the best thing for a wise man to do. This is the position of a radical sceptic.

In order to avoid misunderstandings: The result that no logical foundation of science has been found does not prove that it does not exist, neither does it prove that even if there *is* no logical foundation of science there might not be an objective foundation in other-than-logical terms. Therefore, it is a fallacy to argue that scepticism necessarily follows from the failure to find a convincing argument for a logical foundation of science. The sceptical position is just one possible hypothesis among others, regarding the fact that no logical foundation of science has been found. So, the question is: Why should it be an **adequate** hypothesis? It will be seen that the adequacy of scepticism is highly questionable.

First of all, the sceptical position is self-contradicting. If nothing can be known, how can it be known that nothing can be known? Of course, this problem can be solved by arguing that this is an exception to the rule. Yet, this seems rather arbitrary. Moreover, withholding judgement seems to be inadequate in the

---

44 see Albert, H. (1968), p. 13

45 see Mader (1993a), p. 209-213

46 In Aristotelian terminology: There seem to be no a priori synthetic truths.

47 see Hume cit. Schüllein, Reitze (2002), p. 77

48 It must be stressed that this is not the opinion of Hume but of the Pyrrhonians. Hume is a pragmatic confining his scepticism to theory.

light of the inevitability of action in practical life[49]. By taking purposeful action, people implicitly or explicitly choose a theory. It could be argued from the sceptical point of view that there is no benefit to consciously taking this decision. Indeed, the big merit of philosophy could be to free people from the psychological illusion that science is superior to anything else. Yet, it could be argued that even a psychological illusion has its merit. People demand theories that best calm the mental ***unease*** they experience concerning the uncertainty of the outcomes of their actions. Conscious decision-making would provide the individual with self-transparency, continuity and identity. It is ultimately preferences which decide which theory somebody chooses. By choosing a theory, people reveal preferences. If it is assumed that there is some stability in their preferences, scientists could engage in tailoring scientific statements to these preferences. By doing so, scientists are delivering utility to people. Is this not enough of a justification to pursue science[50]? But then, the ultimate criterion for science would be **subjective appeal**. If this is actually all that science ultimately boils down to, one might be tempted to agree with the sceptical prescription of withholding judgement.

But consider the following thought experiment: If the radical sceptic is taken by his word he should be willing to withhold judgement if asked whether he wants to swallow a cyanide capsule or not and agree to toss coins instead. Yet, it is difficult to imagine many people exhibiting the extent of **fatalism** implied by the sceptical position in a similar situation. Anything else, however, would lead to a **divorce of philosophical conviction and practical decisions**[51].

The radical sceptical (pyrrhonic) position - if immunized against the self-contradiction argument - can be neither proven nor disproved. Yet, its prescription of withholding judgement appears utterly inadequate in the light of the inevitability of theory choice in practical decision making. It leads either (improbably) to fatalism or to a divorce of philosophical conviction and practical decision making.

5.2 Dogmatism

As already implied by the above thought experiment, most people would expect that swallowing a cyanide capsule is not advisable. Similarly, people would distrust a theory based on the statement that stones rise upwards instead of falling

[49] see Hume cit. Mader (1992a), S. 201

[50] In this case it is difficult to judge where scepticism ends and relativism starts.

[51] Hume the foremost proponent of theoretical scepticism advocated pragmatism in real life.

down when "dropped"; but when trying to find a principle of truth they are confronted with the whole range of sceptical arguments.

Taking a dogmatic stance, it could simply be stated that some theories are better than others. After all, this is what motivated the search for the ultimate justification in the first place. Only later did epistemology try to find its principle. If it has not succeed thus far, it should try a little harder. Curiously, it is quite common to continue to think about science as if it was based on something that could ultimately be traced back to simple postulates of reason which are self-evident. Once again, technically speaking, all which has been said does not mean that this is impossible. It just says that all attempts to do so up to now have failed. Still, the question once more is if the dogmatic position is adequate.

The practical consequence of dogmatism is to immunize arbitrarily chosen methodological prescriptions against criticism. If they are not chosen arbitrarily, but because of some specific criterion (e.g. because they are "obviously true"), the question is why no attempt is made to convince others of the quality of this criterion. As a prescription for conducting science, dogmatism leads to a self-contradiction given the fact that science and philosophy of science evolved over time. Dogmatism is dogmatic about things that would never have evolved if dogmatism had been the scientific strategy. Of course, it could unconvincingly be argued that an ahistoric state has now been reached.

Dogmatism is immunizing arbitrarily-chosen methodological prescriptions against criticism. Moreover, it somewhat arbitrarily assumes that an ahistorical state has been reached.

5.3 Common Sense

Discussing the merit of methodological prescriptions, it could be argued that, as common sense has it, some theories are better than others. So, why not name "common sense" the basis of science? The argument could go something like this: Common sense suggests that a theory that has been successful in the past which is plausibly constructed and logically consistent is better than a theory for which all of this does not apply. If this is supplemented by the claim that there exists a specifically human intuition, a new basis for intersubjectivity of scientific statements could be found. In addition, it could be argued that it is justified to be optimistic that a common-sense judgement is not too far off the mark because there is no way how mankind should have survived without a minimum of orientation in the world[52].

Yet, the problem remains: How should conflicts between two parties be settled? Experience shows this supposedly common human feature to lead people almost anywhere. There was a time when people considered empirical evidence to be intuitively unimportant and then the dernier cri.

Still, the convenience of the rational approach and its confidence that anything could be ultimately traced back to basic postulates of reason was based on its claim that anybody, when exposed to the same data, either comes up with the same conclusion or can be convinced to do so; any other option would be called irrational. In truth, however, if human intuitive sensitivity – the whole of human rationality, emotions, senses – is the criterion, two parties could very well disagree with both citing common sense as the basis for their statement.

If two parties could disagree and still cite common sense as the basis for their statement, this approach practically leads to relativism.

5.4 An Axiomatic Approach

If an absolute justification for scientific statements could have been given, such statements could have been labelled "absolutely true". Although such an absolute justification was not found, it was said that some statements could still be better than others. However, the common way to think about truth is that something is either true or false. There is no place for a middle ground. To say that something is more true or less flawed than something else and therefore an approximation of absolute truth amounts to a masquerade upholding the word, devoid of its idea; but as the notion of absolute truth thus defined is an idea without any practical relevance, it should be abandoned. Note that the author is quite pedantic about his insistence on abandoning this notion and not redefining it. This is because the notion of analytical truth, which can be thought of as truth *relative* to stated premises, is very meaningful. There is truth in the sense that everybody is forced to agree in the formal sciences. This very important concept should not become blurred by association with some newly defined "absolute truth" capturing elusive concepts like "superior intuitive appeal". It is therefore suggested to abandon the notion of absolute truth in order to preserve the notion of analytical truth.

---

52 see II4.1

In the previous Section it was deplored that if everybody could cite his intuition as the basis for valid scientific statements, science would ultimately be based on subjective choice. This relativist position has been summed up by *Feyerabend* in the catchy phrase "Anything goes!"[53]. But this does not necessarily mean that any form of objectivity[54] must be abandoned. It could be formally required that a scientific statement is consistent with self-proclaimed criteria. Therefore, even if the criteria for theory appraisal were ultimately subjective, one would actually restrain arbitrariness. Any potential critic could axiomatize the proposed argument and then check for consistency. If the consistency rule is violated, the proposed statement can be rejected. By axiomatising an argument, the critic is actually creating an explicit set of axioms which constitute the first principle of the argument. Anything else can be derived analytically.

Alternatively, one could imagine a group of people explicitly setting a number of basic assumptions. They could fix the criteria that they consider to be necessary for accepting a statement to be valid. They could engage in discussions. Each party could try to persuade others that a given criterion was vital. Yet, in the end, if they agree on a set of axioms, a possible conflict about whether a specific statement is valid or not can be analytically settled. This is extremely convenient.

Therefore, it is proposed for reasons of methodological convenience that a scientific argument should be divided into two spheres: The sphere of first principles, where discussions can be held in terms of persuasion, and a second sphere where statements can be discussed analytically and categories of true and false reapply in the sense that any reasonable man can be forced to agree. This increases transparency of the argument and thereby invites criticism. It also facilitates communication about scientific statements as it allows locating any possible source of disagreement. If people disagree about first principles, they can try to persuade each other. They might eventually decide to refuse entering further discussion, but if people disagree on the implications of first principles they can be confident in resolving the disagreement by means of logic.

In order to facilitate criticism of and communication on theory, it is proposed that theories be presented in an axiomatized form.

---

[53] see Chalmers (1994), p. 135

[54] Recall that objectivity was defined as anything independent of the will, restraining arbitrariness

6 The First Principle[55]: Its Cognitive Status

6.1 Consequences of Relativism

The consistency requirement allows for criticism relative to self-proclaimed criteria. However, if relativism is not overcome, science loses its role as a peaceful arbiter. The question is, therefore, whether or not it is possible to move beyond relativism. The consistency requirement which is embodied by the axiomatic approach helped to preserve a minimum of objective validity by forcing people to live up to explicitly or implicitly self-stated criteria; but what can be said about the first principle itself?

The first principle could be set by everybody individually, but what happens if people disagree? A traditional claim of Enlightenment was that every disagreement can be rationally solved. So, even if disagreements will not always be solved peacefully, peaceful settlement is possible in principle without one party dominating the other. There is **order, but at the same time perfect freedom**. The only law that has to be followed is the natural law[56] of reason which is impersonal. Of course, people could try to reach an agreement based on the first principle, but as soon as agreement is not unanimous there is domination[57]. Another traditional claim of Enlightenment was that it is not important *that* people agree, but rather *why*. One **person could be right while everybody else is wrong,** just because the position of this one person derives its truth from the absolute source of truth. This position must also be given up if it is accepted that there is no absolute justification of science. These are very painful implications.

If objectivity is restricted to the sphere of analytical truth[58], disputes *relative to* but not *about* first principle can be settled. There would be no way to overcome the fundamental relativism of the first principle. This raises the question of whether or not it is possible to move beyond relative truth.

The consistency requirement allows for criticism relative to self-proclaimed criteria. But if relativism is not overcome, science loses its role as a peaceful arbiter. Therefore, the question is whether it is possible to move beyond relativism.

---

[55] This can also be a set of first principles, but in the following the term will be used in its singular. The mathematically-minded reader can think of it as a vector.

[56] see Mader (1992a), p. 102

[57] "Was gemeinsam akzeptiert wird, das ist wahr, wenn und solange es akzeptiert wird" see Platon Theaitetos cit. Mader (1993a), p. 102. – "What is commonly accepted is true, if and as long as it is accepted." (translation by the author)

[58] Confining law to the sphere of analytical truth is at the heart of Kelsen's "Pure Theory of Law".

6.2 Overcoming Relativism

At least the possibility to move beyond relativism cannot be excluded. Even if it is not possible to logically distinguish between good and bad theories, this does not mean that such a distinction does not exist. The point is in the spirit of *Kant*: The existence of absolute truth cannot be proven, but also the non-existence of absolute truth cannot be proven. This **opens the way for metaphysical speculation**. In the following, it shall be attempted to describe what appears to be part of a common human idea of truth.

Every attempt to capture what seems to be the essence of truth takes recourse to parables and a form of "reasoning" which is characterized by an increased level of vagueness. In any case it is **distinct from logical reasoning**. This is the reason why it was suggested to keep the two spheres separated. Interpreted in this way they would correspond to *Kant's* distinction of "Vernunftwissen" and "Verstandeswissen".

The starting point is expressed by a paradox of *Pascal* describing men as "**incapable of absolute ignorance and of certain knowledge**"[59]. The line parable[60] of *Plato* defines the relationship between synthetic truth and analytical truth as equivalent to the relationship between a true opinion and an appearance. *Popper* uses the metaphor that several piles in a swamp can carry a construction, although they do not reach firm ground[61]. Is it possible to further specify this "knowledge" which appears to be a phenomenon between scepticism and dogmatism?

It appears that a **central idea is objectivity** in the sense of something which limits arbitrariness. This becomes obvious in the habit to think from first principle, but also in the reluctance to accept any first principle to be the same. Logical consistency, empirical evidence and plausibility[62] appear to be tightly associated to the idea of objectivity.

---

[59] Pascal (1993), Pensée 434 : « incapables d'ignorer absolument et de savoir certainement »

[60] Plato (1993), Poleteia VI, pp. 194-198

[61] Science does not rest upon rock-bottom. The bold structure of its theories rises, as it were, above a swamp. It is like a building erected on piles. The piles are driven down from above into the swamp, but not down to any natural or 'given' base; and when we cease our attempts to drive our piles into a deeper layer, it is not because we have reached firm ground. We simply stop when we are satisfied that they are firm enough to carry the structure, at least for the time being. (Popper (1959), p. 111)

[62] It can be argued that plausibility is a category of introspection.

A major argument against favouring one first principle over the other was that the danger exists to only formalize some form of **psychological illusion** based on emotionally satisfying fiction. It seems, however, that the idea of objectivity is not based on direct intuitive appeal or attractiveness. Quite to the contrary, there rather seems to be a suspicion of what looks true at first glance and a *willingness to accept indirect arguments.*

Consider the following example: If somebody promises to make sure that the "farmer would receive more for his grain, the worker pay less for his bread, and the baker and grocer have a higher wholesale and retail margin,"[63] a scientist will reject this promise because it is logically inconsistent although it appeals to wishful thinking. Or consider the classic argument of *Hayek* concerning collectivism: It could be argued that collectivism just needs a benevolent dictator to make just decisions. Of course, given the justness of the decision[64], central planning should be implemented. Thus the seemingly uncoordinated activities of people can be rationally coordinated. The wealth of nations can be maximized by avoiding the inefficiencies of the market mechanism. However, it can be argued that it is very difficult to get all the relevant information in time. On the other hand, the market mechanism as a decentralized mechanism can be argued to be more efficient under many circumstances in processing information because decisions are made by persons holding the relevant information (e.g. consumers knowing their preferences or entrepreneurs knowing their cost structure). The case for central planning is another example of an argument which is very attractive at first sight: First of all, one must only flatter oneself into believing that oneself is an example of a benevolent dictator. Then, one would certainly find many instances where the market system produces unjust and inefficient results. Finally, rational planning is very attractive because it suits very well the human mind – especially the mind of the intellectual – which prefers putting things in order. Still, for all its first-hand attractiveness, even socialist scientists like *Lange* are said to have acknowledged the problem of information, although they thought it could be solved.

It could be argued that there is a difference between a merely subjective decision and a subjective decision, which is made in intellectual honesty against the backdrop of the idea of truth[65]. So, the point is not *the fact that* people decide

---

63 see Drucker (1939), p. 18 citing a speech of Goebbels in 1932

64 The problem of aggregation of preferences is ignored here

65 The idea is taken from Kant, who considered "ideas" not to be constitutive but regulative of scientific knowledge. See Mader (1993a), p. 211. This distinction is also what Rousseau had in mind when opposing the "volonté de tous" and the "volonté générale" (see: Rousseau (1762), pp. 30f).

but that they do it with an "opinio veritatis" following a kind of "categorical imperative"[66]. It is suggested that this common idea of truth allows a certain communication context. Honest dialogue could be a means to expose objective criteria analoguous to rational discourse. Yet, this time it is more comprehensive and not just limited to the categories of reason.

James suggests that an acting individual should show a "will to belief"[67] for the premisses that he establishes. If he does not, the theories will do nothing to calm the mental unease of acting. In practice, this will often lead to dogmatism. It is suggested here that the premiss should indeed reflect a belief. One cannot take for granted that others will always share this belief, but one has experienced that by exchanging views with others one is persuading and is being persuaded. So, it should be an open belief drawing not only from personal experience but also from the experiences of others by means of dialogue against the backdrop of the common idea of truth. Still, this dialogue should not be a modus toward achieving a convention that is automatically binding for everybody. It is more a chance to learn from others.

This last point is problematic and requires judgement. It addresses the problem of whether there is a bridge, which the author thinks exists, between the idea of truth and the practical possibility of overcoming relativism by a set of enforceable rules. One can either solve the problem by accepting that the ultimate yardstick is set by convention of the relevant community, or one preserves the anarchist quality of science by providing no such ultimate yardstick. If people could credibly commit[68] to always deciding in good faith, mechanisms as majority rule or a broad consensus within the relevant community could indeed be viable, helping to filter out individual distortions due to error. But there is no way to credibly commit to this[69]. Any mechanism designed to state rules which are binding for everybody therefore balances the need for order against the potential blindness or corruption of power. In scientific practice, it is argued that a strong dose of anarchism should be accepted as long as the individual scientist offers a consistent argument and is open for criticism. This is because of the pragmatic

---

[66] Kant (1786), Was heißt: Sich im Denken orientieren. See Mader (1993a), p. 218

[67] This is the title of a famous essay by James (1896).

[68] The problem of commitment is the fundamental problem of contract theory that will be treated in this thesis.

[69] Indeed, the religious concept of a world hereafter and divine justice can be seen as an "institution" dealing with this problem.

consideration that, in science, more than anywhere else, too much order does more harm than too little[70].

The impossibility to either prove or disprove the existence of an absolute justification opens the way for metaphysical speculation. This is distinctly different from logical reasoning. The notion of scientific validity, however, appears to be tightly associated with the idea of objectivity which is different from direct emotional appeal. Therefore, it is argued, it is possible to distinguish between merely subjective decisions and decisions made against the backdrop of the common idea of truth. This common idea offers a basis for communication. Yet, the willingness to engage in honest dialogue is merely a moral imperative and cannot be taken for granted. Hence, no set of enforceable rules can expose "truth"[71]. Any mechanism that is designed to state rules which are binding for everybody therefore balances the need for order against the potential blindness or corruption of power. In scientific practice, it is argued that a strong dose of anarchism should be accepted, as long as the individual scientist offers a consistent argument and is open for criticism.

7 Methodological Implications

The author was careful to choose phrases like "sharing thoughts" or "inviting others to join" when referring to the discussions about first principle. This might look unnecessarily contrived. The intention, however, is clear: having shown that an absolute basis for science in the strictest sense of the word cannot be proven, some ground shall be regained beyond the notion of relative truth.

The suggested approach of dividing science into two spheres has the following properties: A scientist is willing to name his premisses and thereby invites criticism. This provides at least some objectivity in the sense that he accepts principles which might ultimately become effective against his will. His premisses are nothing else than the criteria relative to which he is willing to have his theories accepted and refuted[72].

---

[70] The need for order is arguably higher in society as a whole, yet the concept of classical liberalism can be viewed as arguing for restraint.

[71] The quotation marks are set, in relation to the earlier argument that the notion of absolute truth should be abandoned.

[72] Of course in many cases, these premisses will be shared by the scientific community.

In order to facilitate theory choice of the individual, it is good to be transparent about the methodological principles underlying the theory that is developed. It is then possible for an individual to easily find out if a theory corresponds to his standards. A scientist does not claim to possess absolute truth. He is not dogmatic. Still he may cling to his principles and refuse to engage into discussion with someone, who does not share the same principles if he cannot be persuaded to adopt them.

By structuring science into two spheres, it is possible to *locate* where people differ in their views. If it is in the sphere of first principle, one will refuse to quarrel in terms of logic. One can only persuade[73]. However, if one is in agreement with first principle one can be confident in resolving the disagreement by means of impersonal rules[74]. This is the merit of keeping the two spheres separated. It is a structured approach to facilitate communication about theories.

By replacing the ultimate justification with a first principle, it is possible to give the idea of the critical role of science at least some room. The scientific undertaking will be based on certain principles. Relative to these principles, there is a meaning to "true" and "false". These principles are made transparent. This facilitates the decision process of whether or not to accept a given theory, but it also provides a structured approach for locating the area of dissent. By explicitly referring to the foundation of science as a first principle, one is also taking a firm stand against dogmatism. Discussion of principles can only be led in terms of persuasion and not in terms of logic. It is proposed here that only these formal criteria be used to distinguish science from non-science.

---

[73] In the sense of Pascal's "The art of persuasion" see e.g. Mader (1993a), pp. 190f

[74] It is always possible to set axioms such that no problem of underdetermination arises.

III The Method of Economics and Contract Theory

1 Introduction

Looking at economic dissertations, one realises that most authors, visibly harassed when asked to reflect methodology, take a “let’s get it over with” approach. They usually declare themselves ardent supporters of this or that author of methodology (mostly resulting in Popperian falsificationism in its most naïve form), bravely ignoring all criticism that has been voiced against it, and – what is even more astonishing – ignoring altogether the newly found champion in methodology when pursuing their own research.

Here, the intention is to not only lay down the principles which are to govern this dissertation, but also to share some thoughts about the merits of this choice. By the way, this choice is not at all revolutionary. It is well within the framework of traditional choices made by many other scientists in the field of microeconomics, although some differences might become apparent along the way.

Kuhn argues that one should not **waste time** thinking too much about methodology. Discussions about methodology rather pertain to a fledgling science. Normally, most scientists within a given discipline have only tacit knowledge of the paradigm they are using, confident that their socialization within the scientific community they grew up in will intuitively lead them in the most generally accepted direction. It can be argued that this is better than to study the philosophical premisses of the paradigm, leaving more time for actual problem solving[75].

If, however, there are **competing paradigms** within a discipline, or if one intends to oppose mainstream thinking, it is justified and even necessary to work out explicitly what that paradigm is all about. *Kuhn* circumvents this by declaring consensus on method[76] constitutive for science. Therefore, by *Kuhn's* definition, it is highly controversial whether social sciences are scientific at all. It is sometimes claimed that in social sciences every scientist is following his own approach. This is certainly an exaggeration. Yet, it is true that there is no generally accepted paradigm[77]. Methodological considerations are therefore more important in the social sciences than in the natural sciences.

---

[75] Chalmers (1994), p. 94f

[76] Chalmers (1994), p. 92f

[77] Although the rational paradigm of economics might be an exception.

As a general rule, explicitly stating one's methodological premisses is all the more important if it is not clear what methodology to expect. This is why a social scientist has to take a methodological stand.

2 Overview

Chapter 3 argues that economic theory, although allowing for some instrumentalism, relies relatively more on the realism of its assumptions than is the case for the natural sciences. This is because predictions are difficult to test and every social phenomenon can ultimately be traced back to human action, opening the way for methodological individualism.

This approach and its specifically economic formulation in terms of rational choice are discussed in Chapter 4. Defending rational choice, it ultimately becomes an empirically empty template, largely upheld for its analytical convenience (4.2.). Section 4.3 makes a brief remark on the properties of game theory stressing that its structural rigidity can be overcome by taking an instrumentalist approach to assumptions. Although economics as a formal science can be defended (4.4), realism of assumptions becomes an issue as soon as statements about reality are made 4.6. Economics is, in principle, not dogmatic about the traditional homo oeconomicus assumption, which assumes pursuit of wealth, opportunism and a high degree of rationality. Still, Section 4.7 discusses reasons why one should be cautious to modify them. In defense of homo oeconomicus it can be shown that phenomena sometimes only appear to contradict assumptions. Moreover, there may be specific situations where these assumptions fit quite well, while still falling short of capturing the whole of human behaviour. Finally, it could be argued that, especially in institutional matters like contracts, it is safer to assume a worst case scenario. A prominent criticism of the homo oeconomicus approach is the high degree of rationality assumed. Section 4.8 presents an evolutionary argument which plausibly argues that agents in institutional economics can be assumed, in some situations, to act unconsciously rational. A methodological programme can be derived from this evolutionary approach. Shortly discussing Popper's piecemeal social engineering in Section 4.9, the objection of historicism against evolutionary concepts is subsequently addressed in Section 4.10.

Chapter 5 makes the case for using introspection in the social sciences in addition to empirical methods. Section 5.1 provides the fundamental rationale: Social sciences ultimately deal with human action. Contrary to the natural sciences wherein observation exhausts the phenomenon, human action has both an external and an internal dimension which cannot be readily observed. In addition, by looking at the internal dimension of human action one can hope to find more stability. Section 5.2 discusses the inflexibility of blackbox models of human behaviour compared to introspection using an example from management theory. In Section 5.3, it is argued that introspection should be considered an independent source of cognition and not just a heuristic. This contradicts the common view that, in the end, only rigorous empirical testing can corroborate a theory. Section 5.4 exposes the fact that the method of introspection rides on the assumption that there is a strong commensurability between the human perceiver and the perceived object, in this case human action. *Mises*' a priorism draws very extreme conclusions from this assumption which are generally regarded as dogmatic. Finally, the method of psychological reduction is discussed, hinting at the different cognitive status of statements derived by this method as opposed to statements of the "exact" sciences.

The issue of the use of empirical methods and the problems associated therein is treated in Chapter 6. Section 6.2 mentions two approaches which can be seen as attempts to defend a unified approach to science (monism). Both dispute introspection as being an independent source of knowledge in the social sciences. The first is the theory of revealed preferences, which claims that the preference structure of individuals can - in principle - be derived by systematic observation. The second is panphysicalism, which claims that everything including psychological processes will eventually be explained in terms of the natural sciences. It is agued that both approaches are not very fruitful. Section 6.3 briefly mentions the role of interviews as a method to explore people's motivation, but also to get hold of facts or make use of their judgement. The last point can be seen as a "market test" for theories. Although controlled experiment has a rather limited role in economics, it is argued in Section 6.4 that it can be used to test microanalytical models, and especially models of human behaviour. Alternatively economics resorts to historical experiment (6.5). In order to make different situations comparable and to isolate relevant factors, econometric techniques can be used; but the multitude of factors and the presence of very little data of low quality make the use of such techniques problematic. Section 6.6 therefore argues in favour of focusing less on the single, formal and decisive test, but rather on a broad range of informal empirical evidence. Having discussed the problems of testing predictions in economics by either controlled experiment or econometrics, it is argued that the validity of economic models relies to a large extent on their microanalytical foundation. Yet, economic phenomena are the product of many interrelated effects. Section 6.7 argues, that due to potentially countervailing qualitative effects, aggregate predictions can only be "derived" by making use of judgement. Aggregation sometimes seems totally unfeasible. In an attempt to avoid both the problem of aggregation and the problem of the multitude of relevant factors, Section 6.8 explores the possibility of focusing on relationships on a macrolevel (between aggregated entities); but even this approach cannot completely ignore demands for providing at least some micro-foundation. The closing Section 6.9 revisits the issue of verificationism vs. falsificationism. This time, however, the focus is not on epistemological problems, as in part I but on the different normative prescriptions that can be derived from these two approaches.

Chapter 7 deals with applied microeconomics. Applied theory is sometimes seen as an art rather than a science. It is argued in Section 7.1 that applied theory indeed has a different cognitive status than pure science. But this does not mean that pure science and applied science should be separated as two entirely different subjects. It is also vigorously disputed that pure science is useless in the social sciences. Applied science is rather judgement within an objective framework, while pure science is the attempt to provide this framework knowing that it will be applied. Yet, this distinction is not as clear-cut as it might seem. In Section 7.2, it is argued that there is a convergence between microeconomic contract theory based on recent microeconomic developments such as economics of information and game theory and German "Betriebswirtschaftslehre", which traditionally is an interdisciplinary theory of the firm rather than just "management theory".

The objective of Chapter 8 is to discuss the approach of optimal contract design. Section 8.1 defines the problem: Institutional design in general examines the choice of constraints rather than the choice within constraints. Stuck in a situation where they only achieve sub-optimal outcome, contracting parties set constraints which will allow them to achieve higher levels of outcome. Solutions are obtained by an exercise of comparative institutional analysis 8.2 or by more general control theory models. The problem favours microanalytical treatment 8.3. As contracting is complex, a major problem will be to find a reasonable level of detail. Theories risk being either too general or too specific. It is argued that the best approach is to switch from the very abstract to the casuistic leaving out the intractible middle ground 8.4.

The closing Chapter 9 shares some thoughts on the relationship between theory and practical life. It is argued that theory and practical action are structurally the same. Therefore, the gap between theorists and practitioners is a problem of different time horizons and a willingness on the part of theorists to engage in the study of very abstract fundamental problems which do not directly lead to better technologies. It is suggested that in some fields the potential value of theory is higher than in others. Still, some unnecessary barriers exist like e.g. the theorist's frequent neglect in making theories more robust to imprecise information.

3 Instrumentalism vs. Realism

3.1 Introduction

The question of whether there is an **outside world** is deemed irrelevant by some rationalists because nothing can be said about it. Yet, there is a simple story which illustrates why brushing aside this question seems problematic: Imagine someone running trough a "forest". He would like to take the shortest way and runs in a straight line. He eventually hits an obstacle. It is not necessary to be able to define or even name the obstacle (although he will probably call it "tree"). The point is that he is running into "something" and that this "something" is independent of his will or knowledge[78]. It is this encounter with things independent of one's will which makes such a strong case for realism.

Different approaches concerning the relationship between the human construction[79] and the world as it is differ to the extent to which they require correspondence between the two spheres[80]. For scientists subscribing to representative realism, which is realism in its strictest form, it is not enough that the single statements derived from a theory or a model are true. A theory or model will only be accepted if its individual elements are true, i.e. correspond to something in the real world. This idea of truth is referred to as the "correspondence theory of truth". Thus, every element of the model is actually seen to be a representation of something real. A structural symmetry between reality and its model is required: Reality and a good model are supposed to be isomorphic.

The extreme counter position referred to as **instrumentalism** maintains that only empirical success of a theory's implication counts no matter which assumptions a theory is based on. The terms in which a theory is formulated depend only on their suitability to organise thinking[81]. A main argument against instrumentalism in this extreme form is that it does not explain why one should be interested in experiments. If theory only links perceptions, why should it be

---

78 The presentation of the basic distinction between realism and instrumentalism is taken from Chalmers (1994), p. 163

79 As was already argued, what the human mind takes as reality is actually a construction of the human mind itself.

80 see Chalmers (1994), pp. 147f.

81 see Chalmers (1994), p. 149

attempted to predict novel facts and then to test them[82]? Irrelevance of assumptions in economics was most forcibly argued by *Friedman*[83].

One particular problem poses itself whenever empirical success of a theory stands in contrast to its unrealistic or at least arcane assumptions. Should a successful theory be discarded because it does not meet the standards of representative realism? So, the question really is: On which levels should a good theory be consistent with empirical evidence, just in its conclusions or all the way from assumptions to conclusions?

A rather unspectacular interpretation of instrumentalism which needs no further discussion is the simple statement that every theory necessarily is an abstraction of reality. Some variables are included and some are left out implying that a judgement is made about the relevance of different variables. There is broad consensus that **abstraction** is a feature of theory. Even *Friedman*, having presented a reductio ad absurdum of slavishly descriptive realism acknowledges that "the notion of a completely realistic theory is in part a straw man"[84] and therefore not worth being argued against. Any attempt to match reality in its complexity is certain to "render a theory utterly useless"[85].

However, the allegation of unrealistic assumptions could also refer to models, which are based on statistically derived entities with no visible connection to the problem. For instance, it is possible that share price models based on some statistical variables yield better predictive results than models which are based on fundamental or macroeconomic variables with larger intuitive explanatory power, although it is unclear why[86].

In the natural sciences, it frequently happens that two models have good predictive success despite their **incompatible assumptions**. This is the case for Newtonian mechanics, the theory of relativity and quantum mechanics[87]. This is

---

[82] Bhaskar, R. (1975) cit. Chalmers (1994), p. 154f and p. 161

[83] see Friedman (1966), pp. 1-16, 30-47

[84] Friedman (1966), p. 32

[85] Friedman (1966), p. 32

[86] see Connor (1995)

[87] Chalmers attributes the use of this example to Kuhn and Feyerabend. see Chalmers (1994), p. 162

also the case for several models in electrical engineering and optics[88]. To make matters worse, none of the models is superior to the others for all purposes. There are, in fact, circumstances where one of these models has better predictive power than the others. So, there is the old problem: If the realist sticks to his view of science he must renounce the use of theories that yield practical results. Often he would still hold on to his view but use the theory nonetheless. Unfortunately, this divorce of theory and practice is quite common.

A milder version of realism called **non-representative realism**[89] addresses this problem. It does not claim an isomorphic relationship between reality and the model. It does not even require models to be compatible in their assumptions. It does, however, require them not to contradict each other in their predictions if they overlap. If there is some contradiction it requires the divergence to be systematic, i.e. it wants there to be a correction rule which is able to transform predictions of one model into the predictions of the other[90].

3.2 Natural vs. Social Sciences[91]

It will be argued here that in the social sciences it is more important for assumptions to be realistic to a certain extent than in the natural sciences. For one thing it will in some instances be quite difficult in economics to test predictions[92]. This is different in natural sciences where controlled experiments are frequently

88 Some models are based on the idea that there are electromagnetic fields. Others assume a substance called aether and still others rely on a concept of flowing electrons (see Chalmers (1994), p. 164). The same applies for optics. Some models rely on a particle flow concept, others assume light waves. These models are clearly incompatible in a realist framework. Light cannot at the same time consist of flowing particles and travel in waves. See Chalmers (1994), S. 156

89 see Chalmers (1994), pp. 161-165

90 A prominent example where this could be achieved is the relationship between Newtonian physics and Einstein's theory of relativity. Newtonian physics can, in many cases, be seen as a pretty good approximation to theory of relativity in their respective predictions.

91 It is argued that this distinction is meaningful, even if it is not mentioned in most text books. "The reason is simple: The hegemony of American social sciences in the post-Second World War period has wiped the slate clean of any trace of an operant distinction between the *Naturwissenschaften* and the *Geisteswissenschaften*."(Mirowski (1994), p. 54). Mirowski continues – in the pages following – to give an overview of the different layers of this discussion. The author's presentation in this dissertation is largely influenced by v. Mises (1949)

92 see Caldwell (1994), p. 146; He claims that also Blaug and Hausman agree on this point.

readily available. Therefore, social sciences can rely relatively less on empirical testing of overall predictions.

This has been vigorously disputed by *Friedman*: "The difficulty in the social sciences of getting new evidence [...] and of judging its conformity with the implications of the hypothesis makes it tempting to suppose that other, more readily available, evidence is equally relevant to the validity of the hypothesis – to suppose that hypotheses have not only "implications" but also "assumptions" and that the conformity of these "assumptions" to "reality" is a test of the validity of the hypothesis different from or additional to the test by implications. This widely held view is fundamentally wrong and productive of much mischief."[93]

Friedman offers a number of arguments that are meant to support his view. The first argument simply reiterates the truism that a theory in order to be useful "abstracts the common and crucial elements from the mass of complex and detailed circumstances surrounding the phenomena"[94]. But as *Friedman* himself earlier acknowledges that nobody seriously advocates slavish realism, this argument is irrelevant and will not be further discussed.

The second argument claims that "the two supposedly independent tests [... on the level of assumptions and on the level of implications] reduce to one test"[95]. This is because "the relevant question to ask about the "assumptions" of a theory is not whether they are descriptively "realistic", for they never are, but whether they are sufficiently good approximations for the purpose at hand. And this question can be answered only by seeing whether the theory works, which means whether it yields sufficiently accurate predictions."[96] Yet, *Friedman* does not take sufficiently into account that there is not only a *negative* reason for increased reliance on the realism of assumptions due to difficulties in testing, but there also is also a *positive* argument for why realism is more important in social sciences than in the natural sciences:

Consider an example of optics[97]: There are models which interpret light in terms of particle flow and others in terms of waves. Yet, nobody has seen these waves or particles. They are merely narratives helping to organize thoughts. One

---

93 Friedman (1966), p. 14

94 Friedman (1966), p. 14

95 Friedman (1966), p. 15

96 Friedman (1966), p. 15

97 see footnote 88

can therefore easily live with the fact that light is interpreted in different terms depending on the situation. As the realism attributed to assumptions is indeed very limited, the only thing that will be demanded is a correction rule or workable delineation of the scope of application of the respective model[98]. This is, however, different in the social sciences. It is an irrefutable fact that all social phenomena, however complex, are the product of individual human action[99]. Human action exists, and one has some very clear ideas about it. This is the rationale of methodological individualism where predictions are derived by aggregating models of human behaviour[100].

What most people advocating "realism of assumptions" actually claim is that they favour assumptions that yield plausible implications on the level of human behaviour. They do not claim to provide an accurate description of the psychological process within the human brain. Later on, it will also be seen that for reasons of analytical tractability some instrumentalism in modeling is accepted[101]. For instance, it is possible in game theory to model behaviour where individuals differently process the same information by assuming that they process information identically but have different information. Thus, in order to keep assumptions about information processing simple, it is assumed that they are exposed to different information. This is an instrumentalist idea. But on the level of the behavioural model, realism is preserved.

Friedman's argument that there is only "one test" is ill-conceived because implications arise on the level of human behaviour *as well* as on the level of aggregated predictions. Representative realism is therefore viable in economics on the level of human behaviour. Thus, in the natural sciences the requirement for realistic assumptions will be lower than in the social sciences. One only has to point to *Friedman's* argument that the question whether "the magnitude of businessmen's costs" or the "color of their eyes" is more important for their decisions can only be tested "by prediction"[102] to see that he utterly ignores the possibility of introspection: If the author asks himself whether he would make

---

[98] This is in the spirit of non-representative realism.

[99] Mises (1949), p. 43

[100] see Hausman (1994), p. 208: "The only methodological principle governing economics and the other social sciences for which one finds much explicit argument is methodological individualism – the insistence that explanatory laws in economics concern features of human beings."

[101] as long as it can be argued to be innocuous

[102] Friedman (1966), pp. 32f

business decisions based on the colour of his eyes he would not have to resort to prediction and experiment to answer this question.

Moreover, *Friedman* argues that the question of what is "realistic enough"[103] and what is too unrealistic can only be answered by considering the phenomenon that shall be explained. He cites the vacuum assumption[104] which is appropriate when throwing a stone but less appropriate when throwing a feather. *Mäki* criticizes that the vacuum assumption is not a peripheral assumption of the model whereas profit maximization which *Friedman* has in mind is a core assumption of economics. So, the correct analogy would have been between profit maximization and gravitational attraction. But it is difficult to see how the argument could be upheld in this setting[105].

In addition, *Friedman's* argument implicitly resides on an unbounded empirical optimism assuming that tests can ultimately attain unambiguous results. His concessions to the contrary[106] thus reduce to pure lip service. It is an unbalanced conclusion to say that realism of assumptions should be abandoned because of methodological difficulties, when at the same time the problems of empirical testing are largely ignored. Why should it be abandoned to assume that altruism will play a larger role within families than among businessmen; or that information asymmetry with respect to legal competence is higher between a private client and a lawyer than between a lawyer and a company[107]? Just because some "test" on the basis of poor data (and economic data is always poor data!) suggests that this information does not matter?

A final point is that, although every social phenomenon can ultimately be traced back to human action, it **does not mean that methodological individualism is the only way** to come to conclusions. Generally speaking, it is also possible to discern **patterns** of behaviour on an aggregated level[108]. Yet, in

---

[103] Friedman (1966), pp. 41

[104] That air resistance can be abstracted from in most cases.

[105] "Friedman's mistake was to defend the core assumption of profit maximization by appealing to an analogy between it and the vacuum assumption, which is a peripheral assumption. The correct analogy would be between it and the core assumption of the gravitational attraction of the earth." (Mäki (1994), p. 146)

[106] see Friedman (1966), p. 40

[107] A large company probably boasts a sophisticated legal department and just hires the lawyer to represent it in court.

[108] It will later be argued that in situations where there is a lot of data and problems of aggregation this will be the method of choice.

the social sciences a minimum requirement would be that these theories can at least be *interpreted* on the level of human action. It seems justified, however, to show some **flexibility** for practical reasons: For predictions, a well-functioning technology, which was repeatedly validated in the past, should be preferred if compared to a technology based on another theory even if this theory's probable correspondence with reality is better. Calculations on the basis of the geocentric concept led to far better results in the initial phase than results based on the heliocentric concept[109]. It is argued here that, even if the imperfections of a model are known, one should continue to use it as long as it yields better solutions; but tension between it and the model, which is closer to reality in its assumptions, should be preserved. This **tension** is a fruitful source for further theory development.

Both the realism of individual model components and predictive success contribute to the quality of a theory. As a general rule, modeling assumptions are relatively more important in the social sciences than in the natural sciences, where convincing experiments can often be set up to test overall prediction and where assumptions are more speculative.

4 Methodological Individualism

4.1 Introduction

It was argued in the last Section that methodological individualism is a possible and potentially fruitful approach in the social sciences. It consists of modeling social phenomena on the basis of behavioural models which are subsequently aggregated. Traditionally, in economics, behavioural models are formulated in terms of **rational choice**. It is assumed that any individual has a preference structure reflecting everything he cares for. Then, in a given situation he chooses the action that maximizes utility (or expected utility in the case of uncertainty) subject to constraints. This is why methodological individualism is also called situational analysis. Mathematically, the preference structure and the situational context are translated into a constrained maximization problem. By solving this problem, behaviour can be predicted[110].

It is doubtful whether rational choice, especially in its variety as a model of choice under uncertainty, is a **realistic model** of behaviour. Defending rational choice by adopting a wider concept of preferences, one will ultimately make it an

---

[109] see Chalmers (1994), p. 72

[110] see Mäki (1994), p. 244 on the centrality of constrained optimization in economics.

empirically **empty concept**[111]. But this does not make it useless. On the contrary: *Because* it is empirically empty it can be universally applied as a template. Every behavioural assumption can be modelled in terms of rational choice. But the fact that any behaviour *can* be modelled in such terms does not automatically suggest that this *should* indeed be done. The criterion for this choice is methodological convenience. Compared with other approaches, there are good reasons for arguing that this approach has many **methodological advantages**. It will therefore be endorsed on normative grounds.

4.2 Rational Choice

4.2.1 Choice under Certainty

Rational choice assumes that all human action is purposeful action. Never does anybody act if he does not think that this leads him to a more preferred state. This seems to be a bold statement. People quite often act in a way which does not seem to serve their best interest. First, it is said that people pursue goals which are against their "objective" interests, negatively affecting their career, health or moral life. Second, they sometimes demonstrate a lack of will, trading in long-term objectives for short-term pleasure, although this long-term objective is much more desirable to them if directly compared to the pleasure derived from not pursuing it. Third, people's actions are sometimes inconsistent with prior action. Finally, actions chosen often seem highly inadequate to achieve a given end[112].

All of these objections are based on the assumption that preferences are objective and stable, or that expectations are not rationally formed. This need not be the case: Of course, normative provisions can be made to dissuade individuals to act according to certain preferences but preferences themselves are intrinsically subjective[113]. In a typical discussion, the concept of utility maximization would be attacked on the grounds of observations that people care for other things than money or even act altruistically. In defence it can be said that this only shows that these people also attribute utility to non-material things like power, respect, love,

[111] Raffée (1974), pp. 40f

[112] Mises (1949), p. 19-22 (4.ed. 1996)

[113] If somebody states a preference, it is possible to argue against it, point to the consequences of such preferences that this individual possibly did not consider, attempt to manipulate his will, but in the end the preference is either there or it isn't. It is mentioned in this context that pan-physical attempts are rejected by the author (see below).

and even the supposed preferences of others in the case of altruism[114]. Also, if an individual has revealed preferences in one instance, it cannot be readily assumed that these preferences will guide his action in the future. This can be modelled by assuming state dependent preferences. Finally, even an action that seems inappropriate need not be irrational per se. It is possible that an individual wants to cure a sick person, but instead of using the treatment suggested by medicine performs a religious rite. This does not automatically suggest that he is irrational but could also establish the fact that this individual expected his behaviour to be more instrumental.

The whole focus is therefore shifted on preferences. For if it is maintained that individuals act on the basis of their rational expectations with regard to the appropriateness of action for the promotion of their own preferences, nothing can be said about why they act in one way rather than in another, as long as no restrictions are placed on preferences.

It becomes clear that if preferences are interpreted in the widest sense, the rational paradigm is empirically empty. Any conceivable behaviour can be modelled if only preferences are duly adjusted. Therefore, the whole focus is shifted on preferences[115].

4.2.2 Choice under Uncertainty

The traditional concept of rational choice under uncertainty is maximization of expected utility. This concept depends on the assumption that uncertainty can be described in terms of simple lotteries[116]. So, whenever there is an uncertain situation, the assumption is that one is able to derive a list of possible states and assign probabilities to each of them.

Moreover, it is assumed – in a basic consequentialist premiss[117] - that the agent is able to reduce complex situations to simple lotteries. Complex lotteries are lotteries which consist of a sequence of simple lotteries. This assumption becomes ever more restricting as situations become more complex. Later on, an

---

[114] Altruism is thus modelled "as if" it did not exist. This is an instance of instrumentalism in modelling which will be discussed later.

[115] see e.g. Blaug (1994), p. 132

[116] Mas-Colell, Whinston, Green (1995), p. 168

[117] Mas-Colell, Whinston, Green (1995), p. 170

evolutionary argument[118] will be presented which argues that the burden of this assumption may be lower than it seems at first sight.

If the agent can establish preference relations among these simple lotteries that are both continuous[119] and satisfy the independence axiom[120], the preference relations can be represented by a utility function[121] which is linear in probabilities[122]. Such a utility function is said to have an expected utility form[123]. The utility of a compound lottery can be calculated as the expected value of the utilities of its individual components. If the outcomes of lotteries are expressed in money terms it is convenient to assume that there is a continuum of outcomes. It can be shown that the concept of expected utility can easily be generalized to the continuous case where the discrete probability distribution is replaced by a density function[124].

---

118 Alchian (1950)

119 Continuity e.g. assumes that if one dollar is preferred to zero, one is also willing to prefer one dollar and a small but positive probability of death to zero. Laboratory experiments suggest that this is not consistent with empirical evidence. But if instead of this artificial experiment, people are asked whether they prefer 10 dollars right away or driving with their car to a location 2 miles away to pick up 200 dollars, many people would prefer to take the trip, although this means objectively increasing the probability of death. Whenever, one is setting up an experiment, one is trying to make something observable, which is not normally observable because of a bundle of simultaneous effects. When trying to isolate a single effect, problems may arise because by setting up the experiment one may unconsciously change relevant factors.

120 The independence axiom assumes, that the ordering of preferences over lotteries is independent of a third lottery with which it is mixed. This axiom is also referred to as the independence axiom. Suppose that a lottery L1 which offers a chance to win a corkscrew is valued less than a lottery L2 which offers the chance to win a bottle of orange juice. If a lottery L3 is imagined that is described by the chance to win a bottle of wine, then a lottery which offers a 50:50 chance of winning L1 or L3 will always be valued higher that a lottery that gives a 50:50 chance of winning L2 or L3. The example was intendedly chosen to show that the independence axiom is a specific feature of choice under uncertainty. If a bundle of goods is compared with another bundle of goods it could very well be assumed that the bundle of corkscrew and wine is worth more than the bundle of orange juice and wine. But in the case of choice under uncertainty one will never be able to consume goods, but just either one or the other.

121 Unique representation is assured by the continuity assumption.

122 Linearity is assured by the independence axiom.

123 see Mas-Colell, Whinston, Green (1995), pp. 171-178

124 see Mas-Colell, Whinston, Green (1995), pp. 183 f

It is important to make a distinction between the utility function defined on lotteries and the utility function defined on amounts of money[125]. The specification of the latter which captures choice behaviour is very important to the analytical power of the expected utility framework. It is assumed to be continuous and increasing[126]. Moreover, due to the St. Petersburg-Menger Paradox[127], it is assumed to be bounded above and below. A common assumption is non-increasing marginal utility of money[128] resulting in a semi-concave function. By Jensen's Inequality this implies that people value an uncertain prospect at or lower than its expected value. This is the definition of risk-averseness[129]. The shape of the utility function can be summarized by the absolute and the relative Arrow-Pratt coefficient of risk-averseness which is a robust measure for concavity[130].

So far it has been assumed that an objective probability distribution was given. But this seems very restrictive. The only concept of probability which arguably is objective is relative frequency[131]. When asked to give the probability that the outcome is "tails" when throwing a coin, most people will probably agree that it is 50%. This is because it can be empirically verified that the relative frequency in a repeated random experiment converges to this number. This will be different in a situation where creditors assess the probability that a given company goes bankrupt. They know that there are two outcomes. They might even have statistical studies on the correlation of balance sheet ratios as leading indicators of insolvency. But still, it is clear that this is distinct from objective probability:

---

125 Mas-Colell, Whinston, Green (1995), p. 171 refer to the first function as the v.Neuman-Morgenstern (v-N-M) function and to the second as the Bernoulli function. But terminology is not consistent across the literature.

126 More money is preferred to less.

127 Assume a game, where the probability of the game ending is 50% after each round but the reward if it continues is 3 powered with the number of the round. It is clear that this is a non-converging sequence. So the value should be indefinite, but nobody would pay an indefinite or even a very high sum for it.

128 People probably value the dollar that buys them food and shelter more than the dollar that buys them the swimming pool for the horses.

129 see Mas-Colell, Whinston, Green (1995) pp. 184f

130 If one wants to model the behaviour of an agent who becomes less risk-averse to absolute gambles with increasing wealth, one has to choose a utility function which has a decreasing absolute risk-averseness. If one wants to model the behaviour of an agent who becomes less risk-averse to gambles proportional to his wealth, one has to choose a utility function with decreasing relative risk-averseness. For a discussion of the Arrow-Pratt coefficient and the issue of robustness see Mas-Colell, Whinston, Green (1995), pp. 190-194

131 see e.g. Camerer, Weber (1992), p. 329; see DeGroot (1970), p. 4 for a short overview on the foundations of probability and references to further literature.

People may disagree. The extreme case would be to assume an urn where it is only known that it contains 100 balls, either black or white, and to ask agents to give a probability that a ball drawn from the urn is black. The two uncertainty situations correspond to the classical Knightian distinction between risk and uncertainty[132], which is why the latter case will be referred to as Knightian uncertainty. So, in the following, the question is how choice will be made under Knightian uncertainty.

Subjective probability theory, also referred to as Baysian decision theory, claims that it is possible to rationalize any choice behaviour under uncertainty in terms of expected utility maximization. So, every decision can be interpreted "as if" utilities were assigned to outcomes, probabilities were attached to states of nature and decisions were made by taking expected utilities"[133]. By systematic observation, (implicit) probabilistic beliefs can be revealed. There are several problematic behavioural assumptions implicit in subjective probability theory. They will be sketched in the following.

As in the case of objective probabilities, there is the consequentialist assumption that requires agents to recognize the underlying structure of complex decision problems[134]. Another assumption is the independence axiom which conflicts with plausible evidence that people try to eschew disappointment[135] and fear taking choices which may lead them to regret[136] not having taken another choice. Another problem is evidence of discontinuous preferences[137] where very important goods are at stake. Moreover, for reasons of tractability the Bernoulli utility function is sometimes specified in a way that does not correspond to plausible behaviour, e.g. the widely used exponential utility function has constant absolute risk averseness, although decreasing absolute risk-averseness often seems more plausible[138].

On a more fundamental level, the very possibility to capture Knightian uncertainty in terms of lotteries is questioned[139]. It was already said that Knight

---

[132] Knight (1921), III, VII, 48

[133] Mas-Colell, Whinston, Green (1995), p. 205

[134] see Mas-Colell, Whinston, Green (1995), p. 171

[135] "Machina Paradox" see Mas-Colell, Whinston, Green (1995), pp. 180f

[136] "Allais Paradox" see Mas-Colell, Whinston, Green (1995), pp. 179f

[137] also called lexicographic preferences.

[138] This is a fair assumption for local approximation.

[139] see Mas-Colell, Whinston, Green (1995), pp. 205f

proposed to distinguish between uncertainty where objective probabilities are given and uncertainty where no such objective probability exists[140]. Subjective probability theory in the Bayesian framework[141] treats these two cases alike[142]. In both cases agents maximize expected utility. The only difference is that under uncertainty people hold subjective beliefs about probabilities and no objective probabilities are given. But this does not accommodate for ambiguity aversion[143] and inertia as suggested by the unwillingness to bet on subjective beliefs whenever they differ[144]. This behaviour cannot be explained by different levels of risk aversion[145].

In general, it is always possible to accommodate criticism "with a theory that defines preferences over somewhat larger and more complex theoretical

---

140 Besides Knightian uncertainty ("true uncertainty" in the words of Knight) there is "sheer ignorance" (see Kirtzner (1997)) which can be interpreted as a consequence of bounded rationality. This is mentioned because the concepts of risk and uncertainty as approaches to formalize uncertainty do not capture sheer ignorance. There are no direct consequences for models of rational choice under uncertainty except the general qualitive caveat that flexibility is important in the face of uncertainty.

141 People explicitly attach subjective probabilities to outcomes. If conditional probability distributions are objectively given prior beliefs are updated as more information becomes available.

142 Bewley (2002), p. 80

143 As suggested by the Ellsberg Paradox (Ellsberg, D. (1961)): Consider two urns denoted R and H. In both urns there are 100 balls. It is assumed that in R 51 balls are black and 49 balls are white. In urn H there is an unknown composition of black and white balls. Now, consider the lottery where one is winning if a black ball is drawn. Which of the two urns would an agent prefer? Many people would prefer urn R. Now consider another lottery where white wins. Here for reasons of consistency people would have to choose urn H. This is because, by choosing R over H in the first experiment they were implicitly assuming that the number of black balls is lower than 51 which in turn means that the number of white balls should be higher than 49. Experiments show, this is not always the case. There appears to be an aversion of ambiguity in the case of urn H.

144 The completeness axiom that is also required for the case of utility maximization, requires people to either prefer one lottery over the other or to be indifferent about them. But if two agents hold different beliefs on the probability of outcomes and the completeness axiom is fulfilled, they should either be willing to change their mind or to bet on the outcome of their belief. But betting does not take place to the extent to which people disagree. The reason, why this is the case may be inertia. Something will only be accepted if acceptance is preferred to rejection.

145 Bewley (2002), pp. 80f

objects[146] than simply the ultimate lottery over outcomes [...] e.g. the decision-maker may value not only what he receives but also what he receives compared with what he might have received by choosing differently. This leads to regret theory."[147] Also, defining state-dependent utilities is a case in point.

Like in the case of utility maximization, the expected utility paradigm can be adjusted to accommodate any possible behaviour; but a tautology is not interesting if no restrictions can be placed on the structure.

4.3 A Remark on Game Theory

Game theory is a mathematical tool which is very useful in modelling choice behaviour in situations wherein people rationally interact with imperfect information and in a specified time ordering in which they carry out their actions[148]. Game Theory requires that all players come to the same conclusions when exposed to the same information, also with respect to probability distributions. If they reach different conclusions, this is only because of different information (Harsanyi Doctrine or common prior assumption)[149]. But this is not as restricting as it seems. If the modeller wishes to model that players reach different conclusions about probabilities, he can do so by adjusting information sets. This is another example of the instrumentalist idea and shows the flexibility of mathematical tools.

4.4 Defending Rational Choice on Normative Grounds

As argued above, if any action can be described in terms of rational choice if only preferences are duly adjusted, the criterion changes: No longer is rational choice intended to be a descriptive theory of choice. It is rather a **template** for the organization of thinking and a means of exposition. It will be argued that using the concept of expected utility maximization as a template is **consistent with the formal rules** of part I.

---

[146] This is a departure from the realist pretension in order to allow for productive speculation (see Chalmers (1994), p. 165) but is consistent with the principle laid down above that realism is maintained only on the level of human behaviour.

[147] Mas-Colell, Winston, Green (1995), p. 180

[148] see Rasmusen (1994), p. 2

[149] see Kreps (1990), p. 111

If someone wants to predict the actions of others, he will be able to cast his assumptions about their likely behaviour into explicit assumptions about their preferences and a description of the relevant situational context. The rest is decision logic. This template is consistent with the author's view of good science: explicit statement of assumptions which are always debatable, and the use of the analytical power of mathematics as a guarantee for truth relative to this set of assumptions[150]. This structuring enhances transparency, facilitates the localization of possible dissent, and predicts the nature of this dissent.

These assumptions will often, indeed, stipulate monetary preferences or behavioural constraints consistent with the classical homo oeconomicus model. Yet, this is because the **modeller has decided** that this describes the behaviour he expects from the acting individuals. If someone else disagrees, he may try to persuade the modeller. If he does not agree, he may construct his own model. However, this can also be done in terms of the (expected) utility maximizing template. In this case, the two models will differ in the sets of assumptions and their disagreement becomes crystal clear[151]: The second modeller might e.g. think that a preference for honesty needs to be taken into account, while the first modeller assumes opportunistic behaviour. If, however, they agree on the same set of assumptions, they can be confident that they will resolve their disagreement by means of logic only. This will assure a maximum of transparency.

Still, especially for choice under uncertainty, some assumptions with regard to incomplete preferences or the independence axiom are very difficult to accommodate within the framework. Some effort will always be made to **translate** behavioural assumptions into the framework[152]. Similarly, existing theories could be reconstructed along the lines of rational choice. Yet, if it becomes too tenuous, it is questionable if this does not outweigh the **analytical convenience** of the expected utility paradigm. The choice of the modeling framework thus depends both on its suitability to accommodate the relevant assumptions and on the availability of alternative concepts[153].

Any behaviour can be described in terms of (expected) utility maximization. Utility maximization is empirically empty but used as a formal template, is consistent with the author's formal rules of good science. It should

---

[150] Simulations are a way to circumvent problems of tractability

[151] Samuelson called that putting one's cards on the table.

[152] Instrumentalism is accepted in the process.

[153] see Gilboa, Schmeidler (1989) and Bewley (2002) for concepts outside the Baysian framework accommodating uncertainty aversion and inertia respectively.

be used if translating relevant assumptions into the framework does not become too tenuous.

4.5 Economics as a Formal vs. Real Science

It was stated above that, if the rational paradigm is empirically empty, the focus is shifted onto preferences. If no claim is made that assumptions are adjusted in a way to make the (expected) utility maximization paradigm a realistic model of human behaviour, microeconomics would be pure decision logic. Purely deductive reasoning is sometimes discarded as fruitless. The argument goes that **no new knowledge** can be found by means of deduction[154].

This is technically true. However, at least in economics, it is not justified to jump to the conclusion that a tautology creates no valuable insights. Indeed, this amounts to the same as claiming that it makes no difference if natural resources exist on the planet or if one is able to extract and use them. In other words: The conclusions derived from deductive reasoning in microeconomics are far from obvious by looking on the assumptions. This is like in Euclidean geometry[155]. The Pythagorean Theorem is contained in the axioms. Still the axioms will probably be to no avail when trying to calculate a triangle. Tautology is valuable because it **enhances relevant knowledge** by making it explicit.

Everybody can choose for himself which assumptions to accept. But as mathematics guarantees truth of conclusions relative to assumptions[156], the scientist is rendering the practitioner a service by figuring out the implications. The rational template of rational choice is nothing else than a transmission belt linking complex phenomena to simple assumptions. It provides people with a decision logic leaving it to them to set behavioural assumptions as it suits them. Or alternatively, if they are to test a given proposition about a phenomenon, it is possible to check its consistency with self-proclaimed behavioural assumptions. So the question is not whether the proposition "*is* true, but rather if it *could* be true"[157].

---

[154] see e.g. Czayka (1991), p. 137

[155] Mises (1949), p. 38 (4.ed. 1996)

[156] A caveat is warranted here: Mathematics also sets constraints. In order to assure tractability the scientist often makes assumption for technical simplification but than claims the results to be general. Often functions are specified. In contract theory many effects assume risk neutrality without giving conclusive proves why this assumption should be innocuous.

[157] see Arrow, Hahn (1971), pp. vi-vii

Another idea on how to avoid making assumptions about preferences is to set up a **prescriptive,** and not descriptive, decision model which would say: Provided that the individual wants to achieve certain aims he should take the recommended action. By using the expected utility framework, it is possible to structure situations of uncertainty and to make decisions according to preestablished consistency rules. Indeed, many people find it difficult to systematically analyse situations of uncertainty. Often there is more information available than is obvious at first sight. Structuring this information and deriving the best[158] action on the basis of present information is helpful[159]. Contingency plans and preliminary assumptions are helpful even in situations where there is Knightian uncertainty or even sheer ignorance. As more information becomes available it can be incorporated into the decision tree by adjusting assumptions. The merit of the Baysian framework as a prescriptive theory can probably best be described by a metaphor: If there is an orchard and **birds** are looking for a place to brood, the chance is high that they choose the tree where a nest already exists. Decision theory is no recipe for creativity. It does not help to catch the birds. But if, by chance, a bird lands, one can make the most of it. The danger with this approach is that people become narrow-minded about information, only taking into account information that was already anticipated[160]. Another problem is that as soon as there are **other agents** involved, prescriptive models must also be descriptive.

Still, it was claimed in part I that objectivity as a common idea about science is often linked to empirical evidence. Therefore, if one is not content to "search for solutions for problems yet to be found" or to engage in a logical pastime, one should try to **plead with the potential user** of the theory that the presented theory tells him something about reality and problem solving. If there is a practical intention it would be absurd if one is not tailoring the assumptions about preferences and situational context to what one thinks to be **relevant behaviour and relevant situations**.

---

[158] Best action relative to subjective believes.

[159] see Mas-Colell, Whinston, Green (1995), p. 178

[160] People are advised to make a map of all their future decisions. In practice, these decisions are not constantly updated. Rather there is a concept and an execution phase. Therefore reactivity to more precise information that was already expected will be high. Contingency plans even tend to increase reactivity because it is possible to immediately put information into context as soon as it arises. But, willingness to deal with unexpected information which one was totally ignorant about might be lower. This need not necessarily be a disadvantage (see Practical Life and Theory in Chapter III9 part III).

In a last attempt, it could be argued that assumptions about preferences of individuals could be avoided if one is taking the **perspective of the government**. It might be interested in the abstract question whether e.g. egoistic behaviour serves the public good[161]. By knowing the consequences of certain behaviour on society, the government can decide whether it is desirable to promote or discourage certain behaviour. But this only seemingly circumvents the problem. The described interest practically implies that the legislator thinks he could **influence his citizen's preferences**, which in turn requires anthropological assumptions[162].

Microeconomics as a purely formal science is useful but too unambitious. As soon as it is intended to pursue economics as a real science the question of the realism of behavioural models cannot be circumvented.

4.6 Realism of Assumptions

Either one wants to show which consequences follow if one accepts certain assumptions. In this case, the model is a pure intellectual pastime. More frequently it will be held by the modeller that the assumptions describe the agent's action reasonably well subject to the restriction that the variety of conceivable preferences must be reduced according to relevance.

To begin with, two things have to be distinguished: On the one hand, it was shown above that (expected) utility maximizing behaviour is a very flexible template. It can be used to model any sort of behaviour if preferences and situational context are duly adjusted. On the other hand, there is the claim - among other things - that people act as if they only cared about money, disliked any effort, kept promises only as long as it suited them, and were able to pursue these aims taking a very sophisticated, far-sighted view, which considered all ramifications of their actions and the actions of others.

Often the homo oeconomicus assumption is taken as a criterion to delineate economics from other social sciences. In the view of the author, this is indeed so when referring to the use of the (expected) utility maximizing template which can accommodate any behavioural assumption but guarantees an argument which is both transparent in assumptions and potentially makes use of the analytical power of mathematics.

---

161 see Sen (1977), pp. 319-322

162 In another context Hutchison (1994), p.29 notes: "Obviously, normative issues [...] are interconnected with positive issues regarding the possibility of their achievement."

With respect to the second interpretation of the homo oeconomicus assumption, which is the traditional interpretation, economics is not in principle dogmatic about this assumption. On the contrary: Especially in recent years, large-scale efforts were made to make assumptions more realistic. There are, however, good reasons to essentially stick with the traditional assumptions or only cautiously enrich them[163].

The homo oeconomicus model comes in two varieties: Fist as a tautology which has to be judged on its methodological merit, and second, as a behavioural model which has to be judged on its suitability in describing relevant behaviour.

4.7 Defending Homo Oeconomicus

4.7.1 Introduction

Given the many doubts about the validity of behavioural assumptions implied in the expected utility maximization concept, there are several possible conclusions that can be drawn. In some cases, the criticism will be accommodated and the behavioural assumptions are modified. Sometimes the criticism only seemingly contradicts the modeling assumptions. In other cases it is real but it can be argued that in the specific situation at hand the problems do not arise. Moreover, it could be argued that, even if it is possible that behaviour is different from the assumptions, in some situations it is safer to assume the worst case scenario.

4.7.2 Relevant Situations

Mill and *Edgeworth* already observed that the homo oeconomicus assumption did not accurately describe all features of human behaviour, but it was sufficient if the captured features were dominant in the situations considered[164]. Therefore, when setting up an economic model, one will not try to create a behavioural model which describes the whole of human behaviour, but rather the features that are held relevant for the purpose of the model. It is, for instance, observed that there is

---

[163] Contrary to the definition of this dissertation, some economists actually define economics as an area of research, where the tradition homo oeconomicus model is valid with slight modifications.

[164] "There is, for example, one large class of social phenomena in which the immediately determining causes are principally those which act through the desire for wealth, and in which the psychological law mainly concerned is the familiar one that a greater gain is preferred to a smaller." Mill (1843): 6.9.3. cit. Hausman (1994), p. 206

altruistic behaviour within families or within small groups. Altruism can be modelled by including the well-being of others in the preference function of the agent. But this will not usually be the case in many business relationships. Therefore, the traditional homo oeconomicus assumption may not be the best description of what happens within families but arguably a better description of what happens in company alliances, top-executive contracting, relationships with suppliers, company transactions involving consultants, investment banks, auditors and lawyers. In brief, following *Edgeworth*, in particular types of activities (war and contract), individuals are, to a good approximation, self-interested[165].

4.7.3 Scope of Concepts

There exist many situations where agents seemingly do not act opportunistically. It may, however, be consistent with opportunism to keep one's promises if there is a long-term relationship, or if there are career concerns. Experience shows that it is far more dangerous to make business as a tourist with a street dealer than with the shopkeeper at home where one is a regular customer. This is not necessarily because the shopkeeper at home is not opportunistic. He could be opportunistic and still act the same way[166].

4.7.4 Robustness – Worst Case

But even if one is not so sure about the correct description, it could be argued that one should always create the mechanism which is "robust [...] designed to survive the 'worst case'"[167]. *Hume* expressed this thought early on by writing: "Political writers have established it as a maxim that, in contriving any system of government, and fixing the several checks and controls of the constitution, every man ought to be supposed a *knave*, and to have no other end, in all his actions, than private interest. By this interest we must govern him, and, by means of it, make him, notwithstanding his insatiable avarice and action, cooperate to public good [...]. It is, therefore, a just *political* maxim, *that every man must be supposed a knave*; though, at the same time, it appears somewhat strange, that a maxim

165 see Sen (1977), p. 318 on why Edgeworth might have portrayed individuals as self-interested although in fact he thinks they are not; see Hausman (1998), p. 69

166 An interesting point can be made here: People often do not like to think about themselves as being opportunistic. So if one asks somebody why he acted in a certain way he will have a high flying moral justification. He is not lying. He has an unrocking belief in what he says (naive opportunist). This might be understood in terms of evolution.

167 Hausman (1998), p. 71 emphasis added by the author

should be true in *politics* which is false in *fact*."[168] A similar argument is brought forward by *Rosenberg* who, although considering economic theory to be predictively empty, upholds it as a "contractarian argument"[169]. *Brennan* and *Buchanan* consent and argue that "using the best estimate of average behaviour leads one systematically to underestimate the welfare loss"[170], implying that rules assuming average behaviour are not robust in the presence of a small number of knaves.

Hausman disagrees on the grounds that "if the outcomes of institutions designed for knaves are much worse than the outcomes designed for actual individuals, and the odds of everybody being a knave were low, then it would be foolish to choose the institutions designed for knaves"[171] and concludes that "economics has normative value in the context of institutional design only if it has predictive value concerning individual behaviour within particular institutions"[172]. Although the issue of robustness is clearly important, as it is plausible to assume that a society of peaceful altruists is very vulnerable to a few aggressive knaves, some would argue that the very assumption of people being knaves is a self-fulfilling prophecy.

There is e.g. the psychological concept of framing[173], which says that people operate in different modes and that the context determines which mode they will be operating in. If the context is one of friendship they will not be opportunistic. If the context is one of knavery they will be knaves. In such a situation, there will be the following dilemma: Either one can take a chance and try to create a friendship context. If one succeeds, gains will be high but losses will also be high in case of failure. Or, one introduces a scheme which is robust to opportunistic behaviour. One can then be rather sure that the intended result will be forthcoming. Of course, it could be that there is a loophole and that the other party feels entitled to be opportunistic if treated like a knave, whereas a greater moral barrier may exist otherwise. However, one could also argue that if an opportunistic party sees that it is treated as a friend it will lose respect and be even more opportunistic.

---

[168] Hume (1741), pp. 40-42 cit. Hausman (1998), p. 67

[169] Rosenberg (1992), p. 20 cit. Hausman (1998), p. 69

[170] Hausman (1998), p. 73 attributes this thought to Brennan and Buchanan (1985), p. 55

[171] Hausman (1998), p. 74

[172] Hausman (1998), p. 77

[173] Lindenberg (2000), pp. 33-38

Weighing the arguments, the author favours the view that descriptive validity is not completely irrelevant to the contractarian problem. Not all situations, however, allow controlling the context in a way suggested by the theory of framing. It will certainly be easier to control the context within an organization than in settings where there is only a one-shot cooperation.

There may be some doubt whether it is appropriate to always assume the worst case in contractarian issues, but it is probably justified to do so in non-relational, inter-firm contracts with high stakes. It will be argued later that mechanisms exist where good cooperation can be assured even in the presence of opportunism.

4.7.5 Instrumentalism in Modeling

The requirement that assumptions should correspond with reality should not be pushed too far. As was argued above, any model will try to keep things relatively simple. So, it will only capture features of behaviour which are relevant in the given situation. It has already been shown that, as a descriptive model, rational choice can be defended at the price of becoming empirically empty: Any behaviour can be formulated in terms of utility maximization. Thus, any behaviour can be modelled "as if" it was the product of maximizing behaviour.

As another example, take the assumption that all human beings are essentially the same. If one observes that there are differences between them one could try to explain these differences by citing situational contingencies. They are different because they have lived through different situations and therefore their preferences will be predictably different. There are a sheer unlimited number of models: A hierarchy of needs or cultural differences due to climate or different experiences in the early years of childhood would all be cases in point. So, in fact, to keep assumptions about anthropologically derived preferences easy, assumptions about the situation are made more complex. This is, incidentally, consistent with the way many people might actually think. When asked to predict the behaviour of others they ask themselves how they would act in their place. This is a mixture of introspection and empathy. Depending on the available information, they will take account of different characteristics of the other person and will be able to put themselves in his shoes. Maybe they know him and do have a view about his character by having observed prior action or knowing his thoughts and values. Maybe there is just circumstantial evidence. So, a profile of his character is constructed by considering, say, his education and probable socialization.

Another example of the instrumentalist idea is how the possibility of one player exhibiting irrational behaviour is modelled in game theory[174]: Irrational behaviour would first be interpreted as rational behaviour by duly adjusting the assumptions about the preference structure (i.e. adjusting the pay-offs for each outcome). Then, uncertainty in forming expectations about a person is not modelled on an individual level but translated into a situation where nature conducts a random experiment. It is clear that this modeling set-up does not reproduce the real situation in an isomorphic way. Take a fighting situation. If somebody picks a fight, although he is likely to get hurt and there is nothing to be gained, it could be said that this is irrational. This behaviour could of course also be interpreted as highly rational if it is assumed that he valued the "honour" he had to defend higher than the prospect of getting hurt. If one player is unsure if the other player will be rational or rather irrational in the sense described above, this could be modelled as a situation where nature chooses a type from a population of agents. This choice of nature is not observed, but composition of types is known to both players. Although the description of the situation would be that there is a single person and that one does not know if he is rational or not, the problem is first altered to the effect that one considers a single person but one does not know how much value he puts on his "honour". In a second step one is not looking at a single person any more but at a situation where there are, say, 10 people who put high value to their "honour" and 90 people who put a higher value to their health. From this group, nature randomly chooses one type. For reasons of convenient modeling, realism is sacrificed.

4.8 Bounded Rationality vs. Unconscious Rationality

4.8.1 Introduction

Often, it is said that economic models presuppose a degree of rationality that most people do not possess. Therefore, they cannot be good descriptions of human behaviour. This argument e.g. assumes that there are situations where people are "intendedly rational, but only *limited* so"[175]. The bounded rationality argument is at the heart of economics of incomplete contracts, and is certainly a problem that should be taken seriously. In the following, however, a defence of rationality shall be mounted, claiming that people are sometimes *superrational but unconsciously so*. It will be argued that in areas where evolutionary forces are strong, people will

---

[174] Also the modelling of different information processing via information sets – mentioned above – would be an example of instrumentalism

[175] Simon (1947), xxiiif.

act rationally even if they just follow the maxims and routines they have learned in a process of socialization[176].

4.8.2 The Evolutionary Mechanism

Evolution of rules and routines is a fact. The crucial part of the argument will be to show that under some circumstances evolution will converge to the rational solution. Therefore, the evolutionary mechanism will have to be described.

The two important prerequisites for evolution are variance and selection. The starting point is that rules and institutions evolve spontaneously within groups and are adopted mostly for their emotional appeal or by chance[177]. These rules come in the form of narratives or maxims. As there are many groups (populations, companies), there will be variance.

The group and with it the rule will only survive if it has a certain degree of success to secure resources. If there is a spectacular failure the old rule will die (reform, death of group, invasion by neighbour). In the end, only successful rules will survive because the groups which have adopted them will prevail in a process of selection (competition among populations, companies). But there could also be a conscious selection mechanism in the form of trial-and-error[178]. A company could try out a sales structure. If it does not work the company will change it. Contract lawyers are transaction specialists. They assist in the formulation of many contracts and advise their clients. They will see that some contracts have worked well while others have created a lot of problems. So, when setting up model contracts, they will sort out the good contracts. In brief, the basic idea is that the "structures we observe have survived because of their merit in coaxing Pareto-efficient behaviour out of agents who do not know what this means"[179].

The selection process will only work for vital rules, i.e. rules which affect performance of the group in a crucial way. The focus of interest here is problems of transactions. Can rules governing transactions be regarded as vital rules? Information asymmetry with respect to effort, choice or quality of product leads to a welfare loss because the hazards of contracting will prevent the parties from

---

[176] see Alchian (1950)

[177] Smith (1991), p. 892 notes that "rules evolve in response to experience, not logical analysis, and policies that are disequilibrating (causing the manager trouble) are altered".

[178] see Smith (1991), pp. 891f for a simple scenario where this might happen

[179] Smith (1991), pp. 894

capturing potential gains of trade. If the kind of product and the business environment leads to information problems, the company that leaves these problems unattended to will make fewer profits than comparable other companies which are more successful in solving this problem. These companies will eventually drive the first company out of business (by buying it or by bidding up resource prices and destroying margins). Of course, companies can be imagined which have such an edge on their competitors that they will survive even if transactions are organized sub-optimally. Selection will therefore be most rigorous where the relevant problem (information asymmetry) is worst and no overwhelmingly strong competitive advantage exists. This will e.g. be true for supply contracts in mature industries.

The evolutionary process converging to the rational result will only take place if the problem that has to be dealt with is of a general nature and will remain stable over time. It will be stronger if the frequency of selection is high. If this is the case, the key implication is that there is convergence to results that are commensurable with rational construction without requiring the agents to make complicated calculations. It is sufficient that they act according to the rules and maxims that they are socialized to use. Thus, contract types can be seen as the product of an evolution, which solved the problem of information asymmetry. If they are used, they are normally not used because of careful analysis but rather because in the given situation the contract type in question is normally used. The basic contract types of private law are a perfect example. In Civil Law countries, they are the codification and systematization of the mostly Roman legal tradition which was available in casuistic form. Dealing with the eternal problems of exchange they can be viewed as the distilled wisdom of more than two millennia.

4.8.3 Method of Evolutionary Economics

The question could be asked why one should bother with these problems when evolution is likely to take care of it. The modest answer would be: In order to understand institutions; the more ambitious, in order to take a short-cut within the evolutionary process much as in genetic engineering. Evolution comes at a price. It is a process of "creative destruction". So, maybe money can be saved, but evolutionary forces are also not equally present in all instances. Maybe there is a situation where evolution did not have a chance to occur because the industry is rather young, so that there has not been much time for evolution to take place. Maybe the learning process by trial-and-error does not work because every project is sui generis, no obvious parallels exist without a theoretical framework (general problem of complex phenomena) and - as a consequence - because the problem is not seen, no centralized and specialized units within organizations will be created; but this is the prerequisite for learning and innovation to take place[180]. Another reason why the process of selection does not work is the absence of competition (department, monopoly). Alternatively, the problem may not be sufficiently severe to make the company fail. Still it can be quite severe or become more severe in the future when the industry becomes mature. Moreover, even if the solution of the problem only gives the company an additional edge it will allow the company to grow faster than its competitors and will therefore be indirectly responsible for its future survival. Less spectacularly, it may just increase profits. The evolutionary approach can very plausibly be defended in many contracting situations. Transactions are omnipresent, and they are crucially important for the welfare of a society based on property rights and characterized by a high degree of separation of labour.

One can probably find most scope for improvement where evolutionary forces are weak. In such a situation, it might be very good to follow the recommendations that where derived analytically. In areas where evolutionary forces are strong, one can try to understand the institutions that have developed. As these are complex, they cannot be understood without a theory. The analytical approach provides such a theoretical framework. Insofar as the predictions of the model do not correspond to the observed institution, one can try to learn from the observed information to make the model better. The methodology of evolutionary economics could be sketched as follows:

1) **Analytically derive the results of human interaction relative to assumptions that are thought to correctly describe human action:** E.g. neoclassical price theory assumes that there are homogenous goods, perfect information and perfect competition. In such a situation, demand and supply functions can be derived from the buyer's utility functions and the seller's cost functions. Horizontal aggregation yields market demand and supply curves. The point where they intersect allows deriving traded quantity and market price in equilibrium. If the economy is not in equilibrium it can be shown that, under some circumstances, the system is stable and tends to equilibrium.

2) **Understand institutions and observable behaviour in terms of this approach:** In the case of neoclassical price theory, the problem is that this theory does not tell anything about the observed institutions, like different kinds of contracts, traders or independent experts offering

[180] Adam Smith has already argued that this was an important ingredient of innovation.

advice. Traditionally, economists therefore assumed that the reason for these institutions was market power, i.e. a divergence from optimal competition.

3) **In an iterative approach, assure consistency between assumptions and observed institutions by adjusting assumptions:** Economics of information changed neoclassical assumptions to the extent that information was assumed to be costly and asymmetric. Starting from these assumptions, it could be shown that, e.g. in the used car market, market failure could arise if no independent traders and experts concerned about their reputation are present. Looking at the car market[181], this seemed to fit quite well.

4) **Predict behaviour and institutions in other areas where evolutionary forces are present:** The same problems exist on the art market. So, it could be predicted that similar institutions would be found there, which is the case. No such problems arise in the market for vegetables. Therefore, it is predicted that no such institutions will be found there[182].

5) **Critically analyse existing institutions:** It is e.g. common in the Anglo-Saxon world that there are punitive damages in private tort law. It is a widespread opinion that this leads to excesses. There are indeed cases where companies paid millions or even billions of dollars to the plaintiff, exceeding the original damage many times over. The US Supreme Court recently ruled[183] that the ratio of awarded compensation and original damage may not be double digit. One might argue that this is unwise: It should rather not exceed the inverse of the probability of detection if the intention is to provide efficient incentives for, say, companies to not pollute the environment. Of course, the argument that the functioning of a system requires measures which unjustly favour one person is not well accepted by many people[184]. A second benefit is that the idea can be used to explain, describe and distinguish different contract types, institutions in company law and insolvency law, etc., by offering an outside perspective. It is a basis for comparative studies of law or a basis for criticism.

---

[181] Akerlof, G; (1970)

[182] Although in times of increased environmental concerns this may and to some extent has already changed.

[183] N.N. (2003), THE ECONOMIST, April 10

[184] Indeed such punishments, if well calibrated, can be argued to be extremely cheap ways to induce compliance with rules (see footnote 344).

6) **Design institutional arrangements from scratch where a new project is undertaken:** If a new company organizing e.g. internet auctions like Ebay is set up, the question for the developers is how they shall organize the internet platform. In such a case it is useful to learn the lessons of information asymmetry and organize the system in a way that helps to record and make available the seller's track-record.

The general idea is to build models starting from plausible assumptions, compare them to institutions that exist in well-established markets, understand these institutions as a product of evolution – at least in areas where it seems plausible that evolution could have occurred (variance, selection!), improve models, make predictions for other areas where evolution occurred. If this prediction is correct, this corroborates the model and suggests that the same approach can be used for social engineering where evolution has not occurred.

4.9 Piecemeal Social Engineering

The evolutionary assumption is in the spirit of *Popper's* "piecemeal social engineering" which is sceptical with respect to total rational reconstruction of reality ("utopian social engineering"). The understanding of organically grown institutions is a source of knowledge of its own. This is because there is the assumption of "concealed wisdom", not because it is old or derived from tradition as in conservatism, but because it must be interpreted under some circumstances as the result of a selection or learning process. This is distinct from the hubris of rationalists who want to redesign everything from scratch.

4.10 Objection of Historicism

There is the criticism that the idea of evolution falls prey to historicism. The historical school tries to find the laws that govern the course of history. The idea is that if it is understood how history evolves, and if it is possible to acertain which stage in this evolution has been currently reached, it can be predicted which stage will follow. Future can thus be predicted[185]. Marxism is a typical example of historicism. The criticism of Popper[186] was that historicist ideas had no empirical content. If the whole history of men must be interpreted as the history of class struggles, any system of moral values, any answer that an acting individual would give concerning the intention of his action will be interpreted as a narrative

---

[185] see the Chapter on the philosophy of August Cieszkowski in Mader (1993b), p. 123

[186] see Blaug (1990), pp. 36f

covering this irrefutable premiss, and indeed any such observation and interview can be interpreted in terms of this premiss. It is a template, not a theory. If somebody who is poor kills somebody who is rich, it can be interpreted as an act of revolt. If he does not kill him it can be interpreted as the consequence of a moral system devised to suppress the poor.

Microeconomics interprets everything in terms of rational choice. This is also a template as was argued above. Therefore, utility maximization has no empirical content of its own, but it can be used to organize thinking about human behaviour. The benefit is transparency of assumptions and the use of mathematics. No such methodical benefit can be seen in Marxist theory unless it is interpreted as a theory with empirical content that predicts e.g. a high chance of social unrest if some social parameters like a certain degree of income inequality and a certain ratio of absolute poverty are present. If it interprets norms and values as reflecting the current state of property rights of productive resources this may be an interesting heuristic. But it only becomes a theory if one predicts how the norms in a certain country will be, given data about property of means of production. If this prediction fails, following Popper[187], there should not be made ad hoc modifications to save the theory. Also, other influences like a common idea of justice, as expressed in the Kantian categorical imperative or in the golden moral rule as expressed in the biblical principle "do not do onto others what you do not want them to do on you", could also be considered as potential sources of the ethical code. Marxist theory is interesting as a heuristic, but more dangerous and less useful than utility maximization as a template.

Now, what about evolutionary theory as applied to social sciences? First, what about evolutionary theory in biology? Evolution is a fact, both in biology and in the social sciences. The composition of genes in the population did evolve over time. Similarly, it can be seen in the history of law that also contractual forms evolved. Quite another thing is the evolutionary mechanism: It is argued in biology that there is selection according to the fitness of a population to survive. In the social sciences, it is argued that rules and institutions survive, if they helped to secure resources in a superior way.

The criticism of historicism is justified if it was said that in history reason is always realised, and that all history has to be seen as the process of revealing reason. If in contrast, the fact is acknowledged that there is evolution and an evolutionary mechanism is described, which yields testable predictions, this is different. E.g. if it can be established that species A was fitter to withstand

---

187 Blaug (1994), p. 112

drought than species B for, say, physiological reasons, and a change in the frequency of drought in a certain area was associated with the expansion of species A and the decline of species B, this would corroborate the theory. In the same way, it could be argued that in the age of industrialization, raising capital and employing professional managers became increasingly important. The rise of the public limited company suggests that there was an evolutionary mechanism at work.

These arguments, however, also reveal a weakness. There obviously is the danger that one is just making theory and evidence fit ex post facto. This will always be a problem with complex phenomena[188] which can only be understood if there is a theory in the first place. This problem can be alleviated if predictions about future events can be made. In fact, the strong competitive dynamic of a globalized economy may be a very interesting laboratory for this purpose.

5 Introspection in Economics

5.1 Internal dimension and Instability

A crucial question is why a behavioural model should be considered to correspond with reality. The standard answer in the natural sciences would be that this depends on whether it is able to make successful predictions. To verify a model one could therefore test predictions by setting up an experiment.

There is, however, one important difference between the natural and the social sciences: In the natural sciences, the fact that a stone falls when dropped can be observed. The observation exhausts the phenomenon. In contrast, human action has both an external and an internal dimension. This internal dimension is the intention of the agent and cannot be readily observed. It could be argued that it is enough to observe the external action and that intention can be safely ignored. The problem, however, is that action always very much depends on the situational context and is therefore unstable; but stability is a basic requirement for systematic empirical methods.

The following example shows that a slight modification of the situational context may totally change the prediction: One could probably find a non-

---

[188] "While it is certainly desirable to make our theories as falsifiable as possible, we must also push forward into fields where, as we advance, the degree of falsifiability necessarily decreases. This is the price we have to pay for an advance into the field of complex phenomena." Hayek (1967), p. 29 cit. Caldwell (1994), p. 144

negative correlation between wealth and the riskiness of people's portfolios. One could argue that people tend to value the dollar which buys them food or shelter more than the dollar buying the swimming pool for the horses. But now consider a poor man who desperately wants to buy a fancy car because he thinks that only by having this car can he impress the woman he is in love with. It would be plausible to assume that he could actually be risk-loving, valuing an investment at or higher than its expected value.

So, for all the empirical data that might have been collected for the average case, one would readily discard the resulting prediction and proceed on the basis of introspection. By looking at the internal dimension of action one can indeed hope to find more stability. This internal dimension can be thought of as the agent's character or his spontaneity of action.

5.2 Blackboxing vs. Qualitative Method

Behavioural models differ from models in the natural sciences. Although there is some scope for quantitative methods both by conducting controlled experiments and by using econometric techniques on available data, qualitative methods are an important basis for behavioural models. This arises from the concern that black box models of human behaviour seem especially problematic, as they prove to be very inflexible. Unfortunately, in management theory these black box models are very popular.

A typical example would be a study claiming that benchmarking has proved to be bad. This result would be obtained by interviewing managers of several listed companies, asking them if they used benchmarking and running a regression looking for is a significant correlation between the use of benchmarking and stock market underperformance. If such a correlation could indeed be found, it would be argued that the hypothesis that benchmarking was bad is consistent with empirical data. It would then be common to argue for a "change of paradigm", replacing benchmarking by another high-flying concept called "reinventing the business process". Even if it is assumed that such a study has taken into account that benchmarking is used more often in mature (and therefore less profitable) industries and did actually compare companies of the same industry, the conclusion is utterly inadequate. A qualitative analysis would have provided the same result and more. If the whole incentive system of the industry is tailored to meet relative performance measures, this will penalize creativity and risk taking. This is indeed a problem if only rival companies in the same industry are benchmarked. Yet, benchmarking companies of other industries (e.g. the electricity company benchmarks the credit card company to see whether its invoicing can be improved or the automatic teller machine company which has to service hardware spread geographically is benchmarking the mobile telephone company which has to service their transmitters) may actually be an important step in "reinventing" the business process. So at best, such studies do not tell anything new and at worst they cheat the reader into believing that something that required so much hard-working data gathering must be correct[189].

5.3 Heuristic or Independent Source?

An intermediary position could be considered allowing qualitative methods for heuristic purposes but insisting on quantitative methods to follow up on them. This is the standard textbook recommendation which can be summed up as: "Develop a formal model; derive a hypothesis and empirically test that hypothesis with technical econometrics"[190]. Of course, one could probably find - with much trouble - a group of people desperately in love and with a slight inferiority complex, run a regression and find that they are disproportionately keen investors in derivatives or a bit less sophisticated in lottery tickets. But what would be gained? It could be argued that by making the test, it was possible to verify if the predicted effect was actually happening. Otherwise, the qualitative approach would tend to be dogmatic[191].

Consider this example from contract theory: Principal-agent models suggest that there is a trade-off between efficient incentive provision and risk-sharing. Still, an empirical study "suggest[s] a positive relationship between measures of uncertainty and incentives rather than the posited negative trade-off"[192]. But this may well be, because risky situations are disproportionably situations where some new project is tried. New projects make it difficult to effectively monitor agents because there is no prior experience which would have allowed the setting up of a production function. If monitoring is not viable, incentive pay is the only way to provide incentives. Alternatively, agents in theses areas could be less risk-averse due to self-selection effects.

---

[189] This epistemic pessimism with regard to empirical studies in microeconomics seems to be shared by Caldwell (1994), p. 147. The reason why this seems so provocative is that "the grip of positivism, with its optimism and, yes, its arrogance about the methods of science, has yet to be completely loosened within economics" (Caldwell (1994), p. 149. This has long been the position of the Austrian subjectivists.

[190] Colander (1994); p. 35

[191] see Czayka (1991); p. 137

[192] Prendergast (2002)

This example suggests that it is always possible to save a hypothesis by generating new hypotheses. *Popper* wanted to restrain these "ad-hoc" hypotheses to statements that could be subjected to a new test. This, however, ignores that introspection might be an independent source of knowledge which can validate a model just as consistency with empirical data could.

5.4 The Hermeneutical Method and a priorism

Especially if one is not concerned with an average agent, but rather with an individual agent in a well-defined and rather unique situation[193], one will probably not discard the information that might be available on this agent as irrelevant and use the behavioural model that was derived in a standard situation in trying to find out what the average agent would do. One would rather try to tentatively model the agent's behaviour using all the available information. There will be empirical facts: There will be information on the agent's background. There may be accounts of his actions in the past. There may even be interviews conducted with this person. The basic idea is that the observer will try to "understand" by asking himself how he would act in the given situation, taking account of the fact that the agent may be a quite different person. However, both are still human beings, so some commensurability can arguably be assumed.

Mises claims that there is complete commensurability between the perceiver and the perceived object in social sciences. He argues that human action is always subject to rationality as the only category available to the human mind. As perceiving subjects, human beings have the same faculty of cognition at their disposal as in their role as acting individuals. So, the rational human being studies the consequences of rationality in human action. It is therefore not by empirical data that human behaviour is predicted but by mere introspection[194]. In the natural sciences this is quite different: There is no a priori commensurability. Perceptions are rationally structured and it is hoped that there is commensurability between

[193] This is precisely the emphasis of game theory, see Rasmusen (1994), p. 2.

[194] "The real thing which is the subject matter of praxeology, human action, stems from the same source as human reasoning. Action and reason are congeneric and homogeneous; they may even be called two different aspects of the same thing. That reason has the power to make clear through pure ratiocination the essential features of action is a consequence of the fact that action is an offshoot of reason. The theorems attained by correct praxeological reasoning are not only perfectly certain and incontestable, like the correct mathematical theorems. They refer, moreover, with the full rigidity of their apodictic certainty and incontestability to the reality of action as it appears in life and history. Praxeology conveys exact and precise knowledge of real things." Mises (1949), p. 39

the human representation of reality and the unanimated world because of the metaphysical assumption of the stability of nature.

Mises therefore argues that, because there is a complete structural symmetry between the perceiving subject and the object of cognition in the social sciences, it is possible to derive a priori synthetic truths by introspection. It was, however, noted that even if the existence of Kantian *a priori* synthetic propositions is acknowledged, "they have a limited power to generate substantive implications for economic behaviour"[195]. In fact, "a number of *a posteriori* auxiliary propositions are also required, such as transitivity or consistency of choices"[196]. This highlights the importance of behavioural experiments.

As was already mentioned, "Understanding"[197] as a method proceeds by "psychological reduction". This is arguably an alternative way of achieving some kind of objectivity other than using controlled experimentation. Basically, it is important for the observer to reflect on his own intentionality, on the context, on grammatical differences, and to fade them out by becoming conscious of them. The objective is to put oneself in the shoes of another person in order to anticipate his behaviour. But, somehow, in the end, assumptions about preferences have to be made. Claiming that these assumptions are true regardless of the empirical evidence make the approach potentially dogmatic[198] or arbitrary. Yet, this need not be the case. "Understanding" is not just, as it is sometimes claimed, a euphemism for arbitrariness. Behavioural assumptions are required to be "critically acceptable"[199]. "The experts may disagree, but only on the grounds of a reasonable interpretation of the evidence available."[200]

---

[195] Blaug (1994), pp. 132f

[196] Blaug (1994), p. 132; It was shown in the Section on rational choice the mere fact that behaviour is purposeful is not enough. A number of additional axioms e.g. the independence axiom has to be assumed. For these assumptions, specifying rationality independent tests can be formulated e.g. like in the experiments that lead to the Allais Paradox. They are therefore *a posteriori*.

[197] "Verstehen"

[198] Czayka (1991), p. 137

[199] Boland (1994), p. 164 argues that many disciples of Popper claim that the notion of "critical acceptance" was much more important to Popper than "falsificationism" which was unduly emphasized by Lakatos and the subsequent discussion.

[200] Mises (1949), p. 52

The historical method[201] is therefore – in the view of the author – an important and independent source of knowledge that is indispensable if the specific agents and not the average agent are considered, as is the case in contract theory. The cognitive status of economics is not only "empirical regularity" as in the natural sciences; but empirical evidence, if available, will always be welcome.

6 Empirical Methods

6.1 Introduction

Having agued that introspection is an independent source of knowledge, the same is true for empirical evidence. These two sources of knowledge do not compete against each other but rather complement each other.

6.2 Reviving Monism

6.2.1 Theory of Revealed Preferences

The theory of revealed preferences tries to show that the preference structure of an agent can, in principle, be derived by systematic observation. This can be seen as part of the neo-positivist programme of only accepting statements that are either directly observable or analytically derived from directly observable statements. If this is possible, it would question the above statement that the cognitive status of economics is – at least in part – introspection.

The theory of revealed preferences, however, requires stability in the form of consistency-like restrictions on rational behaviour that were discussed above in the Section on rational choice; but even if one feels comfortable with assuming stability, which cannot be proven empirically, it will be practically impossible to derive the whole set of beliefs by observation. Therefore, it is more a theoretical possibility than a practical methodology to derive the preference structure.

6.2.2 Panphysicalism

Panphysicalism has the vision to suspend the difference between the social sciences and the natural sciences. If the human being can be interpreted as a

[201] In management this is often somewhat loosely referred to as "relying on (business) judgement".

mechanical creature, it should be possible to model his behaviour by a set of theories from the natural sciences. The light waves from a given object would hit the retina, create a stimulus, would be conducted to the brain, cause chemical processes that eventually conclusively lead to an act of thinking, which in turn might elicit a physical reaction. Human behaviour would no longer be modelled by situational analysis as described above. Everything would be the result of a purely physical, material and mechanical process accessible by the method of the natural sciences and therefore resolving scientific dualism. So far, panphysicalism has shown itself to be fruitless and, even taking a very optimistic outlook, the prospects for it to succeed are low[202].

6.3 Interviews

Interviews can be used to validate models both on the level of behavioural assumptions and on the level of overall predictions. In in-depth interviews, people can be asked about their motivations. So, instead of deriving the preference function by systematic observation as in the theory of revealed preference, one is directly asking people for their preference structure. The problem is that it is not clear if people are reflecting their choices sufficiently in order to be able to answer such questions; and even if they are able they might not be willing to do so. There will probably be much deception and self-deception, which will be difficult to fade out with interview techniques.

Another reason to conduct an interview is to ask about facts. This will be helpful in drawing up the situational setting of a model or in verifying if a model can be applied. So, in contract theory for instance, it is important to know the details of a transaction in order to be able to devise a mechanism that deals with potential problems.

The third motivation for conducting interviews would be to tap business judgement in order to test a theoretical solution. In applied economics it is often the case – as will be argued in more detail later – that there are many different effects which together are relevant to the problem. In this case it will be necessary to apply business judgement in order to weigh the different arguments. Yet, business judgement only arises close to the specific problems of the industry and will often not be available to the modeller. So, he can translate the model into a fictional case study and ask experts whether they think that a problem as described to them is adequately solved[203].

---

202 see Mises (1949), p. 18

203 Kreps (1990), p. 8 calls this the "market test".

6.4 Controlled Experiment

The ideal in the empirical sciences is controlled experiment. Yet, for many economic models, like models of the stock market or models of the economy as a whole, this is not feasible. When it comes to behavioural models, however, such controlled experiments can indeed be made. It is e.g. possible to let people play the prisoner's dilemma or the repeated prisoner's dilemma in an experimental setting. There is evidence that the prisoner's dilemma will be played according to the predictions of game theory, but this is not the case for the repeated prisoner's dilemma with a definite ending. Specifically, the rational prediction in this case is that the game will unravel backwards[204]. Still, people normally cooperate. This leads to the question asked by *Smith*: "Why is it that human subjects in the laboratory frequently violate the canons of rational choice when tested as isolated individuals, but in the social context of exchange institutions serve up decisions that are consistent (as though by magic) with predictive models based on individual rationality?"[205]

In the above case of the repeated prisoner's dilemma with a definite ending, a little detail in the description of the experimental setting can be changed and predictions will fit the evidence. Cooperation is indeed the rational strategy if there is uncertainty about when the game will end[206]. Therefore, the question can be asked whether there are many situations in life where long-term relationships are known to have a definite ending. If this is not the case - as might plausibly be argued – the relevance of the above experiment is put into question. Consider the evolutionary argument that people do not make complicated calculations but live by norms and maxims which arguably converge to the rational result. So, given that there is frequently uncertainty about the ending of long-term relationships, people may just not make the distinction when confronted with artificial experimental settings.

For another example in the same spirit, consider the following: If people are asked to name probabilities under which they prefer a gamble, stipulating 100 dollars or death as possible outcomes, to a gamble offering 10 dollars for sure, many people would refuse to name such a probability, contrary to the continuity assumption implicit in expected utility theory. But, if asked to either accept 10 dollars now or drive to a nearby location where a 100 dollar check is waiting,

---

[204] In the last round, the player defects, which is why there is no reason not to defect in the round before etc.

[205] Smith, V. (1991), p. 894

[206] Kreps (1990), pp. 505f; Gibbons (2001), p. 9 footnote 7

most people would probably get into their car. This, even though driving the car will marginally increase their chances of death[207]. Once again, an artificial experimental setting was created.

Another problem is self-fulfilling prophecies in the social sciences. If, for instance, a model predicting insolvency is widely used among banks, it will probably be very accurate in predicting insolvencies. This, however, does not automatically mean that it is a good model. If the banks act on the presumption that a company will "go bust" then they will call back credit lines and impose other restrictions, thereby actually increasing the chance of insolvency. Nature, on the contrary, does not care about human thinking.

Experiments are interesting empirical checks. There are, however, good reasons to mistrust them in some circumstances. They should therefore be regarded in social sciences as a piece in the puzzle and not as the ultimate yardstick as in the natural sciences.

6.5 Econometrics – Historical Experiment

Conclusions about overall effects cannot be tested in controlled experiments. It is too difficult to reproduce conditions. Only historical experiments are available. The challenge with historical experiments is to find comparable situations. Every situation is unique. Of course, it can be argued that two situations are similar with respect to relevant factors and all other factors can be modelled as white noise, but this approach already presupposes a theory about all relevant factors and is therefore not pure data mining.

Still, even if comparable situations are found, there are often many factors but only little data and low scale levels. Then, econometric methods do not work[208]. When studying capital markets it will be difficult to set up experiments. Yet, a lot of data is available. This makes econometric time series analysis viable. The problem gets more severe for the economy as a whole because, at the macro level, controlled experiment is usually not available as in the financial markets. Furthermore, compared to the financial markets, less data is available and more factors have to be taken into account. The multitude of factors can be reduced by using aggregated entities. This approach will be further explored below.

---

[207] see Kreps (1990), p. 76

[208] There is a general doubt if data in economics is good enough to produce telling tests (see Caldwell (1994), p. 144 who refers to the book "The Inexact and Separate Theory of Science of Economics " of Daniel Hausman (1992)).

In contract theory, econometric tests are basically feasible. The problem is the variety of cases and the large amount of variables that have to be taken care of. Collecting cases will be difficult for confidentiality. Many variables and a small sample is, however, a bad starting point for econometric testing.

6.6 Informal evidence

With respect to econometrics, *Summer* criticized[209] the tendency for ever more complicated formal econometric tests. He claims that they have had little impact on the evolution of macroeconomics and are rather driven by the fact that the cost of computing has dramatically decreased. He argues that it is far more convincing to have a multitude of informal, low-level empirical evidence than to look for the single, formal and decisive test. *Mayer's* argument is in the same vein, when saying that economists focus too much on the strongest links of their reasoning, neglecting the weakest link[210]. It is argued that for theory appraisal it is rather the consistency of the entire picture which matters.

6.7 The Problem of Aggregation

In economics it is rarely possible to determine empirical success in a conclusive way, largely because of the impossibility of controlled experiment and the absence of constant relations. So, economics resides more on methodological individualism than on systematic empirical testing of its predictive success.

The idea is that, if the actions of individual agents can be logically aggregated, it is possible to derive an aggregate prediction. This prediction will have empirical relevance to the extent that the underlying behavioural assumptions are empirically valid and the analytical construction is correct. This is the main idea behind the requirement to make behavioural modeling assumptions realistic.

There is, however, reason not to push too far the requirement of consistency within behavioural models. This is especially true where the thread of causality wears very thin due to problems of aggregation. This is the case for situations where the precision of measurement is too low relative to the sensitivity of the model (see Chaos Theory), but there are also problems of aggregation if there are too many countervailing effects and the scale level of data is low. The predicted

---

209 Summers (1991) cit. Backhouse (1994), p. 15

210 Mayer (1993) cit. Backhouse (1994), p. 15

overall effect often results from a *bundle* of different effects. It is impossible to assign each effect its relative strength. The problem of countervailing effects is quite common in applied economics. Theoretical models often only consider a single effect, but in applied economics it is the problem and not analytical convenience which dictates the scope of effects that have to be considered[211].

Consider the example of a lawyer who is working for a company compared to a lawyer working for a private individual. It is likely that the company is less risk-averse than the lawyer. It is also likely that the company is more sophisticated about legal matters than a private client, and that it can therefore better appreciate the lawyer's qualification. Better knowledge of the law will also allow the company to more effectively monitor the lawyer's performance. Finally, the chance of the company becoming a regular client and its capability to influence the lawyer's reputation in business circles is higher; but which effect was the more important? Could the news spreading capability be important while knowledge of law is unimportant? If it is possible to find a company which is sophisticated about law but for some reason not a likely future client and not well entrenched in business circles, and another company for which this is also the case, but a difference in contracting is found, this would suggest that reputation effects are present. But how many cases can be found where everything is the same except for one variable?

If it is not possible to quantify the different effects, the problem cannot be solved by just taking sums. Unfortunately, predictive precision with respect to time and extent is bad in economics. Economic theories are most often statements of tendency[212]. However tempting[213], creating virtual precision[214] by making strong assumptions will come at the heavy price of a loss of generality. Worse, the transparency of the model will be affected. One possibility is to *circumvent* the problem by only considering cases wherein all effects point in the same direction. If, however, one wants to extend the analysis to other problems, the best possible method to weigh the relative strength of countervailing effects is by making a judgement in the light of specific circumstances. The criterion for this argument will not be strict causality but rather adequacy within the objective framework defined by the model. There will, however, remain ambiguity. This idea is related to the idea of applied microeconomics as an art, which will be treated below.

---

211 "problem orientation", see Colander (1994), p. 44

212 see Hutchison (1994), p. 30

213 There exists "the tendency to oversell the subject" (Blaug (1994), p. 118) to respond to the demands for precision from government and businesses.

214 see Colander (1994), p. 41 who calls this a violation of "the law of significant digits".

One should note that problems of aggregation cannot be expected to be solved by simulation. The advantage of simulation is that it helps to numerically solve a problem for which there is no closed-form solution. Simulations can therefore give models more empirical validity by allowing for more complex and more realistic assumptions. Simulation, however, cannot overcome the problem of countervailing effects in the presence of statements of tendency. The only way this could be simulated is by specifying functions which would create artificial precision.

6.8 Macro modeling: Beyond Methodological Individualism

The alternative to micro-foundation would be to accept a model which rests on black box statistical regularities or patterns which can be found between different entities on the macro-level. If it is e.g. possible to find out that an increase in the money supply is correlated with economic growth and that there is at least some stability in the system, one could build a model around this relationship.

Yet, it must be clear that correlation is different from causality[215]. It was also argued above that, contrary to the natural sciences, it is an irrefutable fact that any aggregated effect is the consequence of human action. Therefore, it is necessary to assume that there is always a fine tissue of interrelated effects on the micro-level that exist, but which cannot be sorted out because of the complexity of the model. Some would argue that there should at least exist the possibility to interpret the model on an individual level[216] without leading to absurd consequences.

A good example of an area where micro-foundation does not look very promising due to problems of aggregation is the prediction of short-term share prices on capital markets. A full scale attempt to model share prices from the perspective of methodological individualism would model the interaction of agents and show how their interaction leads to price formation. Another approach would be to take factors which can be explained to be relevant in order to predict share prices like market-to-book ratio, GDP growth, business or consumer confidence and run a regression to attribute weights to the factors. Assuming

---

[215] There is, however, also a statistical notion of causality. It is used if a potential explinans is not only correlated with the explinandum but also increases the precision of prediction if added to the model (the variance between the model's prediction and the observed explinandum decreases). e.g. Granger (1969) and (1988)

[216] Thus Modigliani's life-cycle hypothesis or Friedman's permanent income hypothesis provide such a microfoundation for Keynes' claim that the marginal propensity to consume is less than 1. see Hausman (1994), p. 209

stability for the future, the model would then be used for prediction. Thus, microeconomic models are used to identify relevant factors but quantification is done by running regressions. Alternatively, one could ask which variables yielded the best ex post facto predictions accepting any variable (i.e. without restraining the list of possible factors to variables which are plausibly connected to the explinandum). Yet, the danger in trying to make the model fit the data is that it will fit this particular data set but nothing else. This is the reason why the obtained relationship must be tested with a control set of data. Only if this produces good results can it be hoped that a general pattern has been discovered.

Evidence from models predicting share prices suggest that purely statistical models derived by data mining are more successful than models based on macroeconomic variables or fundamental company data[217]. This leads to the old dilemma: What should be valued more, past predictive success, which might as well be purely coincidental, or plausible construction? As stated above, tension should be preserved to stimulate further research. The recent surge in behavioural finance can be seen in this context. The phenomenon of overshooting is a good example of this. It can be established by statistical methods that prices tend to overshoot in financial markets, suggesting that trends are self-reenforcing, but the underlying herd behaviour can also be explained on the individual level. It is like choosing between two restaurants. One is recommended in the guide, but maybe in the neighbouring restaurant there are more people. If it is assumed that these people also make choices on the basis of the best information available to them, it is reasonable to distrust the information in the guide. So by interpreting the actions of others, it is rational to go into the other restaurant. But this will shift the bias in favour of that restaurant even more for the next potential guests. So a random choice by the first guests, if interpreted in the described way by subsequent guests, may create herd behaviour.

In situations where aggregation is problematic, statistical correlation between aggregated entities may replace microanalytical modeling, which is causality research in a traditional sense[218].

---

[217] see footnote 86

[218] Caldwell (1994), p. 151 observes that, "it is significant that the field in which economists are most likely to take data seriously is the branch that is most distant from standard microeconomic theory."

6.9 Verificationism vs. Falsifications: A Normative Evaluation

A general point shall be made on empirical methodology: It was shown above that falsificationism, despite its popularity, does not solve the major epistemological problems as it originally claimed. In the following it is analysed in which way falsificationism differs from the verificationist brand of empiricism in its practical prescriptions (as a methodology)[219].

If by falsifiability of theories it is meant that theories which cannot be tested are not scientific, this would be potentially harmful. Testing methods could not be available or theories not yet sufficiently operational. If, however, it is only demanded that theories are falsifiable *in principle*, this is nothing else than asking for theories to say something about reality. This is neither spectacular nor new: A theory that is not excluding a subset of the set of all possible outcomes is apparently useless. This led *Caldwell*[220] to claim that falsificationism, if interpreted narrowly, is too restrictive and, if interpreted broadly, loses its normative value. *Hausman* is even more critical in claiming that "falsificationism as a purely logical relation between theories and basic statements [...] is irrelevant to any important questions concerning science," and that "Popper's relevant views concerning falsificationism as a methodology [...] are unfounded and unacceptable."[221]

It is true that falsificationism circumvents the problem of inductivism. Still, there is not that much difference between the two approaches as it might appear at first sight. A bold new theory is bold and new because it is saying something different about reality than the original theory. So, falsification is just the flipside of verification. If a bold new theory is falsified, this is automatically a verification of the old theory. Obviously, verification of a bold new theory and falsification of an old existing theory are among the more spectacular findings[222]. So, all the fuss made about falsification boils down to the simple prescriptio that a scientist should rather focus on bold new theories challenging the traditional ways of thinking than spend his time finding corroborating evidence for already established theories.

---

219 see Caldwell (1994), p. 144 refers to Hausman (1988,1992) for this two-pronged criticism of Popper (epistemological, methodological argument).

220 Caldwell (1982), p. 236

221 see Hausman (1988), p. 65

222 Chalmers (1994), pp. 56 ff

Is this a wise prescription? Emphasis on bold new theories certainly promotes creativity and change. In fact, repeating the experiments of Galileo all over again in order to prove the law of gravity makes everybody yawn, but emphasis on adapting old theories and making incremental changes sometimes helps fledgling theories to develop to their full potential[223]. It is an often-cited example that, by Popperian standards, the heliocentric theory of *Copernicus* which ultimately led to Newtonian mechanics would have been falsified right away because it initially produced inferior predictions[224]. Fortunately, people like Galileo continued to work on it.

This fundamental criticism was addressed by *Lakatos'* methodology of scientific research programmes. In fact, the heliocentric view would have been falsified because many auxiliary hypotheses that were needed to test it were actually false[225]. This is an example of the so-called Duhem-Quine thesis, which "demonstrates that it is just as difficult to conclusively falsify a hypothesis as to verify it because every test of a hypothesis is in fact a joint test of the hypothesis in question, the quality of the data, the measuring instruments employed, and a host of auxiliary hypotheses"[226] In the event of falsification there is an identification problem: One cannot unambiguously blame the central hypothesis. Therefore, a structured approach to falsification is proposed by *Lakatos*. If e.g. it is stated that information asymmetry leads to market failure and this theory is applied to a client-consultant relationship where information asymmetry exists, and no market failure is observed, one should rather assume that in this case reputation effects did in fact offset the predicted effect than discard the whole theory. In the terminology of *Lakatos*: the "theoretical core" is surrounded by a "protective belt" of hypotheses[227]. If a prediction is falsified, hypotheses in the protective belt should be adjusted but not the theoretical core. By adjusting hypotheses, new testable predictions are made. This is done as long as the theoretical core is "progressive" (i.e. leads to the prediction of novel facts[228]), but glancing through the history of science, this criterion seems difficult to apply[229].

---

[223] Popper admitted that Kuhn had opened his eyes on the importance of "normal" science, which tries to fully unfold the potential of a given paradigm without challenging its central tenets.

[224] see Mäki (1994), p. 254 – Mäki makes reference to Rosenberg (1992), Chalmers (1994), p. 70f

[225] Some planets were not yet discovered, the assumed distance between Earth and the fixed stars was wrong.

[226] Blaug (1994), p. 111

[227] Blaug (1994), p. 114

[228] Blaug (1994), p. 115

[229] see Chalmers (1994), pp. 82f

Popperian falsificationism and the traditional verificationist approach are not as different as they seem. Their difference is merely a difference of emphasis on how science should best be advanced. For a falsificationist the emphasis is on bold new theories, whereas for the verificationist it is on developing the full potential of existing theories.

7 Applied Microeconomics

7.1 Applied Microeconomics as an Art

John Neville Keynes understood applied economics as the formulation of "maxims for practical guidance" and called it an "art"[230]. *Mises* likened it to the historical method of understanding: "Everybody uses understanding in dealing with the uncertainty of future events to which he must adjust his own actions. The distinctive reasoning of the speculator is an understanding of the relevance of the various factors determining future events. And [...] action necessarily always aims at future and therefore uncertain conditions and thus is always speculation. Acting man looks, as it were, with the eyes of a historian into the future."[231] There is an objective framework, but the rest is the careful weighing of arguments. The historian first "analyzes [...] each object of [...his] studies with the aid of the mental tools provided by all other sciences. Having achieved this preliminary work, [...he] faces [...his] own specific problem; the elucidation of the unique and individual features of the case by means of understanding"[232]. The solution is not exact. It is rather rationally acceptable, transparently argued, appropriate and defendable within the objective framework. Therefore, the cognitive status of scientific analysis and practical judgement is different[233]. Judgement involves problem orientation. It is only possible to weigh the importance of the arguments under the specific circumstances. Therefore, the reasoning is close to the specific problem. The process tries to combine analytical reasoning, which provides an objective framework, with judgement. As art starts, where scientific analysis ends and judgement begins, scientific reasoning and judgement should not be separated in applied microeconomics[234].

---

[230] see Colander (1994), p. 35; Keynes, J. N.; (1891), p. 29

[231] Mises (1949), p. 58

[232] Mises (1949), p. 51

[233] see Schülein; Reitze (2001), pp. 192f who make the distinction between "denotative" and "connotative" theories to capture roughly the same issues.

[234] Clausewitz makes some very interesting remarks on this issue in his famous book "On War". Clausewitz (1832), II.2.ii. p. 134 "Schwierigkeit, das Erkennen vom Urteil zu sondern" Note

Schülein/Reitze suggest that the problem of finding an appropriate scientific method for a given field of interest is actually to find an approach which represents the right kind of mixture[235] between the two elements. They argue that in the social sciences there is no scope for fruitful analytical reasoning[236]. The author disagrees: Economic theory developed tools that can be applied to complex social settings. Especially since the 1980's, the advent of game theory led economics to switch from "generalizing" to "exemplifying theory"[237]. Instead of telling what will happen, game theoretic models tell "Stories that Might be True"[238]. This is actually criticized by *Fisher* because by telling different stories, it is difficult to know which of the stories are relevant to the real world[239]. On the other hand, *Rasmusen* points out that "there are also a great many 'Stories that Can't be True'"[240]. Therefore, analytical modeling helps to weed out incoherent descriptions. The most fruitful method of economics, in the view of the author, is to combine pure analytical reasoning, starting from axioms and very specific treatment of real world problems in case studies and leaving out the middle ground.

In the quest for the optimal contract, judgement will be involved at two stages. The first is the subsumption of a real world case under the situational and behavioural assumptions of the model. This is comparable to the analogical reasoning of law[241]. The second is to solve the problem of countervailing effects. The model will allow the derivation of a scorecard of situational variables that will allow the assessment of the suitability of a given project for variable fee contracts. The weighing of the different effects has to be done by judgement: "The historian can enumerate all the factors which cooperated in bringing about a known effect and all the factors which worked against them, and may have resulted in delaying and mitigating the final outcome. But he cannot coordinate except by understanding the various causative factors in a quantitative way to the effects produced."[242] So, the scorecard gives an objective framework, but within

that Graham very inadequately translates „Erkennen" with "perception" which should rather be "cognition".

235 see Schülein, Reitze (2001), p. 203

236 see Schülein, Reitze (2001), p. 197

237 see Fisher (1989)

238 see Rasmusen (1994), p. 3

239 see Backhouse (1994), p. 15 in his interpretation of Fisher's article.

240 Rasmusen (1994), p. 3

241 see Rasmusen (1994), p. 3

242 Mises (1949), p. 56

this framework there is need for arguments "to assign to the various [...] factors their relevance"[243] and to come to a final recommendation. The criterion will be adequacy and not exactness.

It could, of course, be argued that it may well be that there is no better method available for the solving of practical issues, but that such a method could still not be called scientific. Such arguments would define a scientific method (e.g. some sort of econometric test) and subsequently declare every problem that is inaccessible by this method to be situated outside the scope of science. It is certainly fruitless to quarrel about words, but if one believes, like the author, that the main virtue of science is the use of reason, such a narrow definition of science would divulge large areas of interest to irrationality.

7.2 Convergence of Applied Microeconomics and BWL

Microeconomics was traditionally price theory. Starting from assumptions like complete information and perfectly competitive markets, it can be shown that a general equilibrium can be obtained which is Pareto optimal. More realistic assumptions were brushed aside as irrelevant complications. Economists were confident that, in Marshall's words, "natura non facit saltum"[244]. Even if the assumptions did not fully describe reality, it was nevertheless argued that small deviations from the assumption would not change the model. This claim was more a dogmatic credo than a critically reflected insight. However, it was not only unrealistic assumptions that questioned the empirical relevance of microeconomic models; it was also its complete silence concerning important phenomena. Institutions, for instance, could not be explained. Firms were simply summed up as production functions. The standard answer to their existence, if it could not be explained by technological requirements, was the suspicion that they had something to do with market power.

On the other hand, it was the field of management which consisted largely of generalizing practical experience and recording best practice. The German "Betriebswirtschaftslehre" was more ambitious. It set out to create an interdisciplinary science, drawing from all fields that were relevant to the firm with the objective of creating tools while attempting to explain and understand. This also included microeconomic theory, especially for market pricing and production, but otherwise microeconomics could safely be ignored.

---

243 Mises (1949), p. 67

244 see Stiglitz (2000), who recalls the motto on the title page of Principles of Economics, Marshall

The advantage of the microeconomic approach is its formal properties, as was argued above. It is flexible and transparent. Moreover, the analytical power of mathematics can be used. This is achieved by separating the sphere of assumptions and the sphere of analytical truth. The advantage of "Betriebswirtschaftslehre" is its long tradition as an interdisciplinary science and its intricate knowledge of real-world institutions. For the field of contract theory, it is argued that there is a convergence of the two approaches.

Microeconomics has gone a long way over the last two decades. One development has been the economics of information. It was shown that the claim that the assumption about complete information was innocuous could not be upheld. Major discontinuities could be shown to arise for small informational imperfections[245]. The second notable development was the use of game theory, which boosted the use of the rational paradigm in areas outside the impersonal market mechanism. The third development was the interdisciplinary opening of microeconomics. With all these developments, the microanalytical method could be extended to other social sciences like sociology, law and political philosophy[246]. Specifically, a microeconomic theory of the firm evolved. "Betriebswirtschaftslehre" has traditionally been very open to all approaches[247]. At the same time, a certain development can be recognized towards stricter methodological standards.

One major difference between Betriebswirtschaftslehre and theoretical microeconomics is that the latter is often concerned with modeling isolated effects, whereas the former is problem oriented. Problems, however, will not be confined to a single effect. A bundle of different effects has to be considered in order to develop solutions for problems. This creates difficulties for the economic approach as the axiomatic closed-form approach cannot simultaneously capture all relevant effects. Moreover, the status of microeconomic predictions most frequently is that of qualitative[248] statements of tendency. Thus, effects cannot simply be added. Therefore, judgement is required to weigh the relative strength of the different effects.

---

245 "Within information economics discontinuities abound." Stiglitz (2000), p. 1456

246 Major proponents are Gary Becker (sociology), Richard Posner (law) and James Buchanan (political philosophy). This has contributed to the image of "economic imperialism".

247 see e.g. Gutenberg's Production Theory

248 see Blaug (1994), p. 118 who attributes the distinction between "quantitative" and "qualitative calculus" to Samuelson.

By taking the insights of "Betriebswirtschaftslehre" to microeconomics, one can actually increase the empirical relevance of microeconomics. This is because only if recommendations for realistic problems are given, theories can be tested. In addition, by drawing on the large descriptive base of "Betriebswirtschaftslehre" better models can be created, also with respect to micro-foundation.

By taking the approach of microeconomics to "Betriebswirtschaftslehre" it becomes a more rigorous science, which in turn will help to build theories. Contrary to common prejudice, the microeconomic approach is not necessarily reductionist. It is as large or reductionist as the modeller wants it to be. On the other hand, there are problems of tractability. These can partly be overcome by simulation, but in every case where quantification creates artificial precision, it is better to restrict oneself to qualitative modeling.

Therefore, at least with respect to contract theory, it can be said that good applied microeconomics must be "Betriebswirtschaftslehre" and good "Betriebswirtschaftslehre" must be microeconomics.

8 Model of Optimal Contract Design

8.1 Economics of Institutions

Following the standard microeconomic approach, it is possible to analytically derive the behaviour of economic agents starting from their preference structure and assumptions about the situational context. It has been shown above that any behavioural assumption can be cast into this framework. If it is possible to change the situational context, the agent's behaviour can be influenced. This is especially interesting in situations where it can be shown that the agent's behaviour leads to undesirable consequences.

Institutional arrangements like contracts play a special role in this respect. They are part of the situational context, but they are not "given" by nature like other situational parameters. If two parties conclude a labour contract, they cannot change the nature of the job: A salesman will have to move around, making it difficult for his company to monitor his performance. But it is easy to decide to use a variable fee contract instead of a flat fee contract. The main idea in institutional economics is to interpret institutional arrangements as a tool to maximize welfare. The approach is analogous to *Buchanan's* constitutional economic analysis which "attempts to explain the working properties of alternative sets of legal-institutional-political rules that constrain the choices and activities of economic agents, the rules that define the framework within which the ordinary choices of economic and political agents are made.[...T]he whole exercise is aimed at offering guidance to those who participate in discussions of constitutional change [...C]onstitutional economics offers a potential for normative advice to members of the constitutional convention [...] It examines the *choice of constraints* as opposed to the *choice within constraints*."[249] Similarly, the contract is sometimes aptly called the "lex contracta" in legal theory, underscoring that the contracting parties are in the position of the "constitutional assembly", passing the laws applicable to their relationship. Therefore, contract theory, as it is understood in this dissertation, potentially offers counsel to the parties of a contract. Stuck in a situation wherein they achieve only suboptimal outcomes, they strive to set constraints which will allow them to achieve higher levels of outcome. Thus, contrary to what is commonly assumed, writing a contract is not mainly a legal problem. As in all problems "de lege ferenda" economic issues will play a role. For parties concluding a contract, existing law and the judicial system are just some restrictions among others that have to be taken into account[250]. Consider the example of two parties who could realise gains of trade by exchanging goods in their possession. If no mechanism can be found to ensure that the counter party performs once the first party has performed its part, no transaction will take place, resulting in a welfare loss. By concluding an enforceable contract this problem would be solved. Yet, sometimes not just any contract would do the trick. The problem of the optimal contract can thus be defined as the contract maximizing welfare, given situational parameters and the agents' preference structure.

8.2 Solving for the Optimal Contract

There are a multitude of different effects which can lead to problems in transactions and need to be dealt with in order to capture the potential gains of trade. These effects can be captured in models which assume an abstract situational setting and which analytically derive the consequences for given assumptions about the preference structure of the agents involved.

For concreteness, consider the case of "moral hazard with hidden action" which can be summarized in the following story: If A hires B to perform a certain task, it is often plausible to assume that B, whose effort is relevant to the outcome of the project, is better informed about his decisions with respect to effort than A. If A pays B a flat fee, regardless of outcome, it is easy to see that B has no

---

[249] Buchanan (1989), p. 64; emphasis added

[250] Except for the legislator, who can change the law, but also the legislator's problem could be seen as an economic problem. He will, however, also pursue other goals which are not primarily concerned with maximizing welfare.

incentive to exert any effort at all, assuming that he dislikes effort. If no effort is exerted, many projects are likely to result in a loss for A: The pay-off from the project is lower than the flat fee paid to B. A, anticipating low effort, will not hire B at all. The project, however, might be profitable for A and B if only B could commit to exerting effort. This is because, in the situation where B exerts high effort, there exists a salary low enough for A to make a profit and high enough for B to prefer the salary over leisure. Failure to provide appropriate incentives thus prevents the parties from capturing potential gains of trade resulting in a welfare loss. If it is possible to show that a variable fee contract does create incentives for B to exert effort at no extra cost, it can be said that introducing variable fee contracts results in higher welfare. Therefore, variable fee contracts would be better than fixed fee contracts in situations wherein B has private information with respect to his actions.

Effectively in this approach, optimization occurs through a two-step procedure. First, a finite set of candidates for optimal contract is set up. Then, these contracts are ranked and the highest ranking contract is taken as the optimal contract. This is an exercise of comparative institutional analysis. An alternative approach is to mathematically solve for the optimal contract by using control theory models. Yet, it will be seen that only very few general constraints can be imposed on the shape of the optimal contract. Still, a very general result can be derived showing that, in some situations, the optimal contract will be variable fee and flat fee respectively. In order to derive more meaningful constraints additional restrictions are made. To reduce arbitrariness, arguments will be given for these restrictions (e.g. why only linear contracts are considered and others are discarded).

The objective of this dissertation is to identify situations in which variable fee contracts are preferable to flat fee contracts. On an abstract level, the method is therefore straightforward: By inverting the function of the optimal contract, each contract from the set of optimal contracts can be assigned at least one setting for which it is optimal. If all contracts are either flat fee or variable fee, the problem is solved by summarizing the settings associated with flat and variable fee contracts respectively.

Besides "moral hazard with hidden action", other relevant models of contract theory include "moral hazard with hidden information", "adverse selection" and "incomplete contracts"[251].

---

[251] There is no commonly accepted taxonomy of contracting models. Rasmusen (1994), pp. 165f e.g. treats "signaling" and "screening" as separate models, while others treat them under

8.3 The Rationale for the Micro-foundation

In contract theory, problems of aggregation exist, but are significantly less severe compared to stock market models or models of the economy as a whole. Modelled effects are more clear-cut and closer to individual action. Often a limited number of agents interact, so the approach of methodological individualism appears feasible. Especially in the case where a theory of contract design shall be developed, it is important to make use of all the relevant information concerning the specific contract partner and the situation, and not just an average agent and an average situation. As was argued above, this individualization makes it difficult to take recourse to black box models. Methodological individualism is therefore the method of choice. Even if a microanalytical model fails as a predictive model for share prices it can still offer insights into issues involving the microstructure[252] of capital markets, like transaction costs for example.

8.4 A Structured Approach

Contracting problems are very complex. Propositions are therefore either too abstract or too specific[253]. To develop a model for each conceivable situation would not be economical. This problem is familiar to lawmakers. They want to write a text which is concise and rigorous but they face nothing less diverse than a multitude of human relations. Their solution is to switch from the abstract to the casuistic, leaving out the intractible middle ground, and to have legal experts in between who are essentially trained in the method of creating the link between these two poles. Similarly the method used in optimal contract design will follow a structured approach.

Colander suggested that the development of positive theory and applied economics were two entirely different areas. This would allow a separation of labour between the theoretical and the applied researcher. The applied researcher would just have to try to stay up-to-date on the theoretical developments and than apply them to real world problems[254]. The author does not believe that such a separation is sensible. First of all, modeling assumptions have to be clearly understood, especially where the model derives its legitimacy from

"adverse selection". The theory of "incomplete contracts" is often seen as a completely different kind of model as it assumes bounded rationality.

252 see Loistl, Vetter (1999); Casey (2000)

253 see Colander (1994), p. 40: He expresses a similar thought by criticising theory which "is too formal for applied policy work and not formal enough for good positive economic work".

254 Colander (1994), p. 43

microfoundation. Sometimes, searching and understanding among existing models is more time consuming than simply setting up one's own model. Often when studying existing models it is more a given modeling principle than the specific model which is interesting for problem solving. So, the objection that this is like "redevelop[ing] the wheel"[255] is not always warranted. *Colander* objects that the adaptation of the model should follow the more loose methodology of applied economics right from the beginning[256]. This presupposes that theoretical models are robust, but this is unfortunately not the case. One cannot simply take price theory and then somewhat loosely adjust the model to take account of information asymmetry. This would ignore the major discontinuities[257] which can only be understood by analytical modeling. Therefore, analyzing robustness of theoretical models will be an important prerequisite for applying theory[258]. A theorist who loses contact with application will be likely to forget that. So, while agreeing with *Colander* on the different methodological rules to be followed in the two areas, a strict separation of labour is not indicated.

The models restrict attention to a small set of abstract situational variables. Sometimes it is difficult to see how the described effect is relevant to the specific relationship under consideration, like the client-consultant relationship. A solution to this problem is to further specify the situational variables. It is, however, difficult to find a reasonable level of specification. If the exposition is kept too abstract it will be difficult for the reader to see how this thesis can be applied to real world problems. If it is too specific, the exposition becomes long and stuck in tedious detail. As will be seen, already at a general level there is considerable complexity.

In the above example, the situational variable is private information about B with respect to his actions. If the client and the consultant work closely together over the project period, then private information with respect to effort is lower than if the client is absent. Another relevant variable (as will be seen) is risk averseness: Risk averseness measures the extent by which an individual's valuation of a risky project falls short of its expected value. If the size of the consultant firm in terms of equity is smaller than the client firm relative to the downside potential of the project, the consultant firm will be more risk averse than the client firm. This is still very abstract. One could go one step further: If the client is a huge multinational and the consultant a small partnership, and the

---

[255] Colander (1994), p. 38

[256] Colander (1994), p. 44

[257] Stiglitz (2000), p. 1456

[258] Colander himself implies that he considers this as important see Colander (1994), p. 45

project is the launch of a new product line in one division of the multinational, then the consultant is more risk averse than the client. But this is clearly too specific: If the project is no new product line but rather the decision to expand to new markets or to build a new plant, then the consultant would still be more risk averse than his client.

In this thesis an attempt is made to strike the balance by being quite abstract in the general part and to give very specific examples. In the general part, the ultimate goal is to derive a checklist that can be used to design contracts. Therefore, abstract situational variables of the principal-agent argument will be translated into the client/consultant setting, but not any further. In some instances, very specific examples are given purely for ease of exposition. It is indeed a feature of contract theory that some models look daunting if cast in abstract terms but can be motivated by relatively simple examples. The subject is complex enough without trying to make it look even more complex.

The approach of the general part is analytical, but contrary to many technical papers, the emphasis is to give intuitive explanations rather than to add another proof by induction. The author will also refrain from making excessive use of "Ockham's razor" by adding steps which may be "easy to see" for many authors. In the conclusions, a rather specific casuistic approach is taken to somewhat keep the balance. This casuistic treatment is not a mechanical application of the scorecard, but rather a substantial part of actual contract design. The first difficulty is to subsume real world problems under the different effects. The second difficulty is to decide on the trade-offs which cannot be explicitly modeled

9 Practical Life and Theory

If theory is ultimately a guideline to purposeful action, there is no fundamental difference between theory and practical action. Human action, to the extent that it is purposeful, always implicitly uses a theory. Beliefs to the contrary among practitioners are an illusion. In *Schumpeter's* words: "Anyone who wishes may deny the value of theory, but certainly not so the 'practitioner'. For he always practices theory and *his* views are mostly nothing else than theories of 200 years ago."[259]

[259] „Mag wer will den Wert der Theorie leugnen der 'Praktiker' jedenfalls darf es nicht. Denn er treibt immer Theorie und *seine* Anschauungen sind meist nichts andres als Theorien von vor 200 Jahren." Schumpeter (1916), pp. 321f – translated by the author.

In fact, acting individuals, whatever they do, gain experience and assimilate certain combinations of successful behaviour. These "ad hoc" theories are frequently a good approximation to more sophisticated theories. Practical decision rules, maxims and rules of thumb can be interpreted as the product of a conscious learning process or unconscious evolution by group selection. In both cases, better rules are likely to be selected in areas where the environment is stable, the frequency of feedback is high and the cost of failure small. The better the expected rules, the lower the likely benefit of theory and the more theory can learn from working close to practical experience. The benefit of theory would then mostly lie in cautious criticism, creating explicit knowledge as needed for teaching and transfer of knowledge to new situations. If frequency is low, cost of failure is high or situations are highly unstable, then theory will provide the most benefit.

As there is no essential conflict between theory and practical life, the obvious conflict between people who spend most of their time thinking about theories and others who spend most of their time taking action is not necessarily given. There is just a separation of labour between producers and consumers of theories. This being said, it has to be acknowledged that there frequently is a gap between these two groups. Some people mainly concerned with theory tend to overanalyse in situations where time is limited and marginal cost of higher precision exceeds marginal utility. In addition, uneasiness about lack of available data, insecurity, personal hardship and over-toppling events can prove a liability for theorists when confronted with real-life problems.

The most striking difference that was mentioned is different time horizons. In practical decision making it is to a large extent the schedule which dictates the amount of time spent to search for a solution. In science it will be more the problem and standards for adequate problem solution which dictate the time frame, but just as chess and lightening chess will require different talents, both players will play by the rules of chess.

Moreover, theoretical concepts are often very abstract. Application to practical problems is not always obvious. This is partly due to the fact that not every theory has yet achieved the state of technology. While not being directly relevant to practical decisions, it may, however, ultimately lead to better technology. Another reason why theories can become practically irrelevant is if they show too little resistance to limited or inaccurate information owing to an obsession with certain theorists to sacrifice generality for virtual precision[260].

260 Such "overselling" will paradoxically help make theories more popular in the short term but contribute to long-term frustration.

Sometimes the problem is language. Every community tends to create its own way of communicating, sometimes making it difficult for practitioners and theorists to exchange ideas.

Practical decision rules and theory have the same structure and the same ultimate intention. The gap between them cannot be fully avoided due to separation of labour but should, as a rule, not become unnecessarily wide and possibly closed. Therefore, theory should in principle be user friendly: Unnecessarily complicated language, unwarranted abstraction and obsession with artificial precision should be avoided.

IV Analytical Agency Models

1 Overview

In the Section (2.1), a basic model is set up to analyse the situation wherein effort is uncontractible. It will be seen that parties will switch to output contracting. In the third Section (2.2) this very general result will be explicitly modelled by making rather strong assumptions about distributions, utility functions and the structure of the incentive scheme. Subsequently, in Section (2.3) a closer look is taken at risk-sharing, still within this very explicit framework. Section (2.4) will be general again. The intention is to expose the mechanics of the optimal sharing rule. This helps one to understand why relatively strong assumptions are needed to derive meaningful results. Robustness becomes an issue. Section (2.5) discusses some limitations of the presented models. Dealing with these limitations is the objective of subsequent Chapters.

Chapter (3) deals with the consequences of error in judgement and bankruptcy in both input monitoring and output monitoring models. Section (3.1) shows that input monitoring can theoretically achieve first best if harsh enough punishment is feasible and error in judgement can be excluded. Yet, if a bankruptcy constraint is introduced input monitoring will be costly. Alternatively, if error in judgement is allowed for, input monitoring will be costly even if there is no bankruptcy constraint. Section (3.2) deals with shifting support schemes which allow perfectly accurate output monitoring and achieve first best beyond the obvious case of a deterministic production function. Another problem considered will be the **moral hazard with respect to risk** which might arise in output monitoring schemes in the presence of bankruptcy constraints. In both cases the argument is only sketched.

Chapter (4) deals with transaction cost and distortion. Section (4.1) describes sources of direct and indirect transaction cost. Section (4.2) discusses the problem of distortion which arises if there is a tension between what the principal wants and what the agent is rewarded for. It can be shown that distortion can be divided into two components: scaling and alignment. There is conflict with the risk-incentive trade-off as output monitoring is less distortive but generally more prone to error.

Many traditional models of contract theory are one period. The subject of Chapter (5) will be to analyse the effect of time on contracts. The starting point of this discussion is the often stated thesis that time can resolve incentive issues that arise in one-shot relationships costlessly. Four models are presented: The first model deals with the advantage of long-term contracts over short term contracts.

Time allows lowering the cost of incentives by reducing imperfect risk-sharing of output-based contracts (5.2). The second and third model deal with situations wherein relational contracts solve problems of enforcement. The theory of supergames will be used to argue that time may sustain contracts with otherwise desirable properties, which would not be feasible in a one-shot relationship. This is the case wherein contract parameters are observable but not verifiable (5.3). The forth model introduces career concerns which induce the agent to exert effort although choice of effort cannot be contracted on. It will be shown that an implicit contract links the agent's current choice of effort to future pay-off. (5.4). In conclusion, it will be argued that the thesis that time solves incentive issues costlessly cannot be generally upheld. Time merely alters and enriches the insights from one-period models: Conclusions from the one-period models are not necessarily valid in the multi-period settings.

2 The Classical Risk-Incentive Trade-Off

2.1 The Basic Model

2.1.1 Introduction

A model will be set up to study optimal pay incentives in the principal-agent relationship. The following propositions will be derived:

1. If effort is contractible, compensation should not be made contingent on output if it is assumed that the agent is risk-averse and the principal risk-neutral. More generally, if effort is contractible, there is no rationale for output-based schemes in order to avoid shirking. The risk-sharing argument comes fully to bear.

2. If there is a stochastic relationship between effort and output and effort is not contractible compensation should be made contingent on output. Incentives rise in strength as compensation differentials increase.

   2.1. First best can be achieved if the agent is risk neutral. He becomes residual claimant.

   2.2. In the case of stochastic production functions and a risk-averse agent, only a second best solution can be achieved due to the risk-incentive trade-off.

3. In the case of a deterministic production function, output-based schemes achieve first best. A forcing contract can be used.

2.1.2 Modeling Assumptions

It is assumed that there are two output levels, low output x_l and high output x_h[261]. Effort can be chosen on a continuous interval within two bounds, $e \in [e_l, e_h]$. Output stochastically depends on effort. The uncertainty is captured by a probability distribution over output levels[262], $P(x = x_l) = 1 - p$, $P(x = x_h) = p$. Effort e is a parameter of the probability distribution[263], $p = p(e)$. As it is assumed that any outcome is possible under any action, the range of $p(e)$ is the open interval $(0,1)$[264]. It is further assumed that the probability of high output strictly increases with increased levels of effort, but less than proportionately. So, formally, $p(e)$ is a strictly increasing[265] and concave[266] function in e ($p'(\cdot) > 0$, $p''(e) < 0$) on the open interval (e_l, e_h). In order to avoid boundary solutions, $p'(e_l) = \infty$ and $p'(e_h) = 0$. Preferences over lotteries for both the principal and the agent obey the von-Neumann-Morgenstern (v-N-M) axioms[267]. The agent's Bernoulli utility function $u(w,e)$ is known to the principal and depends on the

---

261 The model roughly follows Bester (2001) p. 61-69

262 Note that this implies that either objective probabilities are given or that the principal and the agent hold the same subjective probability beliefs. It was already mentioned above that this is the common assumption in game theory (Harsanyi Doctrine).

263 This is the parameterized distribution formulation of the Agency problem, see Mirrlees (1974, 1976). A more general formulation of this variety will be used in Section 5. There is also the state-space formulation, see Spence, Zeckhauser (1971) which will be used in Section 3.

264 As p(e) is interpreted as a probability, following the axioms of Kolmogorov: $0 \le p(e) \le 1$. As it is assumed, that there is a stochastic relationship between effort and output $p(e_h)$ must be strictly lower than 1 and $p(e_l)$ must be strictly higher than 0. With $p'(e) > 0$, it follows that $0 < p(e) < 1$ for all $e \in [e_l, e_h]$. Otherwise it would be possible, at least for some output levels, to perfectly *deduce* effort.

265 A more general version of this assumption, which also applies to settings with a continuous set of outcomes, would be that increased effort leads to a first-order stochastic increase of output. In the two output case this assumption implies another property, which is a necessary condition for non-decreasing compensation in effort and is called the Monotone Likelihood Ratio Property. In a later Chapter the case of continuous output levels will be studied.

266 In the two output case, concavity of the probability distribution implies the *concavity of the distribution function condition*, which is another necessary condition for non-decreasing compensation in effort (see Kreps (1990), p. 597 and p. 600). Confusingly, this condition is also referred to as the *convexity of the distribution function condition* (see Salanié (1997), p. 120). The reason for this seeming contradiction is that the version as in Kreps captures the more intuitive concept of "probability of higher outcome" which technically is 1 minus the distribution function. In this thesis the terminology of Kreps is followed.

267 In particular, the independence and the continuity axiom (see e.g. Kreps (1990) Chapter 3 or Mas-Colell, Whinston, Green (1995), Chapter 6)

pay level $w_i = w(x_i)$ where $i = \{l, h\}$ and on his effort choice e. It is further assumed that $u(w, e)$ is additively separable[268] in a part that depends on the pay level and another part which depends on his choice of effort and that the agent likes money and dislikes effort. Money utility for both the agent and the principal are given by functions $u(\cdot)$ which are strictly increasing, continuously differentiable and concave, which means that they are either risk-averse or risk neutral. The agent's disutility of effort $d(e)$ is usually assumed to be strictly increasing and convex in e. The principal offers a contract to the agent who will either accept or reject it, in which case the agent's utility is his reservation utility u_0[269] and the principal's utility is 0.

2.1.3 Contractible Effort

The crucial point in the subject of this thesis is to study the effect of asymmetric information on contracting. Contrary to this assumption it shall be assumed – as a benchmark case – that the effort decision of the agent is perfectly observable by both, the agent and the principal and therefore the contract can stipulate effort as a contingency.

If the parties can contract on effort, the principal, when designing his optimal compensation scheme, has to solve the following optimization problem:

$$\max_{\gamma(e, w_l, w_h)} \Pi(\gamma) = p(e)(x_h - w_h) + (1 - p(e))(x_l - w_l) \quad (1.1)$$

[270]

$$\text{s.t. } U(e, w_h, w_l) = p(e)u(w_h) + (1 - p(e))u(w_l) - e \geq 0 \quad (1.2)$$

The **principal is risk-neutral**. He is maximizing expected pay-off. The **agent is assumed to be risk-averse**. Condition (1.2) is called the agent's participation constraint which will hold with equality for the solution because otherwise the principal could lower the compensation for the agent and still

[268] This assumption was shown to be crucial by Gjesdal (1982)

[269] Market forces ensure that the agent can earn his reservation utility elsewhere.

[270] It is common to divide this problem into *steps* (see discussion at the end of the Section). The first step would be to find out the minimum cost incentive scheme to implement any given effort level e. Mathematically, the second step would be to choose the effort level which maximizes net benefit for the principal. For the implication derived in this Section it is sufficient to solve the first step. Therefore, a somewhat easier formulation for the objective function is often seen in literature: $\min_{\gamma(e, w_l, w_h)} w_l + p(e)(w_h - w_l)$ (see e.g. Mas-Colell, Whinston, Green (1995), p. 480.

induce him to accept the contract. For simplicity, e is measured on the scale of disutility and the reservation utility is set to 0 (but could as well be set to any other reservation utility U_0 [271].

Letting μ be the Lagrangean multiplier for constraint (1.2) it can be written:

$$\begin{aligned}&\mathrm{p}'(\mathrm{e})(x_\mathrm{h}-\mathrm{w}_\mathrm{h})-\mathrm{p}'(\mathrm{e})(x_l-w_h)+\\&\mu\left[\mathrm{p}'(\mathrm{e})\mathrm{u}(w_h)-p'(e)\mathrm{u}(w_l)-1\right]\end{aligned} \tag{1.3}$$

$$-\mathrm{p}(\mathrm{e})+\mu\mathrm{p}(\mathrm{e})\mathrm{u}'(\mathrm{w}_\mathrm{h})=0 \tag{1.4}$$

$$(\mathrm{p}(\mathrm{e})-1)+\mu(1-\mathrm{p}(\mathrm{e}))\mathrm{u}'(w_l)=0 \tag{1.5}$$

Rearranging (1.4) yields:

$$\mu=\frac{\mathrm{p}(\mathrm{e})}{\mathrm{p}(\mathrm{e})u'(w_h)}=\frac{1}{\mathrm{u}'(w_h)} \tag{1.4)$'$ ($$

Inserting (1.4)′ in (1.5) yields:

$$(\mathrm{p}(\mathrm{e})-1)-(\mathrm{p}(\mathrm{e})-1)\frac{u'(w_l)}{u'(w_h)}=0 \tag{1.5)$'$ ($$

As $\mathrm{p(e)} \neq 1$, it follows from (1.5)′:

$$\frac{u'(w_l)}{u'(w_h)}=1 \Leftrightarrow \mathrm{u}'(w_l)=u'(w_h) \tag{1.6}$$

For $u''(\cdot)<0$ (risk-averseness as assumed above) it can be followed from (1.6) that:

$$w_l=w_h \tag{1.7}$$

---

[271] The reservation utility is the level of utility that the agent demands in order to be willing to work. It can be thought of as the agent's opportunity cost. It is assumed that any gains from trade are appropriated by the principal. This could be justified by assuming that there are more agents than principals, so that the zero profit condition holds for the agents. In this case, this assumption is taken for purely technical reasons and is totally innocuous. It is just one way to derive a Pareto-optimal result.

If effort is contractible, it is optimal for the principal to provide **full insurance**. He pays compensation independent of output. This is an intuitive result: The effort of the agent can be observed and contracted upon. There is **no need to use the wage system to indirectly induce the agent to exert a certain effort**. A contract can stipulate that the agent receives a certain payment if he is exerting high effort and is punished otherwise. Such a contract is called a forcing contract because the principal can force the agent to choose the desired effort level. In this case the **risk-sharing argument comes fully to bear**. As the principal was assumed to be risk neutral and the agent to be risk averse, it is optimal for the principal to assume all the risk[272] .

Proposition 1: If effort is contractible, compensation should not be made contingent on output if it is assumed that the agent is risk-averse and the principal risk-neutral. More generally, if effort is contractible, there is no rationale for output-based schemes in order to avoid shirking. The risk-sharing argument comes fully to bear.

2.1.4 Uncontractible Effort

If effort is not contractible, the principal has to offer a contract that maximizes his profit knowing that the agent chooses effort in order to maximize his own utility (i.e. if the agent maximizes utility by choosing the lowest effort level he will do it). If the **principal knows the utility function of the agent**, as was assumed, and if he knows the **probability distribution of outcomes conditional on effort**, the principal can perfectly predict the reaction of the agent to any offered compensation scheme. It will be seen that he has to trade off the benefits of inducing higher effort against the cost of providing incentives (the cost of compensating the agent for risk-taking).

The principal has to solve the following optimization problem:

$$\max_{(w_l, w_h)} \Pi(e, w_l, w_h) \tag{2.1}$$

$$\text{s.t. } e \in \arg\max_{e'} U(e', w_l, w_h) \tag{2.2}$$

$$U(e, w_l, w_h) \geq 0 \tag{2.3}$$

272 see The results of Syndicate Theory (Wilson (1968), cit. in Kreps (1990) p. 173f)

The principal's and the agent's pay-off function are the same as in the previous subsection. What is new is condition (2.2). This constraint is the characteristic feature of problems involving hidden action. It reflects the impossibility on the part of the principal to directly influence the agent's effort decision. As the principal cannot observe effort, the agent chooses the effort level that maximizes his own welfare, but the principal anticipates the reaction of the agent. He will choose a compensation scheme that induces the agent to act in the desired way, by providing corresponding incentives. This is why condition (2.2) is called **incentive constraint**[273]. The crucial idea behind this argument is rational behaviour: Even if the effort decision is taken autonomously by the agent, his **rational behaviour** of maximizing expected utility makes him predictable. The principal is effectively choosing a desired effort level which he implements by offering the appropriate compensation scheme. The agent's autonomous decision power is merely adding a constraint. Condition (2.3) is the participation constraint as encountered earlier.

On a technical level, if the action space was finite with n possible actions[274], condition (2.2) translates into a set of n incentive constraints[275]. So, the problem is solved by using the Kuhn-Tucker conditions. If the action space is continuous, as is assumed in this Section, the set of incentive constraints becomes infinite and the described approach becomes analytically intractible[276]. Therefore, as (2.2) is itself an optimization problem, the first order condition for optimization must hold as long as there is no boundary solution (which was excluded in the assumptions under 2.1.2):

$$\frac{\partial U(e,w_l,w_h)}{\partial e} = 0 \Leftrightarrow \mathrm{p}'(\mathrm{e})\left[\mathrm{u}(w_h)-u(w_l)\right]-1=0 \qquad (2.4)$$

Some interesting conclusions can be drawn from the analysis of the first order condition: (2.4) only holds if $\mathrm{u}(w_h)-u(w_l)>0$ as $\mathrm{p}'(\mathrm{e})>0$. But, $\mathrm{u}(w_h)-\mathrm{u}(w_l)>0$, for $u'(\cdot)>0$[277] implies $w_h > w_l$. In addition, for any given level of w_l: $(w_h - w_l)\uparrow\Rightarrow(\mathrm{u}(w_h)-u(w_l))\uparrow\Rightarrow \mathrm{p}'(\mathrm{e})\downarrow\Rightarrow e\uparrow \forall p''(e)<0$. In

---

[273] It is also sometimes called *relative* incentive constraint, to underscore that the action to be chosen by the agent must be made relatively more attractive than all other available actions.

[274] As e.g. in Kreps (1990), p. 577-604.

[275] The optimal solution is also weakly preferred to itself, which is why there are n and not n-1 constraints.

[276] see Kreps (1990), p. 605

[277] It is assumed that more compensation is strictly preferred to less.

words: It can be concluded from the incentive constraint that every optimal compensation scheme in the asymmetric information case involves **wage differentials**. What is more, the higher these wage differentials, the stronger the incentives (the higher e).

Proposition 2: If there is a stochastic relationship between effort and output and effort is not contractible, compensation should be made contingent on output. Incentives rise in strength as compensation differentials increase.

As $U'' = p''(e)(u(w_h) - u(w_l))$ and $p''(e) < 0$ (see assumption under 2.1.2), U'' <0 for all $w_h > w_l$. Thus, the expected utility function $U(\cdot)$ is concave and the first order condition (2.4) is a necessary and sufficient condition for maximization. It can therefore replace the maximization problem of the incentive constraint, considerably simplifying the overall maximization problem[278] :

$$\max_{w_l, w_h} \Pi(e, w_l, w_h) = p(e)\left[(x_h - w_h) - (x_l - w_l)\right] + (x_l - w_l) \quad (2.5)$$

$$s.t. \; p'(e)\left[u(w_h) - u(w_l)\right] - 1 = 0 \quad (2.6)$$

$$p(e)u(w_h) + (1 - p(e))u(w_l) - e \geq 0 \quad (2.7)$$

The participation constraint (2.7) must be binding and therefore holds with equality. Otherwise, the principal could lower compensations w_l, w_h by the same amount, reducing the expected compensation without altering relative incentives (Note that the difference in (2.6) is unaffected.).

Letting μ_1 and μ_2 be the Lagrangean multipliers for (2.6) and (2.7) respectively, it can be written:

$$\begin{aligned} &p'(e)\left[(x_h - w_h) - (x_l - w_l)\right] + \mu_1 p''(e)\left[u(w_h) - u(w_l)\right] \\ &+ \mu_2\left[p'(e)(u(w_h) - u(w_l)) - 1\right] = 0 \end{aligned} \quad (2.8)$$

$$p(e) - 1 - u'(w_l)p'(e)\mu_1 + u'(w_l)(1 - p(e))\mu_2 = 0 \quad (2.9)$$

---

[278] This approach is called the first-order approach (see discussion at the end of the Section). The problem is that the set of incentive constraints of condition (2.2) cannot generally be replaced by the first-order condition. This will only be possible if the agent's v-N-M expected utility function is concave (which was proven above). Generally, concavity is assured if the concavity of the distribution function condition holds, which was garanteed in the assumptions (see footnote 266 for the two output case). Proving non-decreasing wages in e – as was done in the preceding Paragraph – is also sufficient for the first-order approach to be viable (see Kreps (1990), p. 598 Lemma.).

$$-p(e)+u'(w_h)p'(e)\mu_1+u'(w_h)p(e)\mu_2=0 \qquad (2.10)$$

Risk neutral Agent

In the traditional model it is usually assumed that the principal is risk-neutral and the agent risk-averse. For a moment, however, it is assumed that the agent is risk-neutral. An interesting result can be derived for this case from the two constraints:

Risk-neutrality implies that, at any level of compensation, an increase of expected compensation by 1 unit is valued at exactly 1 unit. Inserting $u'(w_l)=u'(w_h)=1$ into (2.9) and (2.10) yields:

$$p(e)-1-p'(e)\mu_1+(1-p(e))\mu_2=0 \qquad (2.9)'$$

$$-p(e)+p'(e)\mu_1+p(e)\mu_2=0 \qquad (2.10)'$$

$$0-1+0+\mu_2=0$$

$$\mu_2=1 \qquad (2.9)'+(2.10)'$$

Inserting $\mu_2=1$ in (2.10) yields:

$$-p(e)+p'(e)\mu_1+p(e)=0$$

$$p'(e)\mu_1=0 \qquad (2.11)$$

As $p'(e)\neq 0$ for $e\in[e_l,e_h)$:

$$\mu_1=0 \qquad (2.11)'$$

From $\mu_2=1$ it can be seen that outcome is efficient. Investing one unit into compensation exactly increases outcome by one unit. **Marginal cost equals marginal product**. Fist best can be achieved. From $\mu_1=0$ it can be concluded that the **incentive constraint is not binding**. The principal can therefore achieve the same profit as under symmetric information.

Another interesting result can be derived by setting $\mu_1=0$ and $\mu_2=1$ into (2.8):

$$p'(e)\left[(x_h-w_h)-(x_l-w_l)\right]+p'(e)\left(u(w_h)-u(w_l)-1\right)=0 \qquad (2.8)'$$

Inserting the first order condition (2.4), this expression simplifies to:

$$p'(e)\left[(x_h - w_h) - (x_l - w_l)\right] = 0 \tag{2.8)''$$

As $p'(e) > 0$ for $e \in [e_l, e_h)$:

$$x_h - w_h = x_l - w_l \tag{2.12}$$

From (2.12) it can be concluded, that the principal's **profit is independent of output**. He is fully insured. The agent effectively buys the project from the principal and is left in a **residual claimant** position. It can easily be seen, that this result also holds for risk-averse principals.

Proposition 2.1.: In the case of a stochastic production function first best can be achieved if the agent is risk neutral. He becomes residual claimant[279]**.**

Risk-Averse Agent

It is now assumed that the principal is risk-neutral and the agent risk-averse. An individual is called risk-averse if he values a project below its expected value. If it is assumed that an individual prefers more to less (positive marginal utility), this implies that the individual attributes an ever smaller extra value to an additional unit of the good consumed (diminishing marginal utility). Formally this can be stated by $u'(\cdot) > 0$, $u''(\cdot) < 0$[280].

Unfortunately, in this case the conditions do not simplify. From $w_h > w_l$ it can be followed that:

$$u'(w_h) < u'(w_l), \tag{2.13}$$

for risk-averse agents $(u''(\cdot) < 0)$. Solving for the two Lagrangean multipliers yields:

$$\mu_1 = \frac{(1 - p(e))(\mu_2 u'(w_l) - 1)}{u'(w_l)\, p'(e)} \tag{2.14}$$

---

279 Rasmusen calls this the "Selling the Shop" Result

280 This assumption was already used above in the case of contractible effort.

$$\mu_2 = \frac{u'(w_h) + p(e)\left[u'(w_l) - u'(w_h)\right]}{u'(w_h)u'(w_l)} \tag{2.15}$$

Rearranging (2.15) yields:

$$\mu_2 u'(w_l) = 1 + \frac{p(e)\left[u'(w_l) - u'(w_h)\right]}{u'(w_h)} \tag{2.15$'$}$$

Inserting (2.15)′ into (2.14) yields:

$$\mu_1 = \frac{(1 - p(e))p(e)\left[u'(w_l) - u'(w_h)\right]}{u'(w_l)u'(w_h)p'(e)} > 0 \tag{2.14$'$}$$

This expression is **positive** for all e^*, because $p(e) \in (0,1)$, $u'(w_l) > 0$, $u'(w_h) > 0$ (positive marginal utility), $p'(e) > 0$ (see assumptions under 2.1.2) and inequality (2.13). It can easily be seen that expression (2.15) is positive for the same reasons.

If the agent is risk-averse, **both the incentive and the participation constraints are binding**. The intuition for this result is the following: In order to induce the agent to exert effort there will have to be a **wage differential**. This implies that the agent is exposed to risk. In order to make the agent's expected utility from the contract meet his reservation utility level, the risk-averse agent has to be compensated for his risk exposure, driving up expected payments by the principal. Naturally, the principal will not want to pay more than necessary. Therefore, he will devise the wage differential so that it **just induces desired behaviour**[281] but no more, since this would mean higher risk exposure for the agent and consequently higher cost for the principal. This is why the incentive constraint is binding.

The reason why the participation constraint must be binding has already been given above: If it was not binding it would be possible for the principal to **reduce the level of payments to the agent for any observed output by the same amount.** This would not affect incentives but would lower cost to the principal. Therefore, this cannot be a property of the optimal incentive scheme.

---

[281] It is a common assumption in agency theory that if the agent is indifferent about two actions he will choose the one that is preferred by the principal. The reason for this assumption is technical: If it is assumed that the principal sweetens the desired choice just a bit, the tool of optimization will not work as there is no "optimal" sweetener. See Kreps (1990), p. 603f on this point.

The fact that the incentive constraint binds implies that expected cost for the principal will be higher than in the symmetric information or risk-neutrality case. The principal's expected net benefit will therefore be lower. As the agent's expected utility remains at the reservation level, **over-all welfare is reduced**. The outcome is therefore second best[282].

Proposition 2.2.: In the case of stochastic production functions and a risk-averse agent, only a second-best solution can be achieved due to the risk-incentive trade-off.

Certainty

In the modeling assumptions (see assumptions under 2.1.2), a stochastic relationship between effort of the agent and output was assumed. Effort was a parameter of the probability distributions of outcome. By choosing his effort level the agent effectively chooses a probability distribution. More specifically, it could not be excluded that output was low although the agent had chosen high effort. If, however, there is a **deterministic relationship** between output and effort, it is possible to deduce effort from output. All that has to be done is to **invert the production function**. So, even if effort may not be observable, which is why this case is treated as a case of uncontractible effort, observing output is equivalent to observing input. Therefore, the analysis of effort contractibility applies to this case. This leads to the following proposition:

Proposition 3: In the case of a deterministic production function, output-based schemes achieve first best. A forcing contract can be used.

---

282 Formally, in the case of observable effort the principal, who wants to implement effort level e_i has to pay the agent: $w^*(e_i) = u(w^*(e_i)) = u_0 + e_i$ in order to fulfil the participation constraint. In the case of unobservable effort, expected utility of the agent must be: $E[u(w(x))|e_i] = u_0 + e_i$. As, by Jensen's inequality, $u[E(w(x))|e_i] > E[u(w(x))|e_i]$ it follows from the above expression that $u[E(w(x))|e_i] > u(w^*(e_i))$. For strictly increasing $u(\cdot)$ this implies $E(w(x))|e_i > (w^*(e_i))$. Therefore, the expected payments from the principal needed to implement any $e \in [e_l; e_h]$ are lower in the case of observable effort than in the case of non-observable effort. see (Mas-Colell, Whinston, Green (1995), p. 486)

2.1.5 Discussion

The analysis in this Section provided some basic results summarized in the propositions. Most importantly, it was shown that if effort is not contractible, compensation shall be made contingent on output. It was also shown that, in this case, welfare levels can never be higher than in the case of observable effort. Barring the unrealistic cases of a deterministic production function and risk neutrality of both the principal and the agent, the optimal compensation scheme leads to a welfare loss due to imperfect risk sharing.

More general models than the one used in this Section can be set up[283] but yield broadly the same results. As this dissertation does not primarily have a technical focus but favours intuitive arguments, the choice of this model seems appropriate.

There is also a different approach to solving the optimization problem than the one used in this Section. This approach was developed by Grossman/Hart (1983)[284] and is called the *three-step procedure* by Fudenberg/Tirole (1990)[285]. First, one searches for the set of contracts that implement e. Then, among these contracts, the contract which is least costly to the principal is chosen. Finally, one settles for the effort level which maximizes net benefit for the principal[286]. Often not all of the steps are needed[287]. Therefore, the approach often allows more simple and elegant analysis[288]. It also stresses the importance of inducing the agent to choose a certain action and the fact that this inducement is costly. On the other hand, the approach used in this Section is more intuitive to set up.

Another methodological choice was the use of the so-called first-order approach which follows from the assumption of a continuous action space[289]. This makes it necessary to replace the (infinite) set of incentive constraints with the

---

283 see Grossman/Hart (1983)

284 Grossman/Hart (1983)

285 see Fudenberg/Tirole (1990)

286 As step 1 and 2 mathematically combine to one (see Rasmusen (1994), p. 176), the approach is also presented in two steps (see Kreps (1990) pp. 587-489).

287 e.g. for the results in this Section, steps 1 and 2 would have been sufficient to drive home the results.

288 see footnote (270)

289 Rasmusen (1995), p. 176 wrongly contrasts the first-order approach and the three-step procedure. The first order approach follows from the continuous action space formulation and in this case must also be used in the three-step procedure.

first-order condition for optimization of the agent's utility. The problem is that this cannot generally be done. It will only be possible if the agent's v-N-M expected utility function is concave[290]. Generally, this is only assured if the concavity of the distribution function condition holds, which is not a totally unproblematic assumption. The advantage is that it considerably simplifies the analysis and is also very intuitive in stressing the autonomy of the agent's decision making if effort cannot be observed. It will therefore be used in many (albeit not all) instances in this thesis. Although Kreps (1990)[291] considers it as pertaining to the "early literature", it is still used - possibly for its intuitive appeal[292].

2.2 Risk-Incentive Trade-off for Linear Contracts

2.2.1 Introduction

In the following model, specific assumptions are made concerning the production function, the agent's utility function and the structure of the incentive scheme[293]. The incentive-risk trade-off can then be explicitly modelled. The following proposition can be derived:

4. If linear contracts are assumed it can be seen that the optimal bonus rate decreases for rising risk-averseness, rising project risk and rising curvature of the disutility function. In the case of a deterministic production function ($\sigma^2 = 0$), all the risk is assumed by the agent (b=1). The forcing contract was excluded by the linear sharing rule, but it can be seen that also a linear contract can achieve first best.

2.2.2 Modeling Assumptions

The project production function is assumed to be linear and disturbed by an error term ε, where y is output, a is effort, measured on the scale of expected project value[294], and ε is a random variable, which is normally distributed with zero mean

---

290 see e.g. Kreps (1990), pp. 605f. and the literature on the first order approach: e.g. Rogerson (1985)

291 see Kreps (1999), p. 604

292 see Bester (2001)

293 see e.g. Gibbons (2001),

294 This is important, because otherwise it would be difficult to interpret negative values for a.

and variance σ^2. Thus, the agent controls the mean of a normally distributed random variable by his choice of effort[295]:

$$y = a + \varepsilon, \quad \varepsilon \sim N\left(0, \sigma^2\right). \tag{3.1}$$

Note that in this model not only the set of possible actions but also the range of outcomes is continuous.

The incentive scheme is linear with a bonus rate b and a base salary s [296]:

$$w(y) = s + by. \tag{3.2}$$

The agent's utility function is an exponential *v-N-M* utility function[297]:

$$U(x) = 1 - e^{-rx}. \tag{3.3}$$

Remark: It can easily be seen that r is a measure of risk-averseness[298]:

$$-\frac{U''}{U'} = r. \tag{3.4}$$

---

[295] This is the state-space formulation of the Agency Problem. see Spence/Zeckhauser (1971). Obviously, the intuition is that higher effort leads to higher mean and with the variance unchanged to a more favourable distribution of outcomes. However, as Stiglitz, Rothschild (1970) have shown, there are examples where a lottery with lower mean and higher variance is preferred by a risk-averse agent. The reason is, that μ, σ-analysis is not generally equivalent to the concept of first/order stochastic dominance. Yet, in the case of a normally distributed error term, it is easy to see that higher effort levels are equivalent to choosing stochastically higher distributions of output.

[296] Linearity is, prima facie, a totally arbitrary assumption. In Sub-Section IV2.4.3 below, reasons are given why it might be justified to constrain the shape of the optimal sharing rule to be linear.

[297] The choice of an exponential Bernoulli function implies that the agent's absolute risk-averseness is constant in wealth x and his relative risk averseness increases in wealth. Yet, it is often natural to assume decreasing absolute risk-averseness and non-increasing relative risk-averseness. Otherwise the agent would e.g. only be ready to invest a constant absolute amount of his wealth into a risky asset. This implies that the share of his wealth invested in the risky asset decreases in wealth.

[298] This shows that the exponential utility function can be fully recovered from the coefficient of absolute risk averseness (also called Arrow/Pratt measure).

The agent's disutility of effort is given by $c(a)$ and is assumed to be strictly increasing and convex in a:

$$c(a) > 0, \; c'(a) > 0, \; c''(a) > 0. \tag{3.5}$$

The principal is risk neutral, which means that he values a project at its expected value. His certainty equivalent CE is therefore:

$$CE = V[E(x)] = E(x). \tag{3.6}$$

2.2.3 The Model

The principal's pay-off for a contract $\gamma = (b,s)$ is:

$$\Pi(\gamma,a) = (1-b)(a+\varepsilon) - s \tag{3.7}$$

The agent's pay-off is:

$$w(a,\gamma,c(\cdot)) = s + b(a+\varepsilon) - c(a). \tag{3.8}$$

The principal's optimization problem is:

$$\max_{\gamma} \Pi(\gamma,a^*) = (1-b)a^* - s \tag{3.9}$$

$$s.t. \; a^* \in \arg\max_{a'} CE(a',\gamma,\sigma,c(\cdot)) \tag{3.10}$$

$$CE(a,\gamma,\sigma,c(\cdot)) \geq 0 \tag{3.11}$$

The principal designs the contract in order to maximize expected profit. As he cannot observe the agent's choice of effort, the agent will choose the level of effort which will maximize his own expected utility. As it is assumed that the principal knows the agent's utility function he will perfectly predict the agent's reaction to a given contract. So, one can think of the principal's problem as designing a contract, keeping in mind that the agent will always optimally adjust his effort (see above). For technical reasons the problem is **stated in certainty equivalent and not in expected utility terms**.

First the maximization problem of the constraint set is replaced by the first-order condition[299] which can be shown to be necessary and sufficient.

It is a well-known result for an exponential utility function and normally distributed output that the certainty equivalent can be written as[300]:

$$CE = \bar{U}\left(E\left(U\left(a,\gamma,c(\cdot)\right)\right)\right) = s + ba - c(a) - \frac{rb^2\sigma^2}{2}. \qquad (3.12)$$

The first-order condition is:

$$\frac{\partial CE}{\partial a} = b - c'\left(a^*\right) = 0 \Rightarrow c'\left(a^*\right) = b, \qquad (3.13)$$

which means that for any incentive scheme the agent maximizes utility by choosing the effort level which sets his marginal disutility equal to the bonus rate. The second-order condition for a maximum is:

$$\frac{\partial^2 CE}{\partial^2 a} = -c''\left(a^*\right) < 0. \qquad (3.14)$$

(3.14) always holds because of the convexity of the disutility function. Therefore (3.12) is convex and the first-order condition (3.13) is necessary and sufficient[301].

Restating the maximization problem, it can be written:

$$\max_{s,b}(1-b)a^* - s \qquad (3.9)'$$

$$s.t.\; c'\left(a^*\right) = b \;\Rightarrow a^* = c'(b)^{-1} = a^*(b) \qquad (3.10)'$$

$$s + ba - c(a) - \frac{rb^2\sigma^2}{2} \geq 0. \qquad (3.11)'$$

---

299 The first order approach once again is needed because of the continuous action space.

300 See appendix to this Chapter.

301 The range of a is R. So one does not have to bother about boundary solutions. It is also assumed that the principal has to offer a contract even if his expected pay-off is negative and cannot set the terms of the contract so that the agent surely rejects it. Otherwise, there would be a problem if cost increase is to steep.

Remark: It can easily be seen from (3.10)′ that **b is positive** as $c'(\cdot) > 0$. It can also be said that **optimal effort is positive,** $a^* > 0$. This is because $c'(\cdot) > 0$ implies $c'(\cdot)^{-1} > 0$.

Inserting (3.10)′ into (3.11)′ gives:

$$\max_{s,b}\,(1-b)a^*(b) - s \tag{3.9'}$$

$$s.t.\; s + ba^*(b) - c\left(a^*(b)\right) - \frac{rb^2\sigma^2}{2} = 0. \tag{3.11''}$$

In addition, the principal will not offer more compensation than is needed to assure the participation of the agent. Therefore, the **participation constraint will be binding**[302]. Letting μ be the Lagrangean multiplier for (3.11)′′ yields:

$$\begin{aligned}\frac{\partial L}{\partial b} &= -a^*(b) + (1-b)a^{*\prime}(b) + \\ &\mu\left(a^*(b) + ba^{*\prime}(b) - c'\left(a^*(b)\right)a^{*\prime}(b)\right) - r\sigma^2 b = 0\end{aligned} \tag{3.15}$$

$$\frac{\partial L}{\partial s} = -1 + \mu = 0 \Rightarrow \mu = 1. \tag{3.16}$$

Inserting (3.16) in (3.15):

$$a^{*\prime} - c'\left(a^*\right)a^{*\prime} - r\sigma^2 b = 0. \tag{3.17}$$

Inserting (3.10)′ in (3.17) and rearranging yields:

$$b = \frac{a^{*\prime}}{a^{*\prime} + r\sigma^2}. \tag{3.18}$$

Differentiating (3.10)′ and solving for a shows that the marginal impact of a higher bonus rate on the level of optimal effort is lower the more convex the disutility function:

[302] As was argued above, it is possible to reduce expected cost of the principal without changing the incentives if the participation constraint is not binding.

$$\frac{\partial}{\partial b} c'\left(a^*(b)\right) = \frac{\partial}{\partial b} b$$

$$c''\left(a^*\right)a^{*\prime} = 1 \tag{3.19}$$

$$a^{*\prime} = \frac{1}{c''}.$$

Inserting (3.19) in (3.18) gives the **optimal bonus rate**[303]:

$$b = \frac{1}{1 + r\sigma^2 c''}. \tag{3.20}$$

Proposition 4.: If linear contracts are assumed it can be seen that the optimal bonus rate decreases for rising risk-averseness, rising project risk and rising curvature of the disutility function. In the case of a deterministic production function ($\sigma^2 = 0$), all the risk is assumed by the agent (b=1). The forcing contract was excluded by the linear sharing rule, but it can be seen that also a linear contract can achieve first best.

Total welfare can be calculated by adding the certainty equivalents of the agent and the principal. Inserting (3.7) into (3.6) and adding with (3.12) gives total surplus in the case of private information:

$$a - s - b(a) + s + ba - c(a) - \frac{rb^2\sigma^2}{2}$$

$$= a - c(a) - \frac{rb^2\sigma^2}{2}. \tag{3.21}$$

In the perfect information case, gains of trade are:

$$\mathrm{a} - \mathrm{c}(\mathrm{a}). \tag{3.22}$$

Subtracting (3.22) from (3.21) gives the welfare loss in the case of private information compared to symmetric information holding the effort level constant:

[303] The same result can be obtained maximizing the joint welfare function of the two parties. This is mathematically more straightforward but less intuitive.

$$\frac{rb^2\sigma^2}{2}. \tag{3.23}$$

One should note that total **welfare loss will be higher**. In the above case, effort levels were held constant. In fact, optimal effort levels in the symmetric information case will be higher[304] but the point here was to show that in the asymmetric information case a welfare loss occurs.

2.2.4 Discussion

The main appeal of the model of this subsection is the existence of a closed-form solution which negatively links the use of variable fee contracts to the agent's level of risk aversion, the level of project risk and the convexity of the disutility function. The weakness of this model is its lack of generality and its unrealistic assumptions as e.g. the constant absolute risk-averseness of the agent's preferences. Especially the linear sharing rule seems to be completely arbitrary. Although an argument in rescue of linear sharing rules will be presented in a later Chapter (see 2.4.3), the main reason why this model was presented is its intuitive appeal and its suitability as a starting point for further analysis.

2.2.5 Appendix

Ad (3.12):
The explicit expression for the following equation is needed:

$$CE = \overline{U}\left(E\left(U\left(a,\gamma,c(\cdot)\right)\right)\right). \tag{3.24}$$

Inserting the utility function, one can write for expected utility:

[304] It is not necessarily the case, that optimal effort levels are lower than in the first best case. This is because there are two sources of loss in the second best equilibrium. One is divergence from the efficient effort level. The other is the cost of separation of different possible actions. These are low if the statistical signal is very strong. Then, it is easy to infer from a certain output level which action was chosen. As the chance of error is lower, and consequently the risk of being innocently punished, the risk premium is lower. Kreps (1990), p. 602f) constructs a simple example to illustrate this point. This will not be the case here, as there is no discontinuity of the likelihood ratios in the model discussed in this Sub-Section.

$$E\left(1-e^{-r(b(a+\varepsilon)+s-c(a))}\right)=1-e^{-r[b(a+\varepsilon)+s-c(a)]}E\left(e^{-rb\varepsilon}\right). \tag{3.25}$$

$E\left(e^{-rb\varepsilon}\right)$ can be written as:

$$E\left(e^{-rb\varepsilon}\right)=\int e^{-rbx}\frac{1}{\sigma\sqrt{2\pi}}e^{-\frac{1}{2}\left(\frac{x}{\sigma}\right)^2}dx=\frac{1}{\sigma\sqrt{2\pi}}\int e^{-rbx-\frac{1}{2\sigma^2}x^2}dx. \tag{3.26}$$

A known rule of integration[305] is:

$$\int e^{-px^2+qx}dx=e^{\frac{q^2}{4p}}\sqrt{\frac{\pi}{p}}. \tag{3.27}$$

Setting $p=\frac{1}{2\sigma^2}$ and $q=-rb$ into (3.27) yields:

$$\begin{aligned}E\left(e^{-rb\varepsilon}\right)&=\frac{1}{\sigma\sqrt{2\pi}}\int e^{-rbx-\frac{1}{\sigma^2}x^2}dx\\&=\frac{1}{\sigma\sqrt{2\pi}}e^{\left(\frac{r^2b^2}{2/\sigma^2}\right)}\sqrt{2\pi\sigma^2}=e^{\frac{r^2b^2\sigma^2}{2}}.\end{aligned} \tag{3.28}$$

Inserting this result into equation (3.25) yields:

$$E(U)=1-e^{-r[ba+s-c(a)]+\frac{r^2b^2\sigma^2}{2}}. \tag{3.29}$$

The certainty equivalent is defined as:

$$CE=\overline{U}\left[E(U)\right]. \tag{3.30}$$

Inverting $U(x): y=1-e^{-rx}$ yields:

$$\overline{U}(x): x=1-e^{-ry}.$$

[305] Rysik, Gradstejn (1965)

Solving for y gives:

$$\bar{U}(x): y = \frac{\ln(1-x)}{-r}. \tag{3.31}$$

Setting $x = E(U)$ in (3.31) gives the certainty equivalent:

$$CE = \frac{\ln(1-E(U))}{-r}. \tag{3.32}$$

Inserting (3.29) into (3.32) yields:

$$\begin{aligned} CE &= \frac{\ln\left(1-1+e^{-r[ba+s-c(a)]+\frac{r^2b^2\sigma^2}{2}}\right)}{-r} \\ &= s+ba-c(a)-\frac{rb^2\sigma^2}{2}.\ q.e.d. \end{aligned} \tag{3.33}$$

2.3 Risk Sharing

2.3.1 Introduction

It was argued above that variable fees may provide useful incentives in situations of hidden action, but also create imperfect risk sharing. Quite apart from any other consideration, a closer look at the **mechanics of risk sharing** is warranted: In the traditional agency models, the principal is always assumed to be risk-neutral, while the agent is assumed to be risk-averse or risk-neutral.

This need not be the case. The assumption that the principal is risk-neutral is often justified by the argument that he is the economically more potent party to the contract. This is largely inspired by the traditional story behind principal-agency models referring to the relationship between a company and its employees. There are several arguments for why the economically more potent party should be less risk-averse: First, it is often plausible to assume that as a person becomes wealthier his absolute level of risk aversion decreases. Second, if the company is held by an entrepreneur, he might be the less risk-averse type of person in the first place. In addition, employees usually only work for one company while the owner might hold many different companies. So, he is probably better diversified. This last point is especially true for publicly held companies. However, in the case of a client and his consultant, things can be different. The small consultant partnership is clearly more risk-averse than its multinational client, but this changes if the big international consultancy firm provides services to a small start-up company through its incubator branch. Clearly, in the setting analysed so far - the case where, say, the principal is risk-averse and the agent risk-neutral - does not appear to be problematic as optimal incentive provision and optimal risk sharing are compatible. But what if there is a bilateral moral hazard problem? To answer this and other questions, one should look at risk sharing in its own right.

In the following, two separate sources of value creation by risk sharing shall be explored: **differences in risk attitudes** which might arise from predisposition or different levels of wealth and **differences in diversification**. This will be modelled in a linear-normal-exponential setting and the following propositions are derived[306]:

5. Without Diversification:

    5.1. If both parties are risk-averse, it will always be optimal to engage in some degree of risk sharing. Each party's share in the risky part of their pay-off equals the ratio of their risk tolerance and overall risk tolerance. The optimal bonus rate thus increases as the agent becomes more risk-tolerant relative to the principal. It does not depend on any specific distributional assumptions.

    5.2. If one party is risk-neutral while the other party is risk-averse, it is optimal for the risk-neutral party to assume all the risk. If both parties are risk-neutral, the choice of the bonus rate does not matter for risk sharing purposes.

---

[306] Technically, in line with the usual instrumentalist flexibility in creating models, it is common to use simple exponential Bernoulli functions, although they exhibit constant absolute risk aversion, even if it is assumed that there is decreasing absolute risk aversion. This is not as big a problem as it seems: In order to model decreasing absolute risk aversion, one is just doing *as if* the wealthy party was less risk-averse by nature and then uses the exponential Bernoulli function to approximate local preferences over lotteries. The same can be done to accommodate for diversification effects. In the case of the publicly held company, shareholders are not actually risk-neutral, but they are diversified. So, collectively, it is in their interest that the company is managed *as if held by a risk-neutral individual* (in the absence of financial distress costs). In this Section, however, diversification effects will be explicitly modelled to highlight the fact that the more risk-averse company might not necessarily be less diversified and vice versa (Take the example of a private-equity partnership).

5.3. It can be seen that the advantage of variable fees over flat fees increases for rising project risk, rising absolute levels of risk averseness and rising relative risk tolerance of the agent and vice versa.

6. With Diversification

6.1. The optimal sharing rule for risk sharing with diversification can be written as the sum of the optimal sharing rule without diversification and a correction term, accounting for the portfolio effects.

6.2. The portfolio effect will increase the optimal bonus rate the stronger the diversification effect in the portfolio of the agent is relative to the principal's diversification effect and vice versa.

6.3. As risk tolerance of the agent relative to the principal increases, the optimal bonus rate always becomes higher if the coefficients of correlation are positive. If adding the project actually lowers portfolio risk of the principal, the optimal bonus rate will possibly decrease for increasing risk tolerance of the agent relative to the principal.

6.4. If the difference between optimal risk sharing and the flat fee case is taken as an indicator for the importance of risk sharing, importance increases for increasing project risk, lower absolute levels of risk tolerance of the parties involved and increasing differentials of "specific risk appetite" which depends on both the relative risk tolerance and the specific way the project interacts with the parties' portfolios.

2.3.2 The Model

In this first subsection, only differences in risk attitudes are considered. Diversification will enter the analysis in the next subsection as an extension to this basic model. Variable fees create value by improving risk sharing if the sum of certainty equivalents of the principal and the agent in the case of flat fees $\left(CE_P + CE_A\right)$ is lower than in the case of variable fees $\left(CE'_P + CE'_A\right)$:

$$CE_P + CE_A < CE'_P + CE'_A . \tag{4.1}$$

An alternative way to think of this condition is that value is created if by moving from flat fees to variable fees the certainty equivalent of the agent (CE_A) is decreasing less than the certainty equivalent of the principal (CE_P) increases:

$$CE_A - CE'_A < CE'_P - CE_P. \qquad (4.1)'$$

The optimal degree of risk sharing is attained if the sum of certainty equivalents is maximized:

$$\max_b \left(CE'_P + CE'_A\right), \qquad (4.2)$$

where b represents the bonus rate of the linear incentive contract.

Staying in the above framework of exponential utility functions and normally distributed outcomes, the certainty equivalents for variable fee contracts can be calculated as follows:

$$\begin{aligned} CE'_P &= \overline{x}_P - (1-b)^2 \frac{r_P \sigma^2}{2} \\ CE'_A &= \overline{x}_A - b^2 \frac{r_A \sigma^2}{2}. \end{aligned} \qquad (4.3)$$

Where $\overline{x}_P, \overline{x}_A$ is the expected value, r_P, r_A is the coefficient of risk averseness for the principal and the agent respectively, and b is the bonus rate. (By setting $b = 0$ it becomes obvious that this formulation comprises the case of flat fees.)

Inserting (4.3) into (4.2) gives:

$$b^* \in \arg\max_b \overline{x}_P + \overline{x}_A - (1-b)^2 \frac{r_P \sigma^2}{2} - b^2 \frac{r_A \sigma^2}{2}. \qquad (4.4)$$

As $\overline{x}_P, \overline{x}_A$ do not depend on b, this can be reformulated as:

$$b^* \in \arg\min_b (1-b)^2 \frac{r_P \sigma^2}{2} + b^2 \frac{r_A \sigma^2}{2}. \qquad (4.5)$$

So, the problem can be thought of as choosing b in order to minimize the risk premium. Differentiating (4.5) yields the first-order condition:

$$b^{*}\sigma^{2}\left(r_P + r_A\right) - r_P\sigma^{2} = 0 \tag{4.6}$$

Both parties are strictly risk-averse

As both parties are strictly risk-averse and the project is risky $\sigma^{2}\left(r_P + r_A\right) > 0$. The objective function is therefore convex and the first-order condition is necessary and sufficient for a global minimum. Solving (4.6) for b^*, it can be written:

$$b^{*} = \frac{r_P}{r_P + r_A} = \left(1 + \frac{r_A}{r_P}\right)^{-1}. \qquad (4.6)'$$

In the literature, this expression can also be found in the form of:

$$b^{*} = \frac{\tau_A}{\tau_A + \tau_P} = \left(1 + \frac{\tau_P}{\tau_A}\right)^{-1}, \qquad (4.6)''$$

where $\tau_i = 1/r_i$ and is called the coefficient of risk tolerance[307]. As this is the more intuitive concept, propositions will be derived in terms of risk tolerance.

Interpreting condition (4.6)'' yields the intuitive result that the optimal bonus rate increases as the agent becomes more risk-tolerant relative to the principal.

$$\left(\frac{\tau_P}{\tau_A}\downarrow\right) \rightarrow \left(b^{*}\uparrow\right) \tag{4.7}$$

In addition, perhaps less intuitively, the optimal bonus rate which reflects the agent's share in the risky part of his compensation equals the ratio of his risk tolerance and the over-all risk tolerance of both parties. Also, note that distributional assumptions play no part in the optimal sharing rule.

---

[307] see Kreps (1990), p. 173

It can also be seen that if both parties are strictly risk-averse it will always be optimal to engage in some degree of risk sharing:

$$0 < b^* < 1. \tag{4.8}$$

One could easily think otherwise: If one party is more risk-tolerant than the other, it will suffer less disutility for taking risk than the other party. So, it seems plausible that it should shoulder all the risk. But this argument is flawed because **the risk premium is convex in b**. Of course, there are situations where b^* is close to zero (for very high τ_P / τ_A) or close to one (for very low τ_P / τ_A).

$$\lim_{\tau_P / \tau_A \to \infty} b^* = 0, \quad \lim_{\tau_P / \tau_A \to 0} b^* = 1. \tag{4.9}$$

Proposition 5.1 : If both parties are risk-averse, it will always be optimal to engage in some degree of risk sharing. Each party's share in the risky part of their pay-off equals the ratio of their risk tolerance and over-all risk tolerance. The optimal bonus rate thus increases as the agent becomes more risk-tolerant relative to the principal. It does not depend on any specific distributional assumptions.

Principal risk-neutral, agent strictly risk-averse and vice versa

Setting $r_P = 0$ the first-order condition in (4.6) becomes:

$$b^* r_A \sigma^2 = 0, \tag{4.10}$$

which means that $b^* = 0$.

Similarly, if the agent is risk-neutral and the principal risk-averse, one gets:

$$\left(b^* - 1\right) r_P \sigma^2 = 0 \tag{4.11}$$

which can only hold true if $b^* = 1$.

Thus, in line with intuition, the risk-neutral party, whether it is the principal or the agent, will assume all the risk. This is the result, underlying the result in subsection (2.1.4) which showed that first-best can be achieved in the case of a risk-neutral agent, even if effort is not observable. The effect of the agent's choice of effort can then be fully internalized, without creating inefficient risk sharing.

Both parties risk-neutral

If both parties are risk-neutral, the sum of certainty equivalents is always the same independent of b .The choice of b does not matter for risk sharing purposes.

Proposition 5.2.: If one party is risk-neutral, while the other party is risk-averse it is optimal for the risk-neutral party to assume all the risk. If both parties are risk-neutral, the choice of the bonus rate does not matter for risk sharing purposes.

Importance of risk sharing

As an indicator for the importance of finding the optimal sharing rule, the difference between optimal risk sharing and the flat fee case is calculated:

$$\frac{r_P^2\sigma^2}{2(r_P+r_A)}=\left(1+\frac{\tau_P}{\tau_A}\right)^{-1}\frac{r_P\sigma^2}{2} \tag{4.12}$$

Proposition 5.2.: It can be seen that the advantage of variable fees over flat fees increases for rising project risk $(\sigma^2\uparrow)$, rising absolute levels of risk averseness $(r_P\uparrow)$ and rising relative risk tolerance of the agent $(\tau_P/\tau_A\downarrow)$ and vice versa.

2.3.3 Model Extension: Diversification

In this subsection, in an extension to the basic model developed above, the effects of different levels of diversification is studied. The crucial idea is that the relevant risk of a project to a party depends on the risk the project adds to this party's portfolio. This might be well below its stand-alone risk and might differ among parties.

The basic method remains the same: First, the risk premium is calculated dependant on the bonus rate b. Then, the optimal bonus rate b* is derived using the first-order condition and checking if it is necessary and sufficient. Finally, as an indicator of the importance of risk sharing, the difference between optimal risk sharing and the flat fee case is calculated. The idea is that risk-sharing arguments should be given more weight if the potential value creation is higher. Interpreting the result, one can show which variables are driving the optimal bonus rate and the importance of risk sharing arguments. It will be seen that the results of the simple model above are special cases of this more general model.

As in the above case, the sum of certainty equivalents is maximized:

$$\max_{b}\left(CE'_P + CE'_A\right). \tag{4.13}$$

The certainty equivalents now reflecting diversification can be calculated as follows (Note that this formulation comprises the flat fee case for $b = 0$.):

$$\begin{aligned} CE'_P &= \bar{x}_{\pi_P} + (1-b)x - s - \frac{r_P\left(\sigma_{\pi_P}{}^2 + (1-b)^2\sigma^2 + 2(1-b)d_P\right)}{2} \\ CE'_A &= \bar{x}_{\pi_A} + bx + s - \frac{r_A\left(\sigma_{\pi_A}{}^2 + b^2\sigma^2 + 2bd_A\right)}{2}. \end{aligned} \tag{4.14}$$

where

$$d_P = \operatorname{cov}\left(\tilde{X}_{\pi_P}, \tilde{X}\right) = \rho_P \sigma_{\pi_P} \sigma_P \tag{4.15}$$

and ρ_P is the coefficient of correlation, x_{π_P} is expected value and σ_{π_P} is variance of the portfolio of the principal and d_A, ρ_A, x_{π_A}, σ_{π_A} defined accordingly for the agent.

Inserting (4.14) into (4.13) yields:

$$\begin{aligned} b^* \in \arg\max_{b}\ & \bar{x}_{\pi_P} + \bar{x}_{\pi_A} - \frac{r_P\left[\sigma_{\pi_P}{}^2 + (1-b)^2\sigma^2 + 2(1-b)d_P\right]}{2} \\ & - \frac{r_A\left[\sigma_{\pi_A}{}^2 + b^2\sigma^2 + 2bd_A\right]}{2} \end{aligned} \tag{4.16}$$

Reformulating (4.16) yields:

$$\begin{aligned} b^* \in \arg\min_{b}\ & \frac{r_P\left[\sigma_{\pi_P}{}^2 + (1-b)^2\sigma^2 + 2(1-b)d_P\right]}{2} \\ & + \frac{r_A\left[\sigma_{\pi_A}{}^2 + b^2\sigma^2 + 2bd_A\right]}{2} \end{aligned} \tag{4.17}$$

For b^* the first order condition must hold:

$$b^*\sigma^2(r_P + r_A) - r_P\sigma^2 - r_P d_P + r_A d_A = 0 \qquad (4.18)$$

Both parties are strictly risk-averse

Checking the second order condition $(\sigma^2(r_P + r_A) > 0)$, it is found that the objective function is concave in b and therefore b^* is a global minimum.

Rearranging, one can write for b^*:

$$b^* = \frac{r_P\sigma^2 + r_P d_P - r_A d_A}{\sigma^2(r_P + r_A)} = \frac{r_P}{r_P + r_A} + \frac{r_P d_P - r_A d_A}{\sigma^2(r_P + r_A)} \qquad (4.19)$$

The above case (without diversification) can of course be shown to be a special case of this more general version by setting $d_P = d_A = 0$.

Setting $d_i = \rho_i\sigma_{\pi_i}\sigma$ (see (4.15)), $\vartheta_i = -\rho_i\sigma_{\pi_i}$, $r_i = 1/\tau_i$ and doing some tedious algebra (4.19) can be written as:

$$b^* = \left(1 + \frac{\tau_P}{\tau_A}\right)^{-1} + \frac{1}{\sigma}\left[\left(1 + \frac{\tau_A}{\tau_P}\right)^{-1}\vartheta_A - \left(1 + \frac{\tau_P}{\tau_A}\right)^{-1}\vartheta_P\right]. \qquad (4.20)$$

τ_i is the party's risk tolerance as above. ϑ_i can be interpreted as follows: $\rho_i\sigma_{\pi_i}$ can be seen as a factor determining the **project's contribution to the principal's overall risk**. If the coefficient of correlation is 1, the project's variance is simply added to the portfolio's variance in order to get the combined risk. If it is less than 1, the combined risk is lower than the sum of variances. In extreme cases (if $\rho_i < 0$), the combined effect can actually lower overall portfolio risk. Generally speaking, the lower this expression the stronger the diversification effect. Therefore, $\vartheta_i = -\rho_i\sigma_{\pi_i}$ can be interpreted as an indicator of the strength of the diversification effect. (Note that the value of ϑ_i is negative as long as the coefficient of correlation ρ_i is positive.)

The effect of diversification can be studied in a first approach by setting $\tau = \tau_P = \tau_A$:

$$b^* = \frac{1}{2} + \frac{(\vartheta_A - \vartheta_P)}{2\sigma} \qquad (4.21)$$

It can be seen that the optimal bonus rate is higher if the diversification effect is stronger for the agent than for the principal. Project risk σ can be interpreted as a **scale variable** of the correction term: The higher the absolute risk, the lower the effect on the bonus rate as small changes already make a big difference.

The assumption of equal risk averseness has been instructive. Now, the more general case will be considered. Rewriting and interpreting (4.20),

$$b^{*} = \left(1+\frac{\tau_P}{\tau_A}\right)^{-1} + \frac{1}{\sigma}\left[\left(1+\frac{\tau_A}{\tau_P}\right)^{-1} \vartheta_A - \left(1+\frac{\tau_P}{\tau_A}\right)^{-1} \vartheta_P\right] \tag{4.20}$$

the following propositions can be derived:

Proposition 6.1.: The optimal sharing rule for risk sharing with diversification can be written as the sum of the optimal sharing rule without diversification and a correction term, accounting for the portfolio effects.

Proposition 6.2.: The portfolio effect will increase the optimal bonus rate the stronger the diversification effect in the portfolio of the agent is relative to the principal's diversification effect and vice versa.

As the agent becomes more risk-toleranton relative to the principal (τ_P/τ_A decreases), the first term on the right hand side of equation (4.20) increases. Analysing the second term is more difficult:

If both coefficients of correlation are positive, ϑ_A, ϑ_P will be negative. So, decreasing τ_P/τ_A will put less weight on the negative and more weight on the positive part of the parenthesized expression. Therefore, the second term will also rise.

If the diversification effect of the agent is so strong that ϑ_A turns positive, then decreasing τ_P/τ_A will put less weight on a positive and less weight on another positive part of the parenthesized expression. So, the parenthesized expression will roughly stay the same. As the agent becomes more risk-tolerant he does not appreciate as much that he can actually reduce portfolio risk by accepting the project, but terms 1 and 2 combined will most likely rise.

If the diversification effect of the principal is so strong that ϑ_A turns positive, then decreasing τ_P/τ_A because the principal becomes less risk-tolerant will actually put more weight on the negative part of the parenthesized expression.

So, it definitely decreases and even turns negative. Therefore, the combined effect of both terms will be low and can even turn negative. In extreme cases, b could even turn negative.

Proposition 6.3.: As the risk tolerance of the agent relative to the principal increases, the optimal bonus rate always becomes higher if the coefficients of correlation are positive. If adding the project actually lowers the portfolio risk of the principal, the optimal bonus rate will possibly decrease for increasing the risk tolerance of the agent relative to the principal.

In this last special case, the portfolio effect would not only reduce the risk contribution of the project below its stand-alone risk, but make the risk contribution negative so that the portfolio of the agent is absolutely more risky before adding the project. The intuition is that the higher the risk averseness of the principal, the more attractive it is for him to add the project to his existing portfolio for its risk-reducing properties. Normally, correlations among projects and the portfolio will be positive, and the only question is if portfolio effects reinforce, mitigate or reverse the general direction reflected by different tolerance of risk.

It is convenient to think of the issues raised here in terms of differentials of "specific risk appetite" between parties. It is specific because it is the appetite for the specific risk of the particular project in question, and not just any kind of risk. It depends on two factors: First, the parties' risk tolerance and second, the diversification effects in the parties' portfolio. One has to be careful to understand how these factors interact. Usually, ceteris paribus the "specific risk appetite" of a party increases as its risk tolerance increases. If, however, diversification effects are so strong that they turn negative, the opposite is the case. The lower risk tolerance, the higher will be the party's "specific risk appetite". This is the case where the project's contribution is not only lower than its stand-alone value but actually negative, i.e. the overall risk of the party's portfolio is decreased by adding the project[308]. So, in the case of diversification, situations may be imagined where the optimal bonus rate is 0 or 1, even if none of the parties is risk-neutral. It can even be imagined that it is lower than 0 or higher than 1. This suggests that

[308] If a savings and loan bank has issued bonds with a fixed coupon and subsequently interest rates go down, the margins of the bank will shrink. At the same time, a property dealer will benefit from the lower interest rates as people will get cheaper financing or switch assets from bonds into property. So, the consultant could counterbalance the risk of doing a variable fee project with a savings and loan bank by acquiring a variable fee project with a property dealer. Usually, however, the consultant will not agree to performance measures that do not take account of such factors.

the parties can gain by swapping payments contingent on project outcome (providing insurance for other risks the counterparty holds)[309].

Principal risk-neutral, agent strictly risk-averse and vice versa

Setting $r_P = 0$ into the first-order condition (4.18) yields:

$$b^{*}\sigma^{2}r_{A} + r_{A}d_{A} = 0. \tag{4.22}$$

Solving for b^{*} and rearranging gives:

$$b^{*} = \frac{\vartheta_{A}}{\sigma}. \tag{4.23}$$

So, for positive coefficients of correlation b^{*} becomes negative. This does not look very realistic. Often b will be bounded to be non-negative, but the following interpretation can be given: If the agent is risk-averse and the risk of the project positively correlates with his portfolio, the parties might be interested to arrange an insurance contract wherein the agent pays the principal to carry not only the risk of the project, but also to provide further coverage for other risks the agent faces.

If the principal is strictly risk-averse and the agent risk-neutral, b^{*} can be written as:

$$b^{*} = 1 + \frac{\vartheta_{P}}{\sigma} \tag{4.24}$$

Analogous to above this time the principal is interested to buy insurance from the agent if the coefficient of correlation is positive.

Importance of risk sharing

The difference between optimal risk sharing and flat fees is given by:

[309] This seems very contrived. A company that wishes to do away with certain risks will probably more likely resort to an insurance policy or a financial engineering product.

$$\frac{\left(r_P\sigma^2 + r_P d_P - r_A d_A\right)^2}{2\sigma^2\left(r_P + r_A\right)} \tag{4.25}$$

Inserting $d_K = d_B = 0$, gives:

$$\frac{r_P\sigma^2}{2\left(r_P + r_A\right)} \tag{4.26}$$

which was exactly the result above in the model without diversification.

Inserting $d_i = -\vartheta_i\sigma$ and $r_i = 1/\tau_i$ into (4.25) rearranging gives:

$$\frac{\tau_A\sigma + \left(\tau_P\vartheta_A - \tau_A\vartheta_P\right)}{2\tau_A\tau_P\left(\tau_A - \tau_P\right)} \tag{4.27}$$

Proposition 6.4.: If the difference between optimal risk sharing and the flat fee case is taken as an indicator for the importance of risk sharing, importance increases for increasing project risk, lower absolute levels of risk tolerance of the parties involved and increasing differentials of "specific risk appetite", which depend on both the relative risk tolerance and the specific way the project interacts with the parties' portfolios.

2.3.4 Discussion

This Section inquired into what is driving perfect risk sharing and highlighted the parties' level of risk tolerance (both absolute and relative to each other), the specific quality of the risk involved as determined by its correlation with existing risk-exposure and the level of project risk.

Part of the results of the first subsection (which excluded portfolio effects) reveals itself to be a special case for 2 individuals of a more general result of syndicate theory[310]: The fact that if a risk-neutral party is involved it carries all the risk; the independence of the sharing rule in each state of the probability assigned to that state; and the fact that the risky part of each party's compensation is

---

310 Syndicate theory is an application of a methodology in the theory of social choice which solves the social choice problem for varying weights of a Bergsonian welfare functional in order to get the Pareto efficient frontier. (see: Kreps (1990), pp. 169-174; the classical reference is Wilson (1968).

proportional to its own risk tolerance divided by the overall risk tolerance of society, if the parties' preferences over lotteries exhibit constant risk aversion (and therefore can be represented by an exponential utility function). In the model presented here, the exponential utility function was assumed right from the beginning. Moreover, a normally distributed output was assumed. The advantage of this set of assumptions - as was proven in the appendix to the previous Section - is that certainty equivalents can be calculated as a simple function of mean and variance. Consistent with the above-cited fact of syndicate theory, distributional assumptions (in this case σ^2) proved to be irrelevant for the optimal sharing rule.

However, this changes as soon as the possibility of portfolio effects is allowed for. In this case, the modeling framework chosen is extremely convenient as it readily admits the use of portfolio theory from finance which is cast in a mean-variance framework[311].

2.4 The Optimal Contract

2.4.1 Introduction

In the above model an important restriction was imposed. Only linear incentive schemes were considered. This assumption is arbitrary, unless it is possible to show that linearity is a feature of optimal contracts. Unfortunately, quite to the contrary, the following propositions can be derived:

7. If effort is **contractible,** the optimal compensation is a flat fee. If effort is **uncontractible**, optimal compensation varies with outcome.

8. If effort is **uncontractible**, optimal compensation depends on outcome through the likelihood ratio. If interpreted in terms of an **inference process,** any outcome that makes the principal revise upwards his beliefs with respect to the probability of high effort will be rewarded.

---

[311] This cannot be taken for granted, because μ, σ- analysis is not generally equivalent to the concept of risk averseness (see Rothschild, Stiglitz (1970)). Another example besides the normal-exponential setting is the quadratic utility function which admits a μ, σ- representation for any distributional assumption but has otherwise awkward properties such as increasing absolute risk averseness (see: Schneeweiß (1967), pp. 95ff.; Feldstein (1968). Better suited is a power function combined with a lognormal probability distribution (see: Schneeweiß (1967), pp. 145 ff).

9. The relationship between the optimal sharing rule and outcome is working through the **information content of outcome** which depends on distributional assumptions. Physical properties of outcome (like quantity) are not interesting as such but only to the extent that they carry information. Therefore, the sharing rule which links compensation to outcome is very contrived and sensitive to distributional assumptions.

10. In conclusion of propositions 7-9, it can be said **that few general constraints** on the shape of optimal incentive schemes can be derived. Utility functions and distributions must be specified in order to arrive at meaningful constraints. What is more, optimal contracts are very sensitive to these assumptions.

11. No natural settings seem to exist for which linearity is optimal. **Linear incentive schemes** can, however, be argued to be relatively **robust** to changing distributional assumptions and to assumptions concerning the richness of the action space. Transaction cost arguments also favor simple incentive schemes.

12. Non-distributional assumptions like **the richness of the action space** affect optimal contracts.

13. For y to be **valuable information,** it must affect posterior assessment. It must be a signal for effort choice without existing information being a sufficient statistic for y with respect to H and L.

The proof for these propositions can only be sketched[312].

2.4.2 Mechanics of the Optimal Sharing Rule

The first step will be to set up a control theoretic model in order to derive properties of the optimal sharing rule. This will lead to a **statistical interpretation** of the basic agency model[313]. This interpretation is key to the understanding of the mechanics of incentive schemes relevant to the following sections, which is why it will be treated at some length. This interpretation gives an intuitive explanation of the above proposition that only very few general

---

312 An excellent review of the following discussion can be found in Hart, Holmström (pp. 79-97, 1987).

313 The statistical interpretation follows the treatment of Hart, Holmström(1987)

constraints can be derived as for the **shape** of the optimal contract, and none of them very meaningful.

The model will be slightly different from the model used above. It is assumed that the agent cannot choose from a continuum of actions but only between two effort levels. Either he can be hard-working or lazy and this time the agent, by choosing his level of effort, is effectively choosing two probability distributions over a continuous support set of signals. This allows studying more closely the effects of distributional assumptions by allowing a much higher variety of distributions.

On a technical level, this leads to the following changes compared to above: As there is a finite action space, the number of incentive constraints will be finite (in this case there is only one incentive constraint) and therefore no first-order approach is needed. The continuity of the set of signals makes it impossible to stipulate that, for any choice of effort, any output arises with positive probability because probabilities then would not add up to zero. Instead, it is assumed that the support sets of signals are the same and that both density functions are strictly positive[314].

As above, the principal has to solve the following maximization problem[315]:

$$\max \int \left(x - s(x)\right) f_H(x)\,dx \tag{5.1}$$

$$\text{s.t. } IC: \int u\left(s(x)\right)\left[f_H(x) - f_L(x)\right]dx - c_H + c_L \geq 0 \tag{5.2}$$

$$PC: \int u\left(s(x)\right) f_H(x) - c_H - u_0 \geq 0 \tag{5.3}$$

where x is the signal (here simply output), $s(x)$ is the sharing rule, $f_H(x)$, $f_L(x)$ are the density functions over output for effort levels H and L respectively. f_H strictly dominates f_L in the sense of stochastic dominance ($F_H(x) > F_L(x)$). c_H, c_L is the disutility of effort for effort levels H and L respectively as measured on the scale of disutility. Both the principal and the agent are v-N-M expected utility maximizers. The principal is assumed to be risk-neutral. The agent is risk-averse. His utility function $u(\cdot)$ is increasing, twice continuously differentiable and concave ($u'(\cdot) > 0$, $u''(\cdot) < 0$). u_0 is the agent's reservation utility.

---

314 see Kreps (1990), p. 604 (he is more formal by stipulating that the "likelihood ratios are uniformly bounded and bounded away from zero)

315 This is the parameterized distribution formulation of the agency problem in a more general version than above, see Holmström (1979). Tirole (2000) also used this formulation.

As above, it can be argued that both constraints must be binding. The incentive constraint must bind because increasing compensation differentials above the level needed in order to induce the agent to implement the high effort would unnecessarily increase the risk exposure of the agent and therefore expected payment by the principal. Also, the participation constraint must hold with equality, because otherwise the principal's expected payment could be reduced by lowering compensation at every signal by the same amount without affecting incentives.

Letting μ and λ be the Lagrangean multipliers[316] for constraint (5.2) and (5.3) respectively, it can be written:

$$\begin{aligned} L(s(x),\mu,\lambda)=\int(x-s(x))f_H(x)+\mu u(s(x))[f_H(x)-f_L(x)]+ \\ \lambda u(s(x))f_H(x)+\mu(c_L-c_H)-\lambda(c_H+u_0)dx \end{aligned} \tag{5.4}$$

As $\partial L/\partial s(x)=0$, it can be written:

$$-f_H(x)+\mu[f_H(x)-f_L(x)]u'(s(x))+\lambda f_H(x)u'(s(x))=0 \tag{5.5}$$

Dividing both sides by $f_H(x)u'(s(x))$ and rearranging yields the following condition for optimal sharing rules:

$$\frac{1}{u'(s(x))}=\lambda+\mu\left(1-\frac{f_L(x)}{f_H(x)}\right) \tag{5.5$'$}$$

If effort is contractible, there will be no incentive problems (as the principal will use a forcing contract). Therefore, the incentive constraint will not bind. From the complementary slackness conditions it can be followed that this implies $\mu=0$. If $\mu=0$, the optimal compensation $s(x)$ will be a flat fee.

If effort is not contractible, there will be an incentive problem. The incentive constraint will bind. If $\mu=0$ the agent will choose L in violation of the incentive constraint. Therefore $\mu>0$. But then, optimal compensation $s(x)$ will vary with outcome x.

---

[316] If constraints cannot be argued to hold with equality, Kuhn-Tucker conditions have to be used.

Proposition 7: If effort is contractible, the optimal compensation is a flat fee. If effort is uncontractible, optimal compensation varies with outcome.

This is the same result as in (2.1), only this time the expression also gives insight into the "mechanics" of the relationship. The sharing rule $s(x)$ depends on x through:

$$\frac{f_L(x)}{f_H(x)}.$$

This expression is familiar from statistical inference and is called the likelihood ratio. "It reflects how strongly x signals that the true distribution from which x was drawn is f_L rather than f_H. A high likelihood ratio speaks for L and a low for H."[317] It can be seen that, in an optimal incentive scheme, the agent is punished for a high likelihood ratio and rewarded for a low likelihood ratio:

$$\frac{f_L(x)}{f_H(x)}\downarrow \Rightarrow \frac{1}{u'(s(x))}\uparrow \Rightarrow u'(s(x))\downarrow \Rightarrow s(x)\uparrow, \text{ for } u''(\cdot)<0.$$

Thus, any outcome that suggests that high effort was most likely chosen is rewarded, which is a quite intuitive result.

It is possible to rewrite (5.5) in a way which stresses even more the analogy to statistical inference. Letting γ be the prior of H and $\gamma'(x)$ the posterior of H if x was observed and applying Bayes' rule gives (see *Exhibit 1*):

$$\begin{aligned}\gamma'(x) &= \text{Prob}(H \mid x)\\ &= \frac{\text{Prob}(H)\text{Prob}(x \mid H)}{\text{Prob}(H)\text{Prob}(x \mid H)+\text{Prob}(L)\text{Prob}_L(x \mid L)}\\ &= \frac{\gamma f_H(x)}{\gamma f_H(x)+(1-\gamma)f_L(x)}.\end{aligned} \tag{5.6}$$

[317] Hart/ Holmström (1987), p. 80

it was a reaction to the inferences of the principal. This interpretation is instructive to understand why there are only few general constraints[318] and none of them meaningful: The relationship between the optimal sharing rule and outcome is working through the information content of outcome. In other words: The physical properties of the outcome (e.g. monetary success of the project) are only interesting to the extent that they carry information about which action was chosen by the agent; but this information content depends exclusively on distributional assumptions. It is not even possible to derive that compensation is always increasing in output. Consider e.g. distribution f_H, f_l where $f_H(x) = f_L(x+1)$. There is stochastic dominance ($F_H > F_L$) but if it is e.g. assumed that f_H, f_l are bimodal then it becomes clear that there is no monotonicity of $s(x)$ in x (see *Exhibit 2*). Of course, it is possible to make the assumption that the likelihood ratio is monotone in outcome[319] to ensure monotonicity of $s(x)$[320].

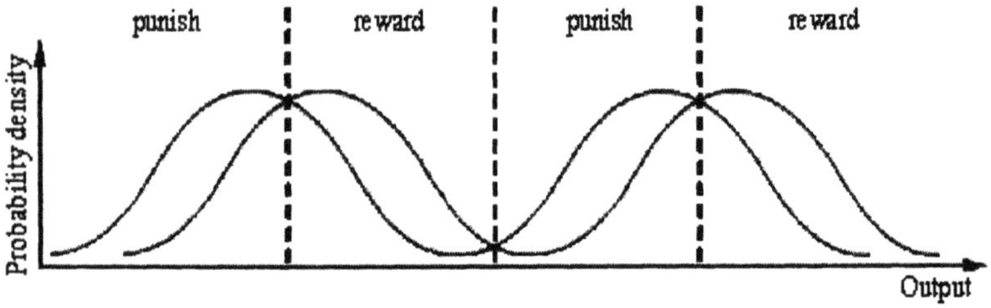

Exhibit 2: No Monotonicity of Compensation in Outcome despite Stochastic Dominance[321]

Proposition 9: The relationship between the optimal sharing rule and outcome is working through the information content of outcome which depends on distributional assumptions. Physical properties of outcome (like quantity) are not interesting as such but only to the extent that they carry information.

---

[318] see Grossman, Hart(1983)

[319] This is called the Monotone Likelihood Ratio Property (MLRP), which is attributed by some to Milgrom (1981) and by others to unpublished work of Mirrlees.

[320] In fact, it was already mentioned above that in the case of more than two available actions another assumption called the "concavity of the distribution function assumption" (see also footnote 266) is needed to ensure monotonicity (see Kreps (1990), pp. 596-598; Grossman, Hart (1983), example 1).

[321] For a very intuitive display of this property see Mas-Colell, Whinston, Green (1995), p. 486.

Therefore, the sharing rule which links compensation to outcome is very contrived and sensitive to distributional assumptions.

Therefore, in order to derive meaningful constraints, **additional distributional assumptions** have to be made. Yet, it becomes clear from the above that derived optimal incentive schemes are very **sensitive** to these distributional assumptions.

Proposition 10: In conclusion of propositions 7-9, it can be said that little general constraints on the shape of optimal incentive schemes can be derived. Utility functions and distributions must be specified in order to arrive at meaningful constraints. Optimal contracts, however, are very sensitive to these assumptions.

2.4.3 The Case for Linear Contracts

The sensitivity of optimal incentive schemes to distributional assumptions suggests a great **variety** of different incentive schemes[322]. This contrasts to the real world experience where only a **few relatively simple incentive schemes** like linear incentive schemes, step-functions and flat fee contracts can be found.

One obvious reason for this conflicting evidence can be **transaction cost arguments**. Optimal contracts can sometimes be rather complex. People tend not to conclude such contracts.

Yet, there are more subtle explanations. One can be the robustness of the incentive scheme: Some schemes may be more **robust to changing assumptions with respect to probability distributions and utility functions**[323] than others. If these distributional assumptions require more accurate information than is practically available, there is an advantage to using schemes which are quite good for a whole range of assumptions. It can e.g. be shown that, for a linear production function and a normally distributed error term (a quite natural formulation), linear incentive schemes are always dominated by **step function schemes** which can approximate first best arbitrarily closely[324]. This is because, at very low outcomes, the likelihood ratio decreases to a point where one can almost act as if non-compliance was determined with zero chance of error. Harsh penalties can be

322 see Hart, Holmström (1987), p.91 n whose line of argument is followed here

323 see e.g. Kreps(1990), p. 612

324 Mirrlees (1974)

inflicted for these outcomes, while the payment is a flat fee over all other outcomes. Therefore, perfect risk sharing can almost be achieved and the agent will choose high effort because low effort will increase the probability of harsh punishment . There are several reasons why this example is **not realistic**. It may not be possible to impose harsh enough penalties because of bankruptcy constraints, or maybe the likelihood ratio is bounded, but this example highlights a more fundamental problem: Step function schemes are an extreme case of **fine tuning**. While they are better than linear schemes in all cases if the range of outcomes for inflicting the penalty and the amount of the penalty are fixed at the optimal level, it is worse than linear schemes in most cases, where the assumptions are only rough estimates as is almost always the case in the real world.

Another robustness argument refers to the **richness of the action space**. It is often observed in economics that measures do not work where the agents have enough options to circumvent them. To capture the intuition it is extremely difficult for a government to tax the extremely wealthy as they can always move their residence to another country. It is also impossible for a company to engage in price discrimination if reselling is permitted. In this case, any price discrimination is arbitraged away. Following the same rationale, it can be shown that **step functions create path-dependent incentives**. If it is assumed that an agent can observe progress while the project is underway[325], he will quite often decide that he does not need to exert effort in the step function case. This is because in many situations he will either conclude that he will not be able to reach the threshold where he is paid or that he has already sufficiently surpassed it. So, he will neither do his best to prevent a bad situation from turning worse nor try to make a good situation even better. This path dependency of incentives does not apply for linear incentive schemes which keep incentives fairly constant. This result "illustrates a more general idea namely, that complicating the nature of the incentive problem can actually lead to simpler forms for optimal contracts"[326].

Proposition 11: No natural settings seem to exist where linear schemes are optimal. Linear incentive schemes, however, can be argued to be relatively robust to changing distributional assumptions and to assumptions concerning the richness of the action space. Transaction cost arguments also favour simple incentive schemes.

---

[325] Note that this is actually a multi-period model. For more on dynamic extensions see Chapter IV5.

[326] Mas-Colell, Whinston, Green (1995), p. 488

It is questionable whether this very general conclusion in rescue of linear incentive schemes is justified given the very restrictive assumptions[327]. It can be argued that the main contribution of this argument was to stress the **importance of non-distributional assumptions such as the richness of the action space**, when deriving optimal incentive schemes. To illustrate the idea, when designing incentives one is actually preparing a path which is meant to channel the behaviour of the agent. Every time he takes the decision, there have to be walls erected to ensure that he stays on the path, otherwise the agent gains control of the game and can manipulate outcome. This, however, poses the problem **of predicting all the relevant options available to the agent**. If one fails to do so, the scheme may break down.

Proposition 12: Non-distributional assumptions, like the richness of the action space, affect optimal incentive schemes.

2.4.4 Valuable Information

A precise result can be derived about **which parameters should enter into an optimal contract** in the first place. Suppose y is another signal besides output x and that the joint density function is $f_i(x,y)$ for $i=L,H$. Then, analogous to (5.5)', it can be written:

$$\frac{1}{u'(s(x))}=\lambda+\mu\left(1-\frac{f_L(x,y)}{f_H(x,y)}\right) \tag{5.8}$$

As $f_i(x,y)=f_i(x)f_i(y)$ the likelihood ratio can be written:

$$\frac{f_L(x)f_L(y)}{f_H(x)f_H(y)} \tag{5.9}$$

If $f_H(y)=f_L(y)$, then they cancel out and the optimal contract should not depend on y. This is an intuitive result: The condition means that y is just unrelated noise with respect to H and L. It is obvious that such a variable would just add noise, increasing cost for the principal who has to compensate the agent for his risk exposure, without carrying any information.

---

[327] Gibbons (2001)

But it was already assumed above that y is a signal. Therefore, $f_H(y) \neq f_L(y)$. Yet, it will be shown that being a signal is just a necessary condition for a contract parameter to provide valuable information.

As the condone probability of y when x was observed is:

$$f_i(y|x) = \frac{f_i(x,y)}{f_i(x)} \tag{5.10}$$

Rearranging gives:

$$f_i(x,y) = f_i(y|x)f_i(x) \tag{5.10)'$$

If $f_H(y|x) = f_L(y|x)$ it can be seen from (5.8) that the optimal contract does not depend on y. This condition says that y is perfectly correlated with x with respect to H and L. All the information about effort choice that is contained in y is already contained in x. So, y offers no additional information. It is also said that x is a sufficient statistic for y with respect to H and L. This leads to the following proposition.

Proposition 13.: For y to be valuable information it must affect posterior assessment. It must both be a signal for effort choice and the information already available may not be a sufficient statistic for y with respect to H and L.

This result is also called the sufficient statistic result or the Holmström informativeness condition[328].

How can this result be interpreted? When designing the incentive scheme of a consultant who makes a cost cutting projectm there is no use in monitoring both the cost saved and the number of workers laid off. There is a deterministic relationship between the two variables. They are perfectly or very closely correlated, but it may make sense to monitor the hours worked by the consultant, formal consistency of the report, the extent and depth of analysis, the amount of relevant empirical material used, the numbers of interviews concluded and the satisfaction of the people involved.

This information is valuable as it increases the ability to separate between high and low effort. It is as if inferences become more precise. Expression (5.8)

---

[328] see Kreps (1990), p. 608; Mas-Colell, Whinston Green (1995), p. 487f; Holmström (1979)

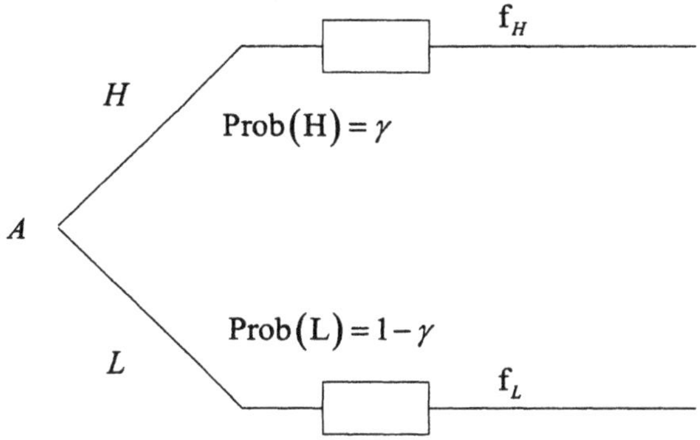

Exhibit 1: Agent chooses a Distribution of Outcomes

Rearranging yields:

$$\frac{f_L(x)}{f_H(x)} = \left(\frac{1}{\gamma'(x)} - 1\right)\frac{\gamma}{1-\gamma}. \tag{5.6)'$$

Inserting (5.6)′ into (5.5)′ yields:

$$\frac{1}{u'(s(x))} = \lambda + \mu\left[1 - \left(\frac{1}{\gamma'(x)} - 1\right)\frac{\gamma}{1-\gamma}\right]. \tag{5.7}$$

Rearranging yields:

$$\frac{1}{u'(s(x))} = \lambda + \mu\left[\frac{\gamma'(x) - \gamma}{\gamma'(x)(1-\gamma)}\right]. \tag{5.7)'$$

It becomes clear that compensation rises if the output makes the principal revise upwards his beliefs with respect to the probability of high effort.

Proposition 8: If effort is uncontractible, optimal compensation depends on outcome through the likelihood ratio. If interpreted as an inference process, any outcome that makes the principal revise upwards his beliefs with respect to the probability of high effort will be rewarded.

It must be stressed that the principal does not in fact infer. He can perfectly predict the actions of the agent, but the optimal incentive scheme is designed as if predicts that as the likelihood ratio decreases the optimal compensation differential is very high. This is because, as inferences are very precise, the chance of error is low and therefore the welfare loss due to imperfect risk-sharing can be kept low in spite of the wage differential. The principal can severely punish the agent if low outcome is observed.

Clearly there is also a cost in obtaining information and often the most valuable information is also the most expensive to obtain. So, directly observing effort would be the most valuable information, but it was assumed that it is uncontractible (read: can only be made contractible at prohibitive cost). If they came at the same cost, one would always prefer to do input monitoring to output monitoring. So, this result on its own only helps to determine the value of information but, in order to decide which parameter should enter the contract, one also has to consider the cost of contracting on it.

The result highlights another important point: It is not only sufficient to look if information is a signal. It must also be analysed whether the signal is not disturbed by the same noise. Beyond the obvious case cited above, this suggests that there is a decreasing marginal utility of information as with a reasonable number of variables considered, probably most of the uncertainty that can be filtered out has been filtered out. The method when considering adding a signal therefore is to ask what the risks are that disturb the relationship between the choice of effort and the signal, and if these risks are of different type and origin than in the relationship between effort and the existing signals. If this is the case, the signal is likely to be valuable.

2.4.5 Discussion

In this Section, a control theory model was set up to determine the optimal sharing rule. It was possible to reprove the results of earlier sections. If effort is contractible, flat fee contracts will be used. If it is not contractible it will depend on output, but contrary to earlier results it was also possible to shed some light on the mechanics of the optimal sharing rule. Compensation depends on output through the likelihood ratio. There are two implications: The optimal sharing rule can be understood quite intuitively as rewarding the agent if the signal makes it likely that high effort was chosen. But it also explains why little general constraints can be derived for the shape of the optimal sharing rule: It is very sensitive to specifications of utility functions and distributional assumptions. Although the optimal contract can only be derived to be linear under awkwardly improbable assumptions[329], there are a number of reasons explaining the practical prominence of such contracts. First, there is the transaction cost argument. Setting up complex contracts is just too expensive. Second, linear contracts are argued to be relatively robust for a large number of settings. So, paradoxically, there are reasons to believe that adding complexity makes contracts simpler. But also non-distributional assumptions, like the number of different options available to the agent, affects the optimal incentive scheme. It was also shown that information is only valuable if it affects posterior assessment of the effort level chosen. Therefore, it must be related to effort choice, but it must also be impossible to perfectly infer the information - to the extent that it is relevant to this assessment - from information on variables already included into the contract. The same results can also be derived for the more general case of a continuous action space and a continuous set of outcomes[330], but this complication offers no additional economic insights[331].

2.5 Limitations and Extensions

A common assumption is that there is a **comparative cost advantage** of output monitoring compared to input monitoring. Why should this be the case? In order to implement input monitoring, the principal has to watch the agent while performing the required task. This causes **opportunity costs** to the principal. Still worse, if the principal does not know the production function of the agent, he may well watch the agent while performing a task but will be **unable to interpret his actions** as to whether they are instrumental to achieve the required output. These costs are amplified by the fact that, usually, the very motivation to hire an agent in the first place was that the principal either did not want or could not perform the task himself. So, either the principal has something else to do, which means that his opportunity costs are high, or the performance of the task requires specialized knowledge that the principal does not possess. The latter case does make it difficult for the principal to monitor the agent effectively. Alternatively, the principal could hire **other qualified agents** to do the monitoring for him, but then it may be difficult to prevent these monitoring agents from colluding with the operative agents. For all these reasons, input monitoring is likely to be very costly in many circumstances. On the other hand, **output monitoring should be very easy**. One has only to look to which extent the required result was achieved, provided that it can be properly defined. So, if a client hires a consultant to

[329] see Hart, Holmström (1987) p. 81

[330] see Kreps (1999). p. 608

[331] see Hart, Holmström (1987), p. 83 who come to this conclusion.

perform a cost cutting project, it will be much easier for the client to evaluate how much cost was reduced than to interpret the wide variety of single measures the consultant takes to achieve his goal.

Having clearly established the intuition for comparative cost advantage of output monitoring compared to input monitoring in a wide variety of situations, it may come as a surprise that **input monitoring can theoretically infinitely approximate first best**. This is because the agent, in his decision on whether to cheat or not, will weigh the benefits of cheating (in the case of shirking reduced disutility of effort) against the expected value of punishment. Therefore, if **harsh enough punishments are announced,** the probability of detection and therefore the number and thoroughness of inspections can be infinitely reduced. This is the first line of attack against the model presented above on the grounds that input monitoring need not be more expensive than output monitoring. In this case, there seems **no rationale for output monitoring**. If it is not cheaper, it will only provide an additional drawback: imperfect risk sharing.

Yet, the second line of attack against the above model disputes just that. It was argued that **input monitoring always establishes the truth**, while output monitoring is prone to error. This is a crucial point, because it was shown above that the **driving force behind imperfect risk sharing** in output monitoring is the possibility of error in judgement and the subsequent punishment of the innocent. If it can be shown that output monitoring can achieve perfect accuracy, or that input monitoring is prone to error as well this distinction breaks down. In fact, both can be shown to be plausible assumptions in some circumstances: Output **monitoring will be perfectly accurate** in the case of deterministic production functions, but also if there is **shifting support**[332]. Indeed, the above argument of Mirrlees on step-functions is in the same spirit. On the other hand, it seems implausible to assume that input monitoring will be able to prove cheating at 100%. There will always be judgement, inferences, circumstantial evidence. Whatever the process, there is a chance of error. Therefore, the above assumption will need to be relaxed to allow for **error in input monitoring**.

These arguments appear construed, and in fact they are. In general, input monitoring will be more costly and output monitoring more prone to error. Ignoring these arguments, therefore, seems to be a justified abstraction, but there is still some merit in taking them seriously. In a nutshell, they say that, regardless of whether one is looking at input monitoring or at output monitoring, there are two relevant issues: **Error in judgement** and **cost of monitoring,** and that under

---

332 see next Section

some circumstances both schemes fare equally well or badly on these two dimensions. By acknowledging that there generally is a distinction between input monitoring and output monitoring, one is actually saying that these circumstances will rarely be present. Understanding why this is the case helps to identify other relevant situational variables which influence the problem of optimal contracting.

Extensions to the classic agency model involve the role of the **bankruptcy constraint**, the **role of error** in the monitoring process which will be treated in Chapter (3), distortive effects of contracting[333] (Chapter 4) and extensions beyond the one-shot relationship[334] (Chapter 5).

3 Error in judgement, Bankruptcy

3.1 Input Monitoring

3.1.1 Introduction

In this Chapter it will first be argued that input monitoring achieves first best if harsh enough punishment is feasible and error in judgement can be excluded. Clearly, these assumptions are unrealistic[335]. Bankruptcy and legal constraints set bounds to the extent of punishment. It will be shown that if a bankruptcy constraint is introduced, input monitoring will be costly. Alternatively, if error in judgement is allowed for, input monitoring will be costly even if there is no bankruptcy constraint. One should note the interesting twist in this argument: The first line of attack against costly input monitoring involves schemes with high punishment. It was argued before that, even if error in judgement cannot be excluded, it is possible to safely abstract from it because its probability is low. As soon, however, as schemes with very high punishments are introduced, even small chances of error will lead to substantial cost due to imperfect risk-sharing.

The following propositions will be derived:

14. Input monitoring can achieve first best if harsh-enough punishments are feasible and error can be excluded.

---

[333] see e.g. Holmström, Milgrom (1991), Gibbons(2001)

[334] see e.g. Bull (1987), Holmström (1999), Levin (2003), Lazear, Rosen (1981)

[335] It is sometimes assumed in behavioural economics that probability of detection may not fall below a certain threshold in order to be effective, regardless of expected value, because otherwise it will not be taken seriously by the agent. Having mentioned it, this criticism will subsequently be ignored.

15. If a bankruptcy constraint is assumed, there is always a welfare loss as the optimal frequency of inspections does not tend to zero, resulting in direct costs of monitoring.

16. If there is a bankruptcy constraint and the cost of the monitoring technology is high enough, "efficiency wages" have to be paid in order to provide incentives. There are situations where no trade occurs, although there are potential gains of trade, resulting in welfare loss. This is because the principal's profit would turn negative.

17. Monitoring cost rises in the scope of cheating (Δ), and decreases in the sum of punishment and compensation ($d+s$). This implies that compensation is a substitute for punishments, and "efficiency wages" are paid where the scope for punishment is limited due to bankruptcy and other legal constraints.

18. Monitoring cost is a decreasing and concave function in agent risk averseness. If it is possible to impose high punishment in situations where potential damage from cheating is high, the cost reduction effect is most powerful.

19. First best can also be infinitely approximated in the case where error is permitted if the agent is risk-neutral and there is no bankruptcy constraint.

20. In the case of a risk-averse agent, there will be a welfare loss if error in judgement is allowed for, even if there is no bankruptcy constraint.

3.1.2 Modeling Assumptions

It is assumed that if the agent shirks he can get a **benefit** of $\overline{\Delta}$ in addition to his agreed-upon **compensation** s. In order to prevent this from happening, the principal installs monitoring technology. If it is established by the monitoring process that shirking occurred, the agent receives no compensation s and has to pay a **fine** d. The fine will almost always be positive. It will be allowed, however, that d is negative. This is the case if legal constraints exist that do not allow the agent to be punished but only make it possible to withhold part of the agreed-upon salary s[336]. But $d+s>0$, because never will the principal have to pay a bonus in excess of salary in the event of punishment.

By choosing the monitoring technology, the principal faces a **cost-quality trade-off**. The quality of a monitoring technology is high if there is a low probability of error. Error occurs if the agent is not punished although he did shirk or if he is punished although innocent. It is assumed that the principal faces a monitoring technology which establishes the truth at a probability of $p(c)$ and errs at a probability of $1-p(c)$, with $c \geq 0$ being the cost of investment in the monitoring technology[337]. It is assumed that the **probability of erring** is the same whether the agent is innocently punished or gets away with shirking[338]. Two cases will be considered. In the first case, the probability of erring will be zero. This is the traditional assumption of input monitoring.

$$p=1,\ c=\overline{c} \tag{7.1}$$

In the second case, the range of $p(c)$ is the half-open interval **between 0,5 and 1**, with 1 as the upper boundary which can be infinitely approximated, but never reached. It is clear that the probability of establishing the truth cannot be less than 0,5. This is because, even if nothing is invested in the technology

336 It can be imagined that if it is determined in court that the agent did shirk, the judge, far from allowing the principal to punish the agent, actually only rules a fraction of the agreed-upon compensation can be withheld.

337 Later, a distinction is introduced between monitoring technology and monitoring scheme. A monitoring scheme is comprises of both monitoring technology and frequency of inspections.

338 **This assumption is not innocent** and needs to be discussed: If the probability of error is 20%, then a shirking agent will get away with it in 20% of the cases and an honest agent has a chance of 20% to be punished nevertheless. If the agent can challenge this decision in court, there may be a problem with monitoring technologies that seem to be very prone to error, especially in a **system obsessed with truth beyond doubt**. So, it could be that, in case a punishment is imposed, the court will only uphold it in 50% of all cases. Then, the probabilities of error would change to 60% and 10%. This raises the interesting problem of the coexistence of private settlement mechanisms and public courts. Parties might agree on a rather error prone monitoring scheme because it is cheap and find some sort of arrangement to compensate for the extra risk, but if the recourse to the courts cannot be excluded, the arrangement might break down. The problem will decrease if monitoring schemes' error comes closer to zero. Another problem arises if the principal controls the monitoring process. He will then have the incentive to always report cheating. Reputation concerns might prevent this, but in a one-shot relationship this clearly is a risk. So, it has to be assumed that the monitoring process is objective and transparent. If necessary, procedural rules can be enforced by the courts. In conclusion, the assumption seems rather strong, but it can be shown that the model does not depend on this in its outcome, so for convenience it is upheld.

($c=0$), it cannot be worse than tossing coins. $p(\cdot)$ Is a positive, strictly increasing and concave function in c:

$$p(c)\in[0,5;1);\ \lim_{c\to\infty}p(c)=1;\ p(0)=0,5;\ p'(\cdot)>0;\ p''(\cdot)<0. \quad (7.2)$$

The principal has a possibility to save cost, other than keeping c low. He can randomize inspections, which means that he carries out inspections only at a fraction α of cases. It is further assumed that all costs of inspection are variable. So the cost of the monitoring scheme will be αc.

It is further assumed that the principal's and the agent's preferences over lotteries satisfy the v-N-M axiom and that the principal is risk-neutral and the agent risk-averse. This is in line with traditional assumptions.

In *Exhibit 3*, the **pay-offs** for the agent and the principal are shown for the different cases. Outcome is written as the vector:

$$\begin{pmatrix}\text{pay-off agent}\\ \text{pay-off principal}\end{pmatrix}$$

One can now proceed to **set up the maximization problem**: The agent will only abstain from shirking if the incentive constraint is fulfilled, i.e. if the expected utility of not shirking is higher than the expected utility of shirking:

$$\begin{aligned}&\alpha[1-p(c)]u(-d)+(1-\alpha[1-p(c)])u(s)\geq\\&[1-\alpha p(c)]u(s+\Delta)+\alpha p(c)u(-d)\end{aligned} \quad (7.3)$$

Rearranging gives:

$$\alpha(1-2p)u(-d)+u(s)-\alpha(1-p)u(s)-(1-\alpha p)u(s+\Delta)\geq 0 \quad (7.3)'$$

The **relevant pay-off** for the participation constraint and the principal's objective function is the pay-off in the case of "no shirking". This is because, otherwise, no incentive constraint would be needed and investment in monitoring would be zero. The agent will only accept the contract if the participation constraint is fulfilled:

$$\alpha(1-p)u(-d)+u(s)-\alpha(1-p)u(s)-u_0\geq 0 \quad (7.4)$$

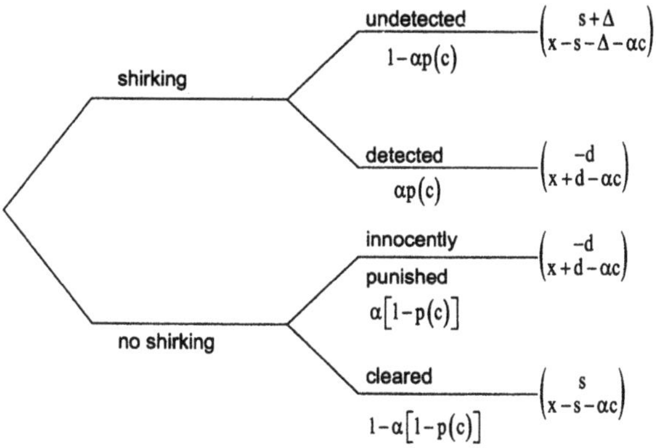

Exhibit 3: Pay-offs in the Input Monitoring Model

The principal's objective function can be written as:

$$\max \alpha(1-p)(x+d)+\left[1-\alpha(1-p)\right](x-s)-\alpha c \qquad (7.5)$$

Rearranging yields:

$$\max \alpha(1-p)(d+s)+(x-s)-\alpha c \qquad (7.5)'$$

Therefore, the **maximization problem** can be set up as:

$$\max \alpha(1-p)(d+s)+(x-s)-\alpha c \qquad (7.6)$$

$$\text{IC}: \ \alpha(1-2p)u(-d)+u(s)-\alpha(1-p)u(s)-(1-\alpha p)u(s+\Delta)\geq 0 \qquad (7.7)$$

$$\text{PC}: \ \alpha(1-p)u(-d)+u(s)-\alpha(1-p)u(s)-u_0\geq 0 \qquad (7.8)$$

3.1.3 Absence of both Error and Bankruptcy Constraint

In the first case that is considered, it is assumed that a **perfect**[339] **monitoring** mechanism exists at a given cost:

$$p(\bar{c}) = 1,\ c = \bar{c} \tag{7.9}$$

It is further assumed that there is **no bankruptcy constraint**. So, any punishment is feasible. The principal's problem therefore is to determine the optimal frequency of inspections α, the optimal salary s and the optimal punishment d.

Inserting (7.9), the **maximization problem** can be stated as follows:

$$\max_{\alpha,s,d} x - s - \alpha\bar{c} \tag{7.10}$$

$$\text{s.t. IC: } -\alpha u(-d) + u(s) - (1-\alpha)u(s+\Delta) \geq 0 \tag{7.11}$$

$$\text{PC: } u(s) - u_0 \geq 0 \tag{7.12}$$

Letting μ_1 and μ_2 be the Lagrangean multipliers for (7.11) and (7.12), the following conditions must hold for an optimal contract:

$$\frac{\partial L}{\partial \alpha} = -\bar{c} + \mu_1\left(u(s+\Delta) - u(-d)\right) = 0 \tag{7.13}$$

$$\frac{\partial L}{\partial s} = -1 + \mu_1 u'(s) - \mu_1(1-\alpha)u'(s+\Delta) - \mu_2 u'(s) = 0 \tag{7.14}$$

$$\frac{\partial L}{\partial d} = \mu_1 \alpha u'(-d) = 0 \tag{7.15}$$

Note that the multipliers have to be non-negative:

$$\mu_1 \geq 0,\ \mu_2 \geq 0. \tag{7.16}$$

The complementary slackness conditions are given by:

$$\mu_1\left[-\alpha u(-d) + u(s) - (1-\alpha)u(s+\Delta)\right] = 0 \tag{7.17}$$

$$\mu_2\left[u(s) - u_0\right] = 0 \tag{7.18}$$

---

339 i.e. zero error probability

Solving (7.13) for μ_1 yields:

$$\mu_1 = \frac{\overline{c}}{u(s+\Delta)-u(-d)} > 0 \qquad (7.13)'$$

which is positive as can easily be seen recalling that $d+s>0$. This also means that the incentive constraint binds.

As $u'(-d) \neq 0$ it can be followed from (7.15) that either α or μ_1 must be 0. μ_1=0 contradicts (7.13)′ and $\alpha = 0$ cannot be true, because it is impossible to induce the agent not to shirk with zero probability of inspections. Therefore, the **Lagrangean conditions cannot hold, which means that there is no optimum for this problem.**

Even if there is no optimum, **interesting implications** can be derived: In order to induce the agent not to shirk, the incentive constraint must hold. Solving the incentive constraint (7.11) for α gives:

$$\alpha \geq \frac{u(s+\Delta)-u(s)}{u(s+\Delta)-u(-d)} \qquad (7.11)'$$

It is evident from the objective function (7.10) that α will always be chosen at the lowest possible level. The **smallest value for** α for which the incentive constraint holds is given by the following condition:

$$\alpha = \frac{u(s+\Delta)-u(s)}{u(s+\Delta)-u(-d)} \qquad (7.11)''$$

Inserting (7.11)′′ into (7.10) yields:

$$x - s - \frac{u(s+\Delta)-u(s)}{u(s+\Delta)-u(-d)}\overline{c} \qquad (7.10)'$$

Assuming the agent to be risk-neutral, (7.10)′ simplifies to:

$$x - s - \frac{s+\Delta-s}{s+\Delta+d}\overline{c} = x - s - \frac{\Delta}{s+\Delta+d}\overline{c} \qquad (7.10)''$$

The **optimal salary** s^* for the principal to offer if he wants the incentive constraint to hold for the lowest possible α must satisfy the first order condition:

$$\frac{\partial \Pi}{\partial s} = -1 - \frac{-\Delta}{\left(s^* + \Delta + d\right)^2}\bar{c} = 0 \tag{7.19}$$

Rearranging gives:

$$\left|s^* + \Delta + d\right| = \sqrt{\bar{c}\Delta} \tag{7.19)'$$

Two cases must be distinguished:

$$\begin{aligned}&(1)\ s^* + \Delta + d = -\sqrt{\bar{c}\Delta}\\&(2)\ s^* + \Delta + d = \sqrt{\bar{c}\Delta}\end{aligned} \tag{7.20}$$

Case (1) is impossible for $d > -s$ and $\Delta > 0$. Solving (2) for s^* yields:

$$s^* = \sqrt{\bar{c}\Delta} - \Delta - d \tag{7.21}$$

The contract must **also satisfy the participation constraint**. Solving the participation constraint for s yields:

$$s \geq \bar{u}\left(u_0\right) = \bar{s} \tag{7.12)'$$

Salary s^* violates the participation constraint if:

$$s^* < \bar{s} \tag{7.22}$$

In this case, the wage is set to the reservation level, making the incentive constraint loose. In other words: Whenever the wage, necessary in order to meet the participation constraint, is higher than is needed to induce the agent not to shirk, the incentive constraint will also hold. Therefore, the chosen wage will be:

$$s^* = \max\left[\sqrt{\bar{c}\Delta} - \Delta - d, \bar{s}\right] \tag{7.23}$$

Inserting into the objective function (7.10)'' gives:

$$\Pi = \begin{cases} x + \Delta + d - 2\sqrt{\bar{c}\Delta} & \text{for } \bar{s} < \sqrt{\bar{c}\Delta} - \Delta - d \\ x - \bar{s} - \dfrac{\Delta}{\bar{s} + \Delta + d}\bar{c} & \text{otherwise} \end{cases} \tag{7.10)'''$$

The optimal d must satisfy the first order condition:

$$\frac{\partial \Pi}{\partial d} = \begin{cases} 1 & \text{for } s < \sqrt{\overline{c}\Delta} - \Delta - d \\ \dfrac{\Delta}{\left(\overline{s} + \Delta + d\right)^2}\,\overline{c} & \text{otherwise} \end{cases} \tag{7.24}$$

It can be seen that $\partial\Pi/\partial d > 0$. Π is **strictly increasing in** d. Therefore, there cannot be a maximum. This is the same result that was obtained with the Kuhn-Tucker conditions above.

As d rises $\overline{s} < \sqrt{\overline{c}\Delta} - \Delta - d$ will not hold. Even in the extreme case where $\overline{c} \to \infty, \Delta \to \infty$ with $d \to \infty$ the condition will be $\overline{s} < -\Delta$. This never holds as $\overline{s} > 0$. Therefore, the other case applies. In other words: **If the participation constraint holds, the incentive constraint will always be loose**: In any case where the agent accepts the contract he will also refrain from shirking.

It was already established that no maximum exists. Yet, it can be shown that there is an upper boundary:

$$\lim_{d \to \infty}\left(x - \overline{s} - \frac{\Delta}{\overline{s} + \Delta + d}\overline{c}\right) = x - \overline{s} \tag{7.25}$$

Therefore, it is possible to **infinitely approximate first best** by infinitely increasing punishment in the case where there is no error in judgement and no bankruptcy or other legal constraints exist.

Proposition 14: Input monitoring can infinitely approximate first best if harsh enough punishments are feasible (no bankruptcy constraint) and error can be excluded.

3.1.4 Bankruptcy constraint

In this subsection, it is still assumed that a **perfect monitoring mechanism** is available at a given cost $\overline{c}$. However, now a **bankruptcy constraint** is introduced. This can have many reasons. The capacity of individuals to absorb losses is limited either by nature or by law (limited liability). Legal provisions do not allow certain kinds of punishment. Therefore, the extent of punishment that can be imposed is limited ($d \geq \overline{d}$).

The result (7.24) of Section (3.1.3) still holds. Π is strictly increasing in d, but d **is bounded** to reflect the bankruptcy constraint, $d \in \left(-s, \bar{d}\right]$. A maximum now exists as a **boundary solution,** $d = \bar{d}$. The maximum amount of punishment will be imposed. But this time, as d cannot rise indefinitely it becomes clear from (7.25) that the frequency of inspections does not approach zero:

$$\alpha = \frac{\Delta}{s+\Delta+d} \square\ 0 \tag{7.26}$$

Thus, it can be concluded that:

Proposition 15: If a bankruptcy constraint is assumed, there is always a welfare loss as the optimal frequency of inspections does not tend to zero, resulting in direct costs of monitoring.

But this is not the only source of welfare loss. In the above argument it could be shown that the incentive constraint was always loose if the participation constraint was met. If there is a bankruptcy constraint it can be seen that:

$$\bar{s} \geq \sqrt{\bar{c}\Delta} - \Delta - \bar{d} \tag{7.27}$$

will not always hold if for a given $\bar{s}$ and $\bar{d}$ the cost of the monitoring technology $\bar{c}$ is high enough. More specifically, the pay level needed to provide incentives not to shirk will exceed the reservation level ("efficiency wages") if situational parameters are such that:

$$\bar{c} > \frac{\left(\bar{s}+\Delta+\bar{d}\right)^2}{\Delta}. \tag{7.28}$$

If, however, the **cost of investment in the monitoring technology is too high**, the contract will not be offered by the principal at all, as his optimal pay-off turns negative. To prevent this from happening, the following condition must hold:

$$x + \Delta + \bar{d} - 2\sqrt{\bar{c}\Delta} \geq 0. \tag{7.29}$$

From $d>-s$[340] and $s<x$[341] follows $d>-(x+\Delta)$ and therefore $(x+\Delta+d)>0$. Thus (7.29) can be rearranged to yield:

$$\bar{c} \leq \frac{\left(x+\Delta+\bar{d}\right)^2}{4\Delta}. \qquad (7.29)'$$

If (7.28) holds as was assumed, (7.29)′ only holds if:

$$\left(x+\Delta+\bar{d}\right)^2 > 4\left(\bar{s}+\Delta+\bar{d}\right)^2. \qquad (7.30)$$

It can be seen that there are situations with potential gains of trade ($x>\bar{s}$) where this condition does not hold.

Proposition 16: If there is a bankruptcy constraint and the costs of the monitoring technology are high enough, "efficiency wages" have to be paid in order to provide incentives. There are situations where no trade occurs, although there are potential gains of trade because the principal's profit would turn negative, resulting in a welfare loss.

3.1.5 Extension: The role of Agent Risk Averseness

In order to study the role of risk averseness, the **utility function will be specified**. It is assumed that the agent's utility function is exponential:

$$u(x) = 1 - e^{-rx}. \qquad (7.31)$$

Inserting (7.31) into the expression for α (see (7.11)′′ and rearranging yields (see *Exhibit 4*)

$$\alpha = \frac{1-e^{-r\Delta}}{e^{r(d+s)} - e^{-r\Delta}}. \qquad (7.32)$$

The sensitivity of monitoring cost α to changes of risk averseness r is given by the first derivative (see *Exhibit 5*):

---

340 It was already argued that otherwise punishment would lose its meaning.

341 Agreed-upon salary will never be higher than the gross outcome.

$$\frac{\partial\alpha}{\partial r} = e^{r(d+s)}\left[(\Delta+d+s)e^{-r\Delta}-(d+s)\right]-\Delta e^{-r\Delta}. \qquad (7.33)$$

The expressions are a bit unwieldy. As the functions were specified, it is convenient to depict the functions to get an intuition of the relationships: It can be seen in *Exhibit 4* that monitoring cost rises with the scope of cheating (Δ), and decreases in the sum of punishment and compensation ($d+s$).

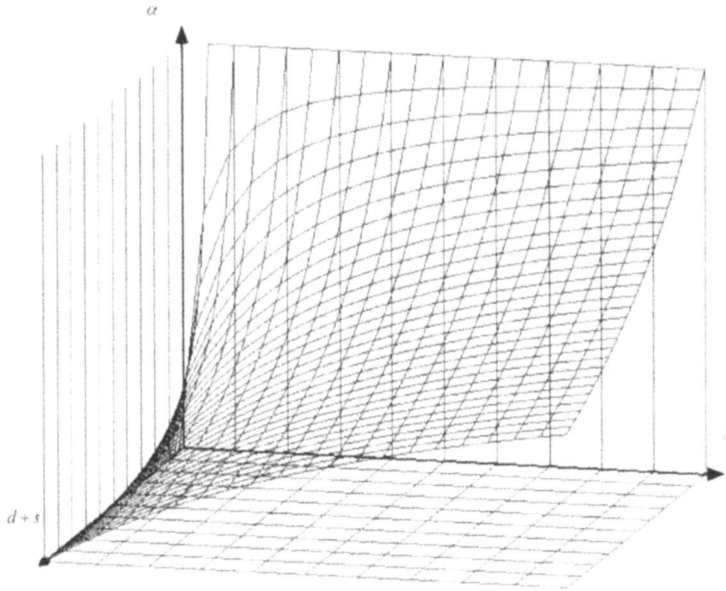

Exhibit 4: Monitoring Cost

This is a quite intuitive result. Perhaps the most surprising is that monitoring cost only depends on the sum of d and s. This is, however, consistent with the result that efficiency wages are paid where the scope for punishment is limited due to bankruptcy and other legal constraints.

Proposition 17: Monitoring cost rises in the scope of cheating (Δ), and decreases in the sum of punishment and compensation ($d+s$). This implies that compensation is a substitute for punishment and " efficiency wages" are paid where the scope for punishment is limited due to bankruptcy and other legal constraints.

The responsiveness of monitoring cost to changing risk averseness is depicted in *Exhibit 5*. It can be seen that the cost of implementing input monitoring decreases as the risk averseness of the agent increases:

$$\frac{\partial \alpha}{\partial r} < 0 \forall d + s, \forall \Delta \tag{7.34}$$

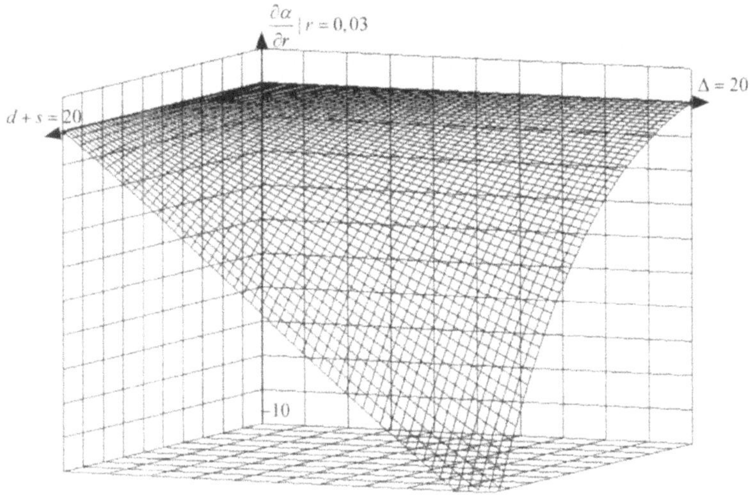

Exhibit 5: Responsiveness of monitoring cost to changing risk averseness.

If it is possible to impose high punishment in situations where potential damage from cheating is high, this effect is most powerful.

In *Exhibit 6* the level of **responsiveness of monitoring cost to changes in risk attitudes** is shown as a function of risk averseness.

It becomes clear that the higher the level of risk averseness to begin with, the higher the decrease of monitoring cost from a small increase of risk averseness will be. Monitoring cost is a decreasing and concave function in agent risk averseness.

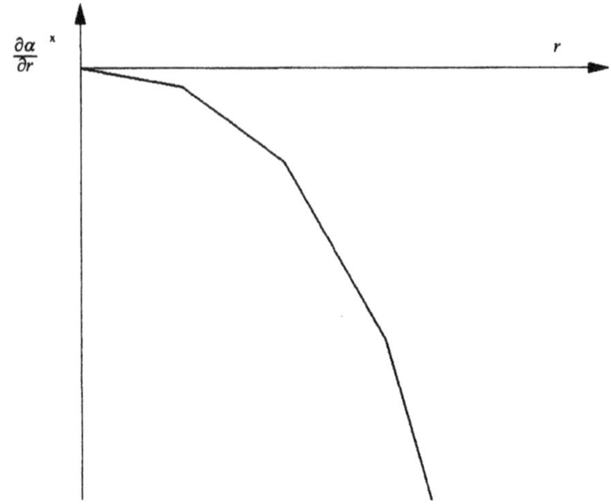

* $(d+2=5, \Delta=2)$

Exhibit 6: Responsiveness of Monitoring Costs to Changing Risk Averseness

Proposition 18: Monitoring cost is a decreasing and concave function in agent risk averseness. If it is possible to impose high punishment in situations where potential damage from cheating is high, the cost reduction effect is most powerful.

3.1.6 Presence of Error

If the possibility of error is allowed for, the maximization problem is a bit more complex:

$$\max_{\alpha,c,s,d} \alpha(1-p)(d+s)+x-s-\alpha c \tag{7.35}$$

$$\text{s.t. } \alpha(1-2p)u(-d)+u(s)-\alpha(1-p)u(s)-(1-\alpha p)u(s+\Delta)\geq 0 \tag{7.36}$$

$$\alpha(1-p)u(-d)+u(s)-\alpha(1-p)u(s)-u_0 \geq 0 \tag{7.37}$$

Letting μ_1 and μ_2 be the Lagrangean multipliers for constraints (7.36) and (7.37), the following conditions must hold:

$$\frac{\partial L}{\partial \alpha}=(1-p)(d+s)-c+\mu_1\left[(1-2p)u(-d)-(1-p)u(s)+pu(s+\Delta)\right] \\ +\mu_2\left[(1-p)u(-d)-(1-p)u(s)\right]=0 \tag{7.38}$$

$$\frac{\partial L}{\partial c}=-\alpha p'(d+s)-\alpha+\mu_1\left[-2\alpha p'u(-d)+\alpha p'u(s)+\alpha p'u(s+\Delta)\right] \\ +\mu_2\left[-\alpha p'u(-d)+\alpha p'u(s)\right]=0 \tag{7.39}$$

$$\frac{\partial L}{\partial s}=\alpha(1-p)-1+\mu_1\left[u'(s)-\alpha(1-p)u'(s)-(1-\alpha p)u'(s+\Delta)\right] \\ +\mu_2\left[u'(s)-\alpha(1-p)u'(s)\right]=0 \tag{7.40}$$

$$\frac{\partial L}{\partial d}=\alpha(1-p)+\mu_1\left[\alpha(1-2p)u'(-d)(-1)\right] \\ +\mu_2\left[\alpha(1-p)u'(-d)(-1)\right]=0 \tag{7.41}$$

Rearranging (7.38) and (7.39), it can be written:

$$d+s-\frac{c}{1-p}+\mu_1\left[\left(\frac{1-2p}{1-p}\right)u(-d)-u(s)+\frac{p}{1-p}u(s+\Delta)\right] \\ +\mu_2\left[u(-d)-u(s)\right] \tag{7.38)'$$

$$-(d+s)-\frac{1}{p'}+\mu_1\left[-2u(-d)+u(s)+u(s+\Delta)\right]+\mu_2\left[-u(-d)+u(s)\right] \tag{7.39)'$$

Adding (7.38)′ and (7.39)′ and solving for μ_1 yields:

$$\mu_1=\frac{p'c-p+1}{p'\left[u(s+\Delta)-u(-d)\right]} \tag{7.42}$$

Rearranging (7.41) and solving for μ_2 gives:

$$\mu_2=\frac{1}{u'(-d)}-\mu_1\left(1-\frac{p}{1-p}\right) \tag{7.41)'$$

It was assumed that the chance of **error in judgement** $1-p$ is a function of the investment in the monitoring technology c. If nothing is invested, the chance of error is 50% (like tossing coins). As the investment is increased, the chance of error decreases, but will never be zero. Therefore, $p(c)$ must be a function which takes the value 0,5 for $c=0$ and asymptotically approaches 1 as $c\rightarrow\infty$.

In order to facilitate the argument $p(c)$ is **specified by a simple function**, fulfilling these properties:

$$p(c) = 1 - \frac{0,5}{1+c} = \frac{2c+1}{2(1+c)}$$
$$p'(c) = \frac{1}{2(1+c)^2} \tag{7.43}$$

Inserting (7.43) in (7.42) and (7.41)′ gives:

$$\mu_1 = \frac{2c+1}{u(s+\Delta) - u(-d)} \tag{7.44}$$

$$\mu_2 = \frac{1}{u'(-d)} + 2\mu_1 c \tag{7.45}$$

Inserting (7.44) into (7.45) gives:

$$\mu_2 = \frac{1}{u'(-d)} + \frac{4c^2 + 2c}{u(s+\Delta) - u(-d)} \tag{7.45)′$$

As $c > 0, d > -s$ and $u'(\cdot) > 0$ it can be followed that both μ_1 and μ_2 are **strictly positive**. From the complementary slackness conditions, it follows that both constraints bind.

At this point a **methodological remark** is warranted: Microeconomic analysis attempts to **isolate effects**. The effect of a bankruptcy constraint was studied above. A perfect monitoring mechanism was assumed in order to make sure that only the effect produced by the bankruptcy constraint is considered: Now, the focus of analysis is the effect of an imperfect monitoring mechanism which allows for error in judgement. In order to isolate this effect it is assumed that **no bankruptcy constraint exists**. Conditions (7.44) and (7.45)′ will therefore be analysed assuming infinite punishment potential ($d \to \infty$).

If the agent is **risk neutral** and because $u(x) = x,\ u'(x) = 1\ \forall x$, μ_1 and μ_2 will simplify to:

$$\mu_1 = \frac{2c+1}{s+\Delta+d} \tag{7.46}$$

$$\mu_2 = 1 + \frac{4c^2 + 2c}{s+\Delta+d} \tag{7.47}$$

It can easily be seen that for $d \to \infty$, $\mu_1 \to 0$ and $\mu_2 \to 1$.

Now the case is considered, where the agent is **risk averse**:

$$\mu_1 = \frac{2c+1}{u(s+\Delta)-u(-d)} \tag{7.44}$$

$$\mu_2 = \frac{1}{u'(-d)} + \frac{4c^2+2c}{u(s+\Delta)-u(-d)} \tag{7.45$'$}$$

As $u(-d) \to -\infty$ and $u'(-d) \to \infty$ for $d \to \infty$, it can easily be seen that $\mu_1 \to 0$ and $\mu_2 \to 0$.

Both the incentive and the participation constraint are binding, but trying to increase d in order to make the incentive constraint vanish ($\mu_1 \to 0$), the **imputed value to the principal of giving an extra unit of income to the agent approaches 1 for the risk-neutral and 0 for the risk-averse agent**.

Therefore, for risk-neutral agents, first best can be infinitely approximated by increasing punishment. In the limit case, investing one unit of utility in the incentive scheme exactly yields one unit of utility to the principal. Marginal utility and marginal cost are the same and the outcome efficient.

Proposition 19: First best can also be infinitely approximated in the case where error is permitted if the agent is risk neutral and there is no bankruptcy constraint.

In the risk-averse case, if d is increased, the marginal utility of one unit invested in the incentive scheme approaches 0. Therefore, **the principal will not choose** $d \to \infty$, but then, the **incentive constraint will be binding and first best can no longer be achieved**. To see why, one can look at the symmetric information case as a benchmark. Here, no incentive constraint has to be stipulated because compliance is assured by a forcing contract. Now, if an incentive constraint is added and it proves to be loose, it means that the same result is feasible as in the symmetric case: First best can be achieved. If it is tight, it means that the **agent has to be compensated for the extra risk**. Inducing the agent not to cheat comes at the price of imperfect risk sharing.

Proposition 20: In the case of a risk-averse agent there will be a welfare loss if error in judgement is allowed for, even if there is no bankruptcy constraint.

The described effect can be interpreted as follows: If there is no bankruptcy constraint, punishment can be made very high. If punishment is very high, the frequency of inspections (α) can be reduced. This means that, holding monitoring cost (αc) constant, it is possible to decrease the chance of error ($1-p(c)$) as the accuracy $p(c)$ is an increasing function in c. In turn, a reduced chance of error decreases the loss due to imperfect risk sharing. Yet, there is a second effect: Holding probability of error constant, higher punishment increases welfare loss due to imperfect risk sharing if the agent is risk averse. There is consequently a direct and an indirect effect, which are countervailing in the case of agent risk averseness.

The resulting trade-off is solved by balancing monitoring cost and risk taking simultaneously on two levels: On the first level, the accuracy of monitoring is an increasing but concave function in cost per inspection (c). Because of concavity there comes a point where it is better to reduce the frequency of inspections and consequently economize directly on monitoring cost than to invest into accuracy, and thereby indirectly reduce the cost of imperfect risk sharing. On the second level there is another problem: With the probability of error held constant, there comes a point where the loss of imperfect risk sharing for increasing levels of punishment is higher than the savings in monitoring cost by reducing frequency.

3.1.7 Discussion

The input monitoring model of this subsection incorporates **bankruptcy constraints**, **monitoring cost**, and **error in judgement**.

It was shown that input monitoring can approximate first best even if it comes at a cost if there are no bankruptcy constraints and no possibility of error in judgement. If there is a bankruptcy constraint, there will be welfare loss because of direct monitoring cost and possibly efficiency wages or complete uncontractibility (no trade). The phenomenon of efficiency wages can be understood by realizing that, for purposes of incentive, provision differentials in agent pay-utility and not absolute pay-levels are relevant. Therefore, in the absence of error in judgement, increasing agent risk-averseness even helps to set up cheap incentive schemes. Yet, if error in judgement is permitted, problems of imperfect risk-sharing arise, requiring the simultaneous minimization of the cost arising from investment in the monitoring technology, the frequency of inspections and the risk premium.

For the sake of tractability, cheating was modelled as a lump sum appropriated by the agent without the consent of the principal. This **leaves no place for different degrees of shirking**. Therefore, in contrast to the output monitoring model, residual loss due to lower effort in equilibrium cannot be captured. The input monitoring model distinguishes two cases: In the first case, there is no input monitoring at all and the principal expects the agent to use his full scope of shirking. Preventing the agent to shirk would be too costly. In the second case, the agent does not shirk at all, but the cost of inducing him to refrain from shirking is modelled. It becomes clear that the **model set-up is coarse** in this respect. **It does not take into account cases wherein the principal is trying to induce the agent to refrain from shirking only to some extent**. This coarseness does not mean that this case is not possible. It is just a technical consequence of the binary formulation of shirking, justified by the emphasis of this model.

3.2 Output Monitoring

3.2.1 Introduction

Error in judgement is a core part of the traditional model for output monitoring described above. Error is inevitable because of the **stochastic disturbance of the production technology**: If compensation depends on output, there is the danger of innocently punishing the agent. Output can be low even if effort was high because of bad luck. The risk-averse agent will want to be compensated for carrying this risk resulting in an incentive-risk trade-off. Input monitoring, on the other hand, was considered to be accurate but costly. Yet, the picture is more complex: Just as input monitoring can have a problem of imperfect risk-sharing because of the pitfalls of the monitoring process, there are **situations where output monitoring is perfectly accurate** and can achieve first best beyond the obvious case of a deterministic production function. This will be the case for shifting support schemes[342]. Another problem considered will be the **moral hazard with respect to risk** which might arise in output monitoring schemes in the presence of bankruptcy constraints.

21. Output monitoring can achieve first best if **shifting support** sets are assumed and harsh enough punishment is feasible relative to the actionable portion on the joint support set.

22. The bankruptcy constraint makes variable fee schemes, which are not already asymmetrical in design **de facto asymmetrical**. This creates a new moral hazard problem with respect to choice of risk.

---

[342] This means that the above assumption that density functions are defined on the same support sets is relaxed (see: IV2.4.2).

3.2.2 Shifting Support

It was said that output-based compensation leads to imperfect risk sharing if the agent is risk averse and the production function is stochastic. This is only true if it is assumed that choice of effort affects the density function but leaves the support set unchanged. If, however, different effort levels make the support set shift so that **ranges of outcomes do not perfectly overlap** for different effort levels, very harsh punishments can be announced. These schemes are called shifting support schemes or "boiling-in-oil contracts"[343]. First best can be achieved. The intuition is that if certain very bad outcomes can only happen if effort is lower than desired by the principal, the threat of a harsh punishment for these outcomes will induce the agent to refrain from shirking[344].

Once again the crucial point is to exclude the possibility of error in judgement. This solution combines the **best of two worlds. Low cost** output monitoring and **no error** as in traditional input monitoring. There are, however, two problems:

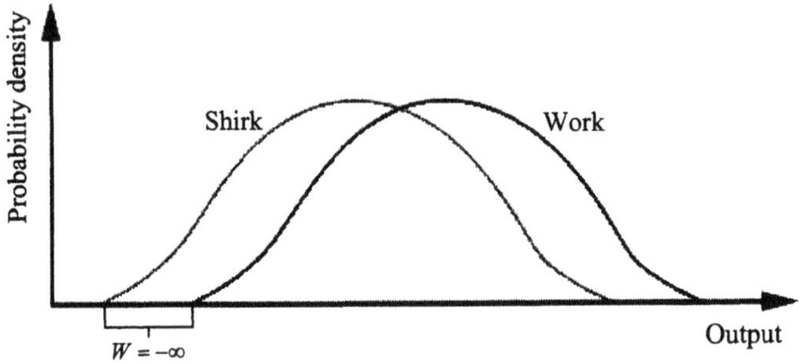

Exhibit 7: Shifting Support Scheme[345]

First, as for input monitoring, the introduction of **bankruptcy** and other legal constraints is harmful to the feasibility of shifting support schemes, although

---

[343] Rasmusen (1994), p. 180

[344] This result is similar to the result of Mirrlees that step-function schemes are always better than linear incentives. It is also the basis for the idea, that if society wants to enforce compliance with rules at low cost it must impose punishments out of proportion with harm (see: Becker (1968) for criminal law and Polinsky, Che (1991) for tort law). As was mentioned above (see footnote 183), the US. Supreme Court recently ruled on this matter and drew some criticism from economists. At the same time, there are certainly moral issues involved. A quite different critical argument was mentioned in footnote 335.

[345] Rasmusen (1994), p. 180

the problem is **less severe** than in the case of input monitoring, where the objective was not just to create incentives for showing effort but also to drive down monitoring cost by decreasing the frequency of inspections.

The second problem is more severe: It is difficult to imagine many situations where shifting support occurs. And if it occurs, the problem will be to **predict the portion** where the support sets of the two density functions do not overlap[346]. Given the severity of the consequences this is crucial. Otherwise, the problem of **imperfect risk sharing** reappears. Maybe there is a portion on the joint support set where one can say that it is possible to infer with 100% certainty that low effort was exerted. Yet, these portions, which will be called "**actionable portions**", **tend to be very narrow**. The narrower they become, the looser the bankruptcy constraint must be in order to provide appropriate incentives.

Proposition 21: Output monitoring can achieve first best if shifting support sets are assumed and harsh enough punishment is feasible relative to the actionable portion on the joint support set (a narrow "actionable portion" requires a high bankruptcy constraint).

3.2.3 Moral Hazard with respect to Risk

The bankruptcy constraint makes monitoring in general more costly. This applies for fixed and variable fee contracts. In the case of a fixed contract, limited possibility to impose punishment drives up inspection cost. In the case of a variable contract, there is the danger of unilateral increase of risk. This may require putting a **cap** on the upside of incentive schemes, which **limits their effectiveness**.

For an intuitive explanation, one can look at the case of the stochastically disturbed linear production function and a linear sharing rule. If the agent not only controls the mean but also the risk (variance) of the project, he can improve his position by increasing the risk above the optimal level. This is comparable to somebody holding a **call option**. He benefits if the risk of the underlying increases. For low enough expected compensation of the agent, it is preferable for him to choose **a high risk project even if expected pay-off is lower**. This causes potential damage to the risk-neutral principal, not only the equity holder but also the creditors. If e.g. the owner-manager also has limited liability, there could be

---

346 This argument is analogous to the "fine tuning" – argument against step function schemes (see IV2.4.3).

collusion between the consultant and the client at the expense of the creditors who are the principal's principal[347].

Proposition 22.: The bankruptcy constraint makes variable fee schemes, which are not already asymmetric in design, de facto **asymmetrical.** ***This creates a new moral hazard problem with respect to choice of risk, which may require putting a cap on the upside of incentive schemes, limiting their effectiveness.***

3.2.4 Discussion

In this Sub-Section it was shown that shifting support schemes create first best solutions for output contracting even if the agent is risk-averse. Yet, such schemes are often unrealistic because of bankruptcy constraints (legal, moral, economic) and the problem of fine tuning, already encountered earlier in the case of step functions. Another point made was the asymmetry of incentive schemes due to bankruptcy constraints, which create problems as the agent will have the incentive to choose very risky projects even if they have a lower expected value than alternative projects.

4 Transaction Cost, Bonding, Distortion

4.1 Transaction Cost and Bonding

The following propositions will be motivated in this subsection:

23. **Direct transaction costs** arise for input monitoring and for output monitoring, though it will often be plausible that they are **lower for output monitoring**.

24. **Indirect transaction costs** arise from provisions which are designed to lower direct transaction costs. The goal is to **rationalize monitoring** or to **directly influence the agent's disutility function**. This leads to inefficiencies because production technology is prescribed from top to bottom in a way that is known to be inefficient. In addition, innovation from bottom to top is stifled. This is a distortive effect.

---

347 This is an example of a chain of principal-agent relationships and the problem of colluding. This can often be encountered in the real world and is a fundamental problem of corporate governance.

One of the parameters of the input monitoring model was the **direct transaction cost** for putting in place the monitoring device. Inspections have to be carried out either simultaneously or ex post. Not only input monitoring but also output monitoring may cause such extra transaction cost, though it will usually be lower: Required output has to be defined and provisions have to be made to record output thus defined, sometimes resulting in extra accounting expenses.

Less obviously, there are **indirect costs** of monitoring: **Bonding costs** arise when the agents have to abide by certain strict rules. Such measures can have two purposes: Either they **influence the disutility function** by reducing distraction, or they **rationalize monitoring**. Surfing the internet, phoning privately, walking through the park during office hours might be prohibited. If a consultant is required to work on site in an office assigned to him, his disutility function is influenced by reducing distraction (it is not very interesting to sit in the office looking out of the window, while it may be very attractive to sit down and watch TV). In addition, it is easier to monitor his actions in the office than in the field. Another example is a private investor instructing his banker not to make certain kinds of investments. He may forgo profit opportunities (e.g. by not allowing him to exceed a certain leverage), but also protects himself against the hazards of excessive risk taking. This actually comes close to **prescribing production technology** from top to bottom, potentially stifling innovation and forcing people to use inefficient technology. On the other hand, it helps to circumvent situations that are difficult to monitor. Bonding is thus conditioned by the monitoring device but it also has features of **distortion**, which will be treated below.

4.2 Distortion

4.2.1 Introduction

The discussion so far focused on parties who want to contract on effort but may decide to contract on output. This is because they expect the advantage of observability and verifiability to outweigh the potential disadvantage of imperfect risk sharing[348], due to the increased importance of the external factor. In fact, the above models of output monitoring and input monitoring serve to derive **optimal contracts stipulating contingencies upstream in the case of input monitoring and downstream in the case of output monitoring. In a next step the two optimal contracts can be compared**. In a situation where the optimal output monitoring contract dominates the optimal input monitoring contract, more

---

[348] If the agent is relatively more risk-averse.

downstream performance measures will be chosen and vice versa. As a by-product of the analysis, much is said about how to specify the resulting contract.

But, so far, one important problem was ignored: If the **principal switches to alternative measures of performance because total contribution cannot be contracted upon** (or only at prohibitive cost), there will not only be the potential problem of imperfect risk-sharing: There will also be a **tension between what the principal desires and what the agent is rewarded for**. This problem, called **distortion**, was highlighted by *Kerr*, when he described the "folly of rewarding A while hoping for B"[349]. The rational and opportunistic agent only has the incentive to perform the tasks he is rewarded for and therefore will not serve the best interest of the principal, or in Kerr's words: "What you measure is what you get". *Kerr* attributes this problem to the "fascination with objective performance measures". Therefore, "if you can't measure what you can, you end up wanting by what you can measure"[350].

But, the discussion above showed that there is more to this problem than a simple **psychological trap**, easily avoided by cool-headed rational thinking. What is wanted just may not be contractible. If this problem is unattended to, many potential gains of trade cannot be realised because people will not trade. So, if a related alternative performance measure can be found that can be contracted upon, some of the gains can be realised by going for this **second best solution**. So far, imperfect risk sharing, residual loss due to shirking, and direct cost of the monitoring mechanism were mentioned. Now, another source of loss must be added: distortion. The following propositions will be derived:

25. If the weights measuring the effect of the different actions on the performance measure are generally higher than the weights reflecting the contribution of these actions to the principal's value, the bonus rate will be small.

26. If the incentives are well aligned with the ultimate goal, distortion will be low and the bonus rate will be high.

---

[349] Kerr (1975)

[350] Gibbons (2001), p. 4

4.2.2 The Model

If **total contribution** y, or "everything the principal cares about except for wages"[351] is not contractible, the agent's incentive will depend on an **alternative performance measure** p. "The essence of the incentive problem, is the **divergence** between the agent's incentive to increase p and the principal's desire to increase y"[352]. To clarify the effect, a model will be introduced.

If $y = a + \varepsilon$ and $p = a + \phi$, and the contract specifying compensation is $w = s + bp$, there will be no such distortion. The agent, by trying to increase his compensation also increases the principal's utility y. It can, however, be imagined that **two actions** (or "tasks") are required in order to promote the principal's interest. Consider a client who might be interested in **cutting his cost** in order to enhance his long-term profit perspectives. Thus, the tricky task for the consultant is to cut costs without decreasing the capability of the client to produce valuable products and services to his customers; it is normally straightforward to observe and verify cost cutting while less obvious to assess the implications on the company's capabilities, which will show much later, if at all. To formalize this situation, y is modelled to depend on two tasks $y = a_1 + a_2 + \varepsilon$ (in the example a_1 would be cost cutting and a_2 the observance of the restriction that capabilities must be maintained). The performance measure will be $p = a_1 + \phi$. It can easily be seen that the agent's incentive to perform one task or the other depends on the way a_1 and a_2 affect the performance measure p and on the bonus rate b. Therefore the agent will promote a_1, but not a_2.

Another case is where $y = \alpha_1 + \varepsilon$ and $p = a_1 + a_2 + \phi$. The agent will have an incentive to perform both tasks a_1 and a_2 although a_2 creates no value at all for the principal. An example would be the problem of "**impression management**". Agents will sometimes devote considerable resources to improve the impression the principal gets from them instead of pushing forward with the real task. Even if the agent does not know by which criterion he is evaluated, he will overemphasize highly **visible tasks**. There are some performance criteria that are good indicators of performance as long as they are not used as incentives. In order to evaluate a teacher, students' performance on standardized tests may be a **good indicator**. As soon, however, as this is used as an incentive, teachers will try to "**teach to the test**". The principal (in this case the parents or the government) may fail to get the good education for their children they ultimately desire.

---

[351] Gibbons (2001), p. 5

[352] Gibbons (2001)

The extreme case, $y = a_1 + \varepsilon$ and $p = a_2 + \phi$, is where the agent only performs a_2, not creating any value at all. The models dealing with these problems are called "multi-task models"[353]. A tractable example will be presented in the following[354]:

It is assumed that the **value** created to the principal is given by:

$$y = f_1a_1 + f_2a_2 + ...f_na_n + \varepsilon = \vec{f}\vec{a} + \varepsilon. \tag{7.1}$$

And the **measured performance** is given by:

$$p = g_1a_1 + g_2a_2 + ...g_na_n + \phi = \vec{g}\vec{a} + \phi. \tag{7.2}$$

The principal offers the agent **a linear contract** contingent on p,

$$w = bp + s. \tag{7.3}$$

The agent accepts the contract if compensation is high enough to cover his **costs** which are assumed to be:

$$c(\vec{a}) = 1/2\vec{a}^2. \tag{7.4}$$

He will choose his actions $\vec{a}$ unobserved by the principal. The principal determines p[355] and pays the compensation as specified by the contract. Even if the principal cannot observe $\vec{a}$, given the terms of the contract he can perfectly predict the choice of the utility maximizing rational agent. Against this backdrop, he has to choose the contract terms maximizing his own utility. This is the **familiar agency model** where the principal maximizes his expected pay-off subject to an incentive and a participation constraint. For simplicity it is assumed that both principal and agent are risk neutral, so that both maximize expected value E_P, E_A. The maximization problem can therefore be set up as follows:

$$\max_{b,s,\vec{a}^*} \vec{f}\vec{a} - b(\vec{g}\vec{a}) - s \tag{7.5}$$

---

353 These models were originated by Holmström/Milgrom (1991)

354 The model presented is a slightly more general version than the model presented by Gibbons (2001). Gibbons refers to more elaborate models: see Feltham and Xie (1994), Kulp, Datar, and Lambert (1999), and Baker (2000).

355 Whether or not he observes y is irrelevant in the one-shot relationship.

$$\text{s.t. IC: } \vec{a}^* \in \arg\max_{\vec{a}} b(\vec{g}\vec{a}) + s - \frac{1}{2}\vec{a}^2 \tag{7.6}$$

$$\text{PC: } b(\vec{g}\vec{a}) + s - \frac{1}{2}\vec{a}^2 \geq 0 \tag{7.7}$$

The incentive constraint is a maximization problem. Therefore, the **first-order** condition must hold.

$$\text{Grad}(E_A) = 0 \Leftrightarrow b\vec{g} - \vec{a} = 0 \tag{7.8}$$

Replacing the maximization problem of the incentive constraint by the first-order condition requires it not only to be **necessary but also sufficient**. It can easily be seen that:

$$\frac{\partial E_A^2}{\partial a_i^{\,2}} = -1 \text{ and } \frac{\partial E_A^2}{\partial a_i \partial a_j}\ (i \neq j) = 0 \tag{7.9}$$

Therefore, the quadratic form is negative definite and E_A is concave. The first-order condition can therefore replace the maximization problem of the incentive constraint.

Inserting (7.8) and **restating** the maximization problem gives:

$$\max_{b,s,\vec{a}^*} \vec{f}\vec{a} - b(\vec{g}\vec{a}) - s \tag{7.5}$$

$$\text{s.t. IC: } b\vec{g} - \vec{a} = 0 \Leftrightarrow \vec{a} = b\vec{g} \tag{7.6$'$}$$

$$\text{PC: } b(\vec{g}\vec{a}) + s - \frac{1}{2}\vec{a}^2 = 0 \tag{7.7}$$

Solving (7.6)′ for $\vec{a}$ and inserting into (7.7) gives:

$$b^2\vec{g}^2 + s - \frac{1}{2}b^2\vec{g}^2 = 0 \tag{7.7$'$}$$

Solving (7.7)′ for s yields:

$$s = -\frac{1}{2}b^2\vec{g}^2 \tag{7.7$''$}$$

Inserting (7.7)'' and (7.6)' into (7.5) gives:

$$b\vec{f}\vec{g} - b^2\vec{g}^2 + \frac{1}{2}b^2\vec{g}^2 = b\vec{f}\vec{g} - \frac{1}{2}b^2\vec{g}^2 \qquad (7.5)'$$

The **first-order** condition for an optimal b is therefore:

$$\vec{f}\vec{g} - b^*\vec{g}^2 = 0 \qquad (7.10)$$

Solving for b^* yields:

$$b^* = \frac{\vec{f}\vec{g}}{\vec{g}^2} \qquad (7.10)'$$

As $\vec{f}\vec{g} = |f||g|\cos\varphi$ and $|g| = \sqrt{\vec{g}^2} \Leftrightarrow \vec{g}^2 = |g|^2$:

$$b^* = \frac{|f||g|}{|g|^2}\cos\varphi = \frac{|f|}{|g|}\cos\varphi, \qquad (7.11)$$

where φ is the angle between the vectors $\vec{f}$ and $\vec{g}$ and $|f|$, $|g|$ the length of the vectors.

It becomes clear from the model that the optimal bonus rate depends on two important factors: **scaling** and **alignment**[356].

If the weights[357] $\vec{g}$ measuring the effect of the different actions on the performance measure p are **generally higher** than the weights $\vec{f}$ reflecting the contribution of these actions to the principal's value y, it means that p is relatively more sensitive to higher levels of action than y. One would therefore expect the bonus rate to be small. This is exactly what is expressed in the model.

Proposition 25: If the weights measuring the effect of the different actions on the performance measure are generally higher than the weights reflecting the contribution of these actions to the principal's value, the bonus rate will be small.

---

356 Gibbons (2001) p. 7

357 By analogy one could speak of marginal products

Besides the overall scale of the weights, a relevant feature is the extent to which the weights of y and p have a **similar pattern**. If the pattern is similar, the distortive effect by "rewarding A, while hoping for B" will be small. This is because there will not be many instances where a particular action has a strong effect on p but not on $\underline{y}$. For intuitive illustration, consider the graphical interpretation of vectors $\vec{f}$ and $\vec{g}$, representing the weights on y and p respectively. In fact, the **cosine of the angle between them summarizes the extent of pattern similarity**. If the angle between them is small (and cosine will be high), they roughly point in the same direction. They are well "aligned". In these cases, one would expect the bonus rate to be rather high since **distortive effects are low**. This is exactly what is shown in the model: **The lower the angle, the higher $\cos\varphi$ and therefore the higher the bonus rate.**

Proposition 26: If the incentives are well aligned with the ultimate goal, distortion will be low and the bonus rate will be high.

4.2.3 Discussion

Distortion arises if there is a tension between what the principal wants and what the agent is rewarded for. Often it is not possible to eliminate this tension. What the principal wants just might not be contractible. As was shown in this subsection, distortion can be divided into two components: scaling and alignment. scaling refers to the relative sensitivity of the two measures to changes in the drivers, and alignment to the similarity of driver patterns. If a university rewards a scientist (by promotion or resources) according to the number of articles published during a certain period of time (driver), there will be a problem of alignment if the university cares about both quantity and quality. Indeed, the researcher would have the incentive to publish many articles in low quality journals. If no ranking of journals to account for quality is available, rewards should not depend too much on the number of published articles. Now, considering different departments it could be that a typical researcher in, say, marketing has 5 times as many publications than a typical researcher in, say, mathematics. If the basis for the bonus is the number of published articles, a scaling argument suggests the bonus rate for marketing researchers to be one-fifth of the bonus rate for mathematicians.

As will be elaborated later in more detail, it is obvious that there is a conflict with the risk-incentive trade-off. This model suggests that the bonus rate should be high if the observed variable is relatively undisturbed[358]. This will be the case

[358] see Proposition 4

for upstream parameters, but these will be the most distorted which suggests that the bonus rate should be low.

5 Dynamic Extensions

5.1 Introduction

Up to now, the analysis has been largely one period. Only in one instance did a dynamic idea sneak into the argument; namely, when it was argued that non-linear incentive schemes – in particular the step function scheme – create **path-dependant incentives**[359]. This was taken as a favourable feature of linear incentive schemes. Yet, there is a more general point to be made about dynamic extensions.

Many traditional models of contract theory are one period. The subject of this Chapter will be to analyse the effect of time on contracts. The starting point of this discussion is the often stated thesis that time can resolve incentive issues that arise in one-shot relationships costlessly, or at least can significantly reduce incentive costs[360]. Four models will be presented here to discuss this question. The first model deals with the advantage of long-term contracts over short-term contracts. Time allows lowering the cost of incentives by reducing imperfect risk sharing of output-based contracts (5.2). The second and third models deal with situations wherein relational contracts solve problems of enforcement. The theory of supergames will be used to argue that time may sustain contracts with otherwise desirable properties, which would not be feasible in a one-shot relationship. This is the case where contract parameters are observable but not verifiable (5.3). The fourth model introduces career concerns which induce the agent to exert effort, although choice of effort cannot be contracted on. It will be shown that an implicit contract links the agent's current choice of effort to future pay-off. (5.4). In conclusion, it will be argued that the thesis that time solves incentive issues costlessly cannot be generally upheld. Time merely alters and enriches the insights from one-period models: Conclusions from the one-period models are not necessarily valid in the multi-period settings.

---

[359] see Sub-Section IV2.4.3

[360] Fama (1980)

5.2 Income smoothing

5.2.1 Introduction

Whenever parties are unable to contract on what they are really interested in, they are forced to switch to alternative performance measures. Output monitoring was shown to be relatively cheap and undistorted, but input monitoring created less exposure to the external factor leading to better risk sharing.

The Mirrlees argument[361] on the superiority of step functions over linear incentive schemes and the "shifting support" argument both attempted to combine the best of two worlds: Perfect risk sharing in the presence of output monitoring. These solutions were mainly attacked on practical grounds. It could be established that such schemes were an extreme case of fine tuning[362].

Time alters this argument. If many periods are observed, the law of large numbers filters out uncertainty and it becomes easier to distinguish shirking from bad luck. The intuition is simple: In a one-shot relationship, if the project fails and the agent is punished, there is a considerable risk that he is punished innocently. If a project fails repeatedly, the risk of this being due to bad luck decreases. Thus, the cost of imperfect risk sharing is lower than in the multi-period case[363]. In practice, the principal can offer the principal a long term contract wherein the decision on bonus or punishment is made towards the end of the contract. Until then he is paid a low but regular income. If the principal can commit to such a scheme, the agent knows that if he is not shirking he will receive the bonus. In this Section, the following proposition will be illustrated:

27. Long term contracts can provide cheaper incentives than a sequence of short term contracts if the agent has saving and borrowing constraints.

5.2.2 The Model

In order to further illustrate this argument, a simple model is constructed: It is assumed, that the agent can choose two levels of effort a_l and a_h representing the mean of a normal distribution ($\tilde{Y}_l = a_l + \varepsilon$ and $\tilde{Y}_h = a_h + \varepsilon$, where $\varepsilon \sim N(0,\sigma)$, $a_h > a_l$). In the one-shot relationship the distribution of outcomes contingent on effort is therefore:

---

[361] Mirrlees (1974)

[362] Hart, Holmström (1987), S. 90/91

[363] Radner (1981)

$$\tilde{Y}_l \sim N(a_l, \sigma)$$
$$\tilde{Y}_h \sim N(a_h, \sigma) \quad (12.1)$$

The n-period relationship is modelled as the sum of n identically distributed, independent random variables (actions are uncorrelated):

$$\tilde{Y}_l' = n\tilde{Y}_l$$
$$\tilde{Y}_h' = n\tilde{Y}_h \quad (12.2)$$

Applying the law of large numbers, the distribution of $\tilde{Y}_l'$ and $\tilde{Y}_h'$ respectively can be calculated to be:

$$\tilde{Y}_l' \sim N\left(na_l, \sqrt{n}\sigma_l\right)$$
$$\tilde{Y}_h' \sim N\left(na_h, \sqrt{n}\sigma_h\right) \quad (12.3)$$

Obviously, the distance of means increases proportionately, while the standard error increases less than proportionately with time. Thus, separation between the two distributions becomes better. This will be shown in *Exhibit 8*, where the density functions of shirking vs. non-shirking in the one-shot and in the multi-period case are depicted:

In the area where the chance of punishing the honest agent is infinitesimal, harsh punishments can be inflicted without additional monitoring or review procedure. The portions where this is the case are called "actionable range" in *Exhibit 8*. It becomes clear that the shirking agent expects a probability of punishment of about 5% in the one-shot relationship under such a scheme, whereas he expects a probability of punishment of about 50% in the long-term relationship. 5% may be enough if punishment can be high enough, but bankruptcy constraints are likely to render such a scheme unfeasible. Therefore, either imperfect risk-sharing has to be accepted or ex post monitoring (in the form of a revision process) has to be introduced.

The cost of monitoring is determined by the monitoring technology and the probability that the monitoring process is triggered. It will be assumed for simplicity that ex post monitoring is accurate and comes at a given cost. So, the probability of revision taking place is the only cost driver. For concreteness, it is assumed that punishment can be made high enough to make the agent choose "not shirking" if the probability of detection is 66%. It becomes clear that the monitoring process is triggered in 50% of the cases (see area ABC) in the one-shot relationship and in about 8% of the cases (see area DEF) in the multi-period relationship. The range of outcomes triggering the revision process is referred to in *Exhibit 8* as "control range".

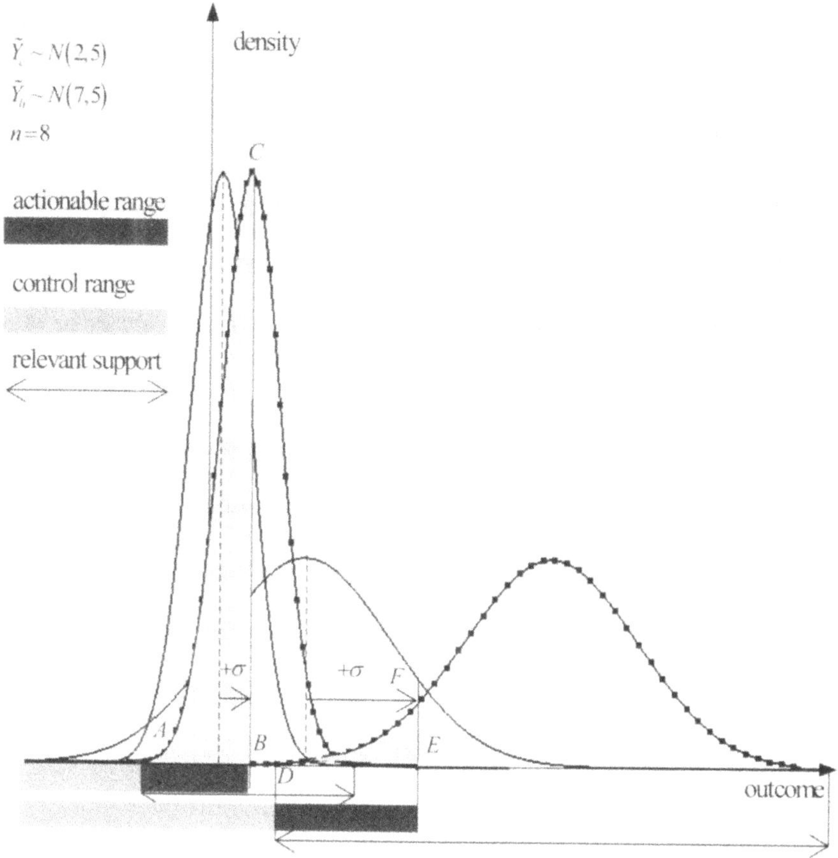

Exhibit 8: Shirking/Non-Shirking: One-shot vs. Long-term

If it is assumed that in the one-shot relationship the actionable range will never be sufficiently wide to implement first best at realistic bankruptcy constraints, there will have to be an ex-post monitoring process. If there is a chance of error, punishment cannot be too high. The control range will have to be rather wide relative to the relevant support set (if "not shirking" is implemented, the relevant support set is that of "not shirking"). In the multi-period case, the "actionable range" may be wide enough to achieve first best at realistic punishment levels. If additional monitoring is needed to avoid imperfect risk-sharing, the control range will be small relative to the relevant support set. Therefore, in the multi-period case "punishment can be made harsher and the control range tighter"[364].

5.2.3 Discussion

Thus, shirking can be dealt with more cheaply in the multi-period relationship, because the principal can engage in income smoothing for the agent. This, however, will only be of value to the agent if he has saving and borrowing restrictions which is not necessarily the case[365]. Still, information problems of an outside party suggest that the principal of the primary relationship will often be the privileged counterparty for such transactions. Therefore:

Proposition 27: Long term contracts can provide cheaper incentives than a sequence of short term contracts if the agent has saving and borrowing constraints.

One should understand the nature of this transaction in order to preclude any misunderstanding. Saving and borrowing enables people to shift the present value of their business relationships in time. It is just the possibility for the agent to borrow if he knows that by bad luck he received less as he would normally receive and to save if he has a windfall profit higher than his effort would normally justify. This is no case of insurance. There is almost certainty about the present value, because in equilibrium the agent will not shirk, which will ultimately be seen by the principal[366].

---

[364] Holmström, Hart (1987)

[365] Allen (1985)

[366] Of course, if one allows for the agent to default then there might be a moral hazard if too much borrowing is permitted and the incentive scheme breaks down. This will also happen if insurance in its proper sense is possible for the agent. In this case, the agent will receive the same utility whatever the circumstances. In such a situation, there would be no incentives for the agents to exert effort. But normally, such insurance would never be offered. A well-known case where this might happen nevertheless is if the agent can securitize the present value of his claims from his business relationship and sell them. This happens when managers receiving stock options for incentive reasons sell these stock-options in the market in order to reduce Exposure, which is why there are normally restrictions to such sales in stock-option schemes.

5.3 Reputation Effects in Supergames

5.3.1 Introduction

In the last Section, time was built into an explicit long term contract and allowed to lower the cost of incentives by reducing imperfect risk sharing of output-based contracts. Output-based contracts were an answer to the uncontractability of input parameters.

It was already argued that contractibility presupposes the knowledge of the production function, observability and verifiability. An especially interesting case is where parties can observe a performance measure that will not be verifiable by a third party like a court. There are certain situations wherein a self-enforcing mechanism – also referred to as an implicit contract – exists, sustaining a contract based on such subjective performance measures. The fundamental reasoning for these mechanisms is that if one of the parties makes a promise, it must be able to commit to this promise. Otherwise, the promise is worthless and cannot create incentives. In other words, it must be clear that at the moment when the party will have to make good on its promise it must be in its interest to do so. Otherwise, it can hold up the other party. Thus, the centre of interest is the decision rule of the party[367].

Consider, for instance, a situation where effort is observable but cannot be objectively verified. The principal cannot commit to paying a bonus contingent on effort because it will always be in his interest to renege later. So, maybe he commits on something else that constrains his future action space in such a way that it will be in his interest to make good on his promise. The tournament mechanism[368] is a case in point. The principal facing many agents commits based on the total amount of bonuses paid out. By taking away the option of saving money by reneging, he can also credibly commit to paying the bonus as promised if only an infinitesimal preference for honesty is assumed. In this Section, it is shown that long term relationships actually are able to create circumstances in which parties find it easier to commit.

The basic intuition is simple: If one party has experienced that the other party acted opportunistically, it will stop doing business with this party. However, if the other party values the ongoing trade relationship, it will, anticipating this decision, not let its business partner down in the first place. It is therefore argued

---

367 see Gibbons (2001)

368 see Lazear(1981)

that long term relationships can in some circumstances support contracts that may otherwise not be feasible by reputation effects created between the parties[369].

In the following subsections, two models will be presented: The first model (5.3.2) deals with a situation where effort is observable but not objectively verifiable. It was argued that in such cases, parties will switch to output-based bonus contracts. Yet, reputation effects may make a flat fee contract based on observed effort feasible. This is because the agent will not engage in shirking because his reputation is at stake.

The second model (5.3.3) deals with a situation where effort is not observable. Parties therefore switch to output monitoring, but now it is assumed that it is output which cannot be objectively verified, although it is observable to both parties. In such a case, it can be argued that it was impossible to create incentives because the principal cannot commit on the bonus payment. Again, reputation effects can make such an arrangement feasible because the principal might refrain from reneging because of reputation concerns. The following propositions will be derived:

28. It can be seen that the agent will be less likely to renege if gains of trade are high (low β), the agent's discount rate is low (high δ), the agent's expected growth rate for the value of the trade relationship is high (high ϕ) and the bargaining power of the agent is high (high γ). If the growth rate is zero ($\phi = 1$), it can be seen that condition (12.8)′ always holds for a discount rate approaching 0 ($\delta \rightarrow 1$) if the agent gets at least a tiny fraction of the gains of trade, as was stipulated in the assumptions ($\gamma \in (\beta, 1]$). In this case, first best will always be feasible

29. Reputation effects are more likely to sustain a bonus contract if the value of the trade relationship ($\Delta = H - L$) is high and the principal's discount rate (r) is low.

30. The strong assumption of indefinite repetition can be relaxed by assuming uncertainty with respect to game's conclusion.

---

[369] The classic reference is Bull (1987)

5.3.2 Observable but Uncontractible Effort

The basic idea of reputation effects is that present action influences not only pay-off in the current period, but also in future periods[370]. Thus, in any period the agent has to take into account the payment of this period and of the following $t > \tau$ periods. It is assumed that the agent can decide whether to choose high or low effort (a_L, a_H), which stochastically determines output $(y_i = a_i + \varepsilon_i$ with $i = L, H)$. The disutility of effort is assumed to be a linear function of effort $(\beta a_L, \beta a_H)$[371]. The principal will commit to paying a flat fee that will be between the expected cost to the agent (βa^e) and the expected value of output (a^e). The exact distribution of the gains of trade will be determined by bargaining, and depend on the bargaining power[372] (γ):

$$\beta a^e < \gamma a^e \leq a^e \Rightarrow \gamma \in (\beta, 1] \tag{12.4}$$

Profit for the agent will therefore be:

$$\gamma a^e - \beta a_i, \tag{12.5}$$

which depends on the principal's expectations (a^e) and on the agent's choice of effort (a_i). Independent of whether or not the principal agrees to a low or a high flat fee, the agent will profit from choosing low effort. Therefore, the principal will have low expectations $(a^e = a_L)$. The profit for the agent will thus be $a_L(\gamma - \beta)$. Because $a_L(\gamma - \beta) < a_H(\gamma - \beta)$, profit would be higher for the agent if he could commit to choosing high effort (a_H). This is impossible in the one-shot relationship.

However, if the parties are playing a repeated version of this one-shot game this might change. It is assumed that the principal plays a trigger strategy. He expects the agent to choose high effort until he observes that he is choosing low effort. In this case he will assume low effort forever after.

---

370 This model is inspired by a model of Bester in an unpublished script.

371 Disutility is usually modelled as a convex function in effort. In this model, there is another focus and a linear disutility function is assumed for ease of exposition.

372 There are some models (e.g. Rubinstein 1982, see Kreps 1990, 556n) where the outcome of bargaining depends on the process of bargaining. An alternative to a bargaining solution would be to assume that the market mechanism determines a market price. It is common e.g. to assume that many principals compete against each other, driving the profits down to zero. As it is intended to apply the models to the client-consultant relationship where services are normally very specific to the relationship, a bargaining approach is taken.

The agent's discount factor[373] is assumed to be δ and the growth rate of the expected gains of trade ϕ. The growth rate is introduced to model the agent's expectation that the business relationship with the client will increase or decrease in value over time. Then the agent's pay-off for choosing high effort (a_L) in period τ is:

$$\sum_{t=0}^{\infty} \delta^t \phi^{t+\tau} (\gamma - \beta) a_H \tag{12.6}$$

Doing some algebra[374] this can be written as:

$$\phi^\tau \frac{a_H(\gamma - \beta)}{1 - \delta\phi} \; for \; \delta\phi \neq 1 \tag{12.6'}$$

On the other hand, the pay-off from defecting will result in a higher pay-off in the first period but in lower pay-offs forever after:

$$\phi^\tau (\gamma a_H - \beta a_L) + \sum_{t=1}^{\infty} \delta^t \phi^{t+\tau} (\gamma - \beta) a_L \tag{12.7}$$

Again, doing some algebra[375] yields:

$$\phi^\tau \left[\gamma (a_H - a_L) + \frac{(\gamma - \beta) a_L}{1 - \delta\phi} \right] \tag{12.7'}$$

The agent will choose high effort if pay-off (12.6)′ is bigger than pay-off (12.7)′:

$$\phi^\tau \frac{a_H(\gamma - \beta)}{1 - \delta\phi} > \phi^\tau \left[\gamma (a_H - a_L) + \frac{(\gamma - \beta) a_L}{1 - \delta\phi} \right] \tag{12.8}$$

This condition can be simplified[376] to:

$$\beta < \delta\phi\gamma \tag{12.8'}$$

---

[373] The agent's reputation is at stake here.

[374] See Mathematical Appendix at the end of this Paragraph.

[375] See Mathematical Appendix at the end of this Paragraph.

[376] See Mathematical Appendix at the end of this Paragraph.

Proposition 28: It can be seen that the agent will be less likely to renege if gains of trade are high (low β), the agent's discount rate is low (high δ), the agent's expected growth rate for the value of the trade relationship is high (high ϕ) and the bargaining power of the agent is high (high γ). If the growth rate is zero ($\phi = 1$), it can be seen that condition (12.8)′ always holds for a discount rate approaching 0 ($\delta \to 1$) if the agent gets at least a tiny fraction of the gains of trade, as was stipulated in the assumptions ($\gamma \in (\beta,1]$). In this case, first best will always be feasible.

Mathematical Appendix

Footnote 374:

$$\sum_{t=0}^{\infty} \delta^t \phi^{t+\tau} (\gamma - \beta) a_H = \phi^\tau \sum_{t=0}^{\infty} \delta^t \phi^t (\gamma - \beta) a_H$$
$$= a_H (\gamma - \beta) \phi^\tau \sum_{t=0}^{\infty} (\delta\phi)^t = \phi^\tau \frac{a_H (\gamma - \beta)}{1 - \delta\phi}$$

Footnote 375:

$$\phi^\tau (\gamma a_H - \beta a_L) + \sum_{t=1}^{\infty} \delta^t \phi^{t+\tau} (\gamma - \beta) a_L$$
$$= \phi^\tau (\gamma a_H - \beta a_L) + \phi^\tau (\gamma - \beta) a_L \left[\frac{1}{1 - \delta\phi} - 1 \right]$$
$$= \phi^\tau (\gamma a_H - \beta a_L - \gamma a_L + \beta a_L) + \phi^\tau \frac{(\gamma - \beta) a_L}{1 - \delta\phi}$$
$$= \phi^\tau \left[\gamma (a_H - a_L) + \frac{(\gamma - \beta) a_L}{1 - \delta\phi} \right]$$

Footnote 376:

$$\phi^\tau \frac{a_H (\gamma - \beta)}{1 - \delta\phi} > \phi^\tau \left[\gamma (a_H - a_L) + \frac{(\gamma - \beta) a_L}{1 - \delta\phi} \right]$$

$$0 > \phi\left[\gamma(a_H - a_L) + \frac{(\gamma-\beta)(a_L - a_H)}{1-\delta\phi}\right]$$

$$0 > \phi\left[\frac{\gamma(a_H - a_L)(1-\delta\phi) - \gamma(a_H - a_L) + \beta(a_H - a_L)}{1-\delta\phi}\right]$$

$$0 > \phi\frac{-\delta\phi\gamma(a_H - a_L) + \beta(a_H - a_L)}{1-\delta\phi}$$

$$0 > \frac{\phi[\beta - \delta\phi\gamma]}{1-\delta\phi}$$

$$\beta - \delta\phi\gamma < 0$$

5.3.3 Observable but Uncontractible Output

If effort is uncontractible, parties might switch to output-based compensation. However, output could be observable to the parties while not objectively verifiable. This raises the possibility that the principal reneges on the promised bonus. He might, however, decide not to renege for reputation concerns[377].

Two possible levels of outcomes are assumed: "low outcome (L)" and "high outcome (H)". Effort ($a \in [0,1]$) is interpreted as the probability of "high outcome (H)". Therefore, expected outcome is:

$$aH + (1-a)L = L + a(H-L) \quad (12.9)$$

The efficient effort choice, maximizing joint utility and used as a benchmark is:

$$\max_a L + a(H-L) - c(a) \quad (12.10)$$

Taking derivatives, one can write:

$$b^{*} - c'(a) = H - L \quad (12.11)$$

[377]see Bull (1987), Levin (2000), Gibbons (2001)

The principal promises the agent to pay a base salary s plus a bonus b in the event that he observes high outcome (H). If the principal honours the contract when high outcome is observed, his pay-off will be:

$$H-s-b \tag{12.12}$$

If he reneges his pay-off will be:

$$H-s \tag{12.13}$$

If the agent expects the principal to honour his promise his expected pay-off will be:

$$s+ab-c(a) \tag{12.14}$$

If he expects the principal to renege:

$$s-c(a) \tag{12.15}$$

The disutility of effort for the agent is a strictly increasing convex function in a:

$$c(\cdot)>0,\ c'(\cdot)>0,\ c''(\cdot)>0\ \lim_{a\to 1} c(a)="\infty" \tag{12.16}$$

It is assumed that the agent is playing a trigger strategy: he expects the principal to honour his contract until he defects. In this case he assumes defecting forever after, but if the agent expects that he will not be paid a bonus, he will not exert effort ($a = 0$) and outcome will be low in certainty. In this case the principal knows that his pay-off will be:

$$L-s \tag{12.17}$$

An additional assumption will be included here: The project will only be profitable in the event of high outcome:

$$L-c(0)-w_a<0, \tag{12.18}$$

where w_a is the agent's reservation utility. Consequently, the principal will not be willing to offer a contract $s \geq c(0)-w_a$. But, any other contract would violate the agent's participation constraint and would therefore not be accepted: No trade takes place and pay-off is zero for both parties.

Thus, if the principal defects in period τ, he will have a higher pay-off in this period but zero pay-off for periods $t > \tau$. If he does not renege, his expected pay-off for periods $t > \tau$ will be $L + a(H - L) - s - ab$.

Therefore, reputation concerns will induce the principal not to renege, if the following condition holds:

$$(H - s) + 0 \leq (H - s - b) + \frac{L + a(H - L) - s - ab}{r} \qquad (12.19)$$

The agent's incentive constraint if he thinks that the principal will honour the contract is:

$$a \in \arg\max_{a'} s + a'b - c(a') \qquad (12.20)$$

Replacing the maximization problem by the first order condition (which can be shown to be necessary and sufficient) yields:

$$b = c'(a) \Rightarrow a = a^*(b) \qquad (12.21)$$

Using (12.21), agent's participation constraint is given by:

$$s + a^*(b)b - c(a^*(b)) \geq w_a \qquad (12.22)$$

Using (12.22) and rearranging, (12.19) can be written as

$$b \leq \frac{a^*(b)[H - L] + L - c(a^*(b)) - \bar{W}}{r}$$
$$\text{or } b \leq \frac{V(b)}{r} \qquad (12.23)$$

Exhibit 9 shows this relationship (for $c(a) = -a/a - 1$, and $L - w = 0$). The shaded area represents the contracts satisfying the reneging constraint condition (12.23) i.e. contracts that can be sustained by reputation concerns of the principal. The function $b^*(a)$ represents the efficient bonus rate maximizing joint utility (see (12.11)).

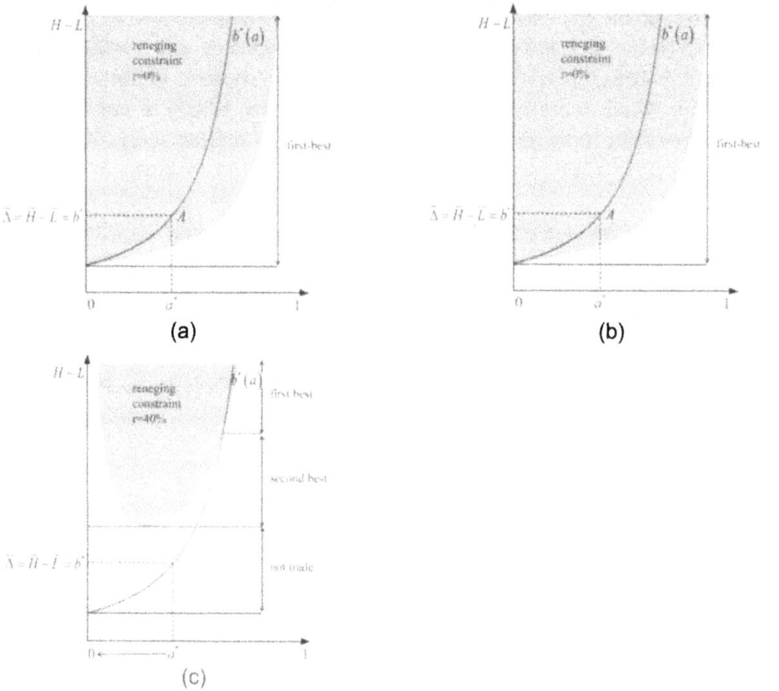

Exhibit 9: Reputation Effects: a) First best incentives b) Second best incentives c) No trade

It can be seen that, for a given differential between high and low outcome ($\bar{\Delta} = \bar{H} - \bar{L}$), first best incentives are possible at a low discount rate *(Exhibit 9 (a))*. From condition (12.11), it follows that the efficient bonus rate b^* equals the differential between high and low outcome $\bar{\Delta}$. If the principal is offering b^*, the agent will perform the efficient effort a^*. He anticipates that the principal will honour his promise because the reneging constraint is loose (point A is within the shaded area). In other words: As not honouring the contract would hurt his long-term interests, the principal can provide efficient incentives which are credible to the agent. As the discount rate increases, this may no longer be the case.

In *Exhibit 9 (b)*, the principal cannot commit on the efficient bonus rate b^*. If the principal was to offer b^* the agent believes that he will renege on his promise (point A is outside the shaded area) and will therefore not exert any effort. The principal, anticipating that, will try to induce the highest effort level $a' < a^*$, not violating the incentive constraint. At the given outcome differential $\bar{\Delta}$, a' is constructed by moving from A parallel to the abscissa until reaching B, which is just within the shaded area, and then projecting down onto the axis to find a'. The second best bonus level is found by moving upward to C, which lies on $b^*(a)$. Moving to the ordinate gives the bonus level $b' < b^*$, which is needed to induce a'. Thus, second best incentives can be created. If the discount rate becomes very high, there may not be any bonus rate, which is small enough to satisfy the reneging constraint[378]. This is the case in *Exhibit 9 (c)*. No trade will take place.

It can also be seen that if the discount rate is close to zero, first best incentives can always be provided at any output differential Δ (even if there is a small value to the trading relationship); but if the discount rate increases, first best contracts may still be possible if there for very high Δ.

Proposition 29: Reputation effects are more likely to sustain a bonus contract if the value of the trade relationship ($\Delta = H - L$) is high and the principal's discount rate (r) is low.

5.3.4 Reinterpretation of the Discount rate

In both models, one assumption was infinite repetition of the basic one period game in order to create reputation effects. Assuming that the relationship ends after t periods, clearly in the last period t, the dominant strategy will be to defect; but then there will be no value to the trade relationship in the last period, meaning that also in period t-1 the optimal strategy will be to defect, etc. The game will thus unravel backwards and the argument breaks down. Indefinite repetition, however, seems to be a very strong assumption.

Fortunately, the models can be saved if it is assumed that the game is not infinitely repeated but instead concludes at an uncertain date[379]. In fact, the discount *factor* δ in Section 5.3.2 and the discount *rate* r in Section 5.3.3 can be reinterpreted as a combination of the actual discount factor [rate] and the probability of the game ending after each period played. If the probability of ending is q, the probability of the game continuing in the next period is $1-q$. Thus, if the actual discount factor [rate] of the party whose reputation is at stake is μ $[s]$, the present value of a regular pay-off V is given by:

---

[378] In fact, for $a^* = 0$, no contract will be offered. The intercept (D) is just the bonus that would minimize losses to the principal if he offered a contract.

[379] Gibbons (2001)

$$\sum_{t=0}^{\infty}\mu^t(1-q)^t V=\frac{1}{1-\mu(1-q)}V \tag{12.24}$$

Thus, the discount factor δ can be reinterpreted as follows:

$$\delta=\mu(1-q) \tag{12.25}$$

The relationship between the discount factor and the discount rate is given by:

$$\delta=\frac{1}{1+r},\mu=\frac{1}{1+s} \tag{12.26}$$

Inserting (12.26) into (12.25) yields:

$$\frac{1}{1+r}=\frac{1}{1+s}(1-q) \tag{12.27}$$

Solving for r and rearranging gives the reinterpretation for r[380]:

$$r=\frac{s+q}{1-q} \tag{12.27'}$$

Therefore:

Proposition 30: The strong assumption of indefinite repetition can be relaxed by assuming uncertainty with respect to the the game's conclusion.

It seems plausible that this is very often the case in business relations, where parties can express their judgement of the relationship continuing rather in terms of probabilities than in terms of definite dates of conclusion[381].

---

[380] e.g. see Gibbons (2001), p. 9 footnote

[381] Still, experiments suggest that parties will often find some way of cooperating in games with finite repetition, contrary to the logic of the presented argument. Having mentioned this behavioural evidence for something like a "trust mechanism" it will be ignored in the following as this thesis stands firmly on the grounds of rational decision making and opportunistic behaviour in its formal part. Still, as the reinterpretation of the rational model for uncertain ending shows, ignoring behavioural ideas does not come at such high a price as is often suggested.

Another advantage of this reinterpretation is that it actually enriches the model with a further variable. It is not only the discount rate (sometimes very aptly called "patience" rate) of one party whose reputation is at stake, which is relevant, but also the probability of the relationship's continuity, which is a judgement involving the relationship and thus both parties.

5.3.5 A Multiparty Extension

A common multiparty interpretation for the models presented is to assume that, in the relationship between an employer and his workers, workers live for one period but pass their experience on to fellow workers, who will in turn act in the following period as if the experience of their colleagues were their own[382].

This can be easily extended to the case where the workers live more than one period, but are spreading the news to their fellow workers. This can be modelled by adding a growth rate in the spirit of Section 5.3.2., reinforcing the reputation effect.

This is only one step short of assuming that there is a market reputation effect. The only difference, indeed, is that it is implicitly assumed in the case of the workers that the spreading of news is in some way facilitated by the fact that they work within the same organization. This highlights the importance of some kind of news-spreading mechanism.

It can very well be imagined that e.g. in the consultant-client relationship, observed shirking or reneging can play a role beyond the original relationship. If the project is highly visible, public interest will make sure that judgements are spread, possibly by press coverage. If the client or the consultant is very well entrenched in business circles, they will also have plenty of opportunity to spread around their experience. The mechanisms in place require close scrutiny which is probably more a sociological task. From an economic perspective, it can be asked, what motivates parties to spread news. The threat to do so can help in contractual relationships, but the same threat can be used for blackmailing. Therefore, the credibility of such comments is questionable.

Yet, the point is an important one. Consulting companies insist that their business is done very much on recommendation. Therefore, the argument goes, concerns for reputation make bonus contracts redundant. It does not, however, seem plausible that this argument is true to the same extent for all cases. There

---

382 see e.g. Gibbons (2001), p. 9 footnote 6

clearly seems to be a difference if the client is a large multinational company or a small start-up, if the consultant is a small one person firm or a big international consultancy, if the project is highly visible or not.

5.3.6 Discussion

First best can be achieved if utilities are not discounted in an infinitely repeated version of the basic one period model[383]. The intuition behind this argument is that players start by cooperating, but if one party starts to defect, they will defect forever after. If this is accepted to be the strategy of the players, the dominant strategy is to cooperate. The immediate gain from defecting is always overcompensated by the loss in later periods.

The main criticism is that infinite repetition and no discounting are very unrealistic assumptions. This argument breaks down as soon as there is an end to the game. Then, the dominant strategy in the last period will be to defect. The game will unravel backwards. If games are finite, first best cannot be achieved because of backward unravelling.

If there is a discount rate and conclusion of the game is uncertain, first best can only be sustained in special cases. In some cases there will also be a second-best solution. As a general rule, the reputation effects are more likely to sustain contracts if the discount rate of the party whose reputation is at stake is low, if the judgement of this party attributes a low probability to the scenario that the relationship is discontinued, and if the gains of relational trade are high and possibly expected to rise.

The two models discussed above can be seen as complementary: If effort is not contractible, but can be observed, reputation concerns of the agent can support flat fee contracts based on effort. If this is not possible, parties may switch to output-based bonus contracts; but these contracts may not be feasible if output is just observable and not contractible. Reputation concerns of the principal may solve this problem. This suggests a sequence of analysis: Only if agent reputation effects are too low or observability limited will bonus contracts be considered.

The reputation mechanism may work beyond the original bilateral relationship. A "news-spreading mechanism" has to be assumed in these cases. Often it is not explicitly modelled. The relevant variables will be project visibility and the parties' position and credibility within the relevant community.

---

[383] see Radner (1981)

5.4 Career Concerns - Learning

5.4.1 Introduction

So far, two different kinds of arguments have been presented: First of all, it was shown that time can help to write explicit multi-period contracts which can reduce imperfect risk-sharing compared to one-period contracts.

Then, it was argued in the theory of supergames that reputation concerns might allow parties to contract on contingencies which are observable but not verifiable. Although an explicit contract would not be enforceable, an implicit contract ties observed effort to future pay-offs. Pay-offs will be lower if one party defects because the counterparty stops trusting, which reduces the future gains of trade. Thus, parties may be able to eschew switching to alternative performance measures which induce imperfect risk-sharing or are more distorted.

Another such implicit contract which ties current effort to future pay-offs is described by the model of career concerns. The intuition, as formulated by Fama[384], is that there is no need for explicit contracts, because the market can effectively police agents. This is because the agent's career will depend on his performance track record. The market monitors past performance and only agents who achieve high performance levels will be promoted. So, they will exert effort in order to positively affect their career chances.

This intuition is formalized by Holmström[385]. He shows that Fama's conclusion that career concerns can provide efficient incentives will only hold under very special assumptions. Major inefficiencies can arise both in the short and in the long run.

The model allows important insights into incentive effects in a setting where the market monitors the agent's output in order to learn about his productive capabilities. The following propositions will be derived:

31. It can be seen that incentives are high if the discount rate is low, if the precision of the production technology is high, and if the disutility of effort does not increase too fast.

---

[384] Fama (1980)

[385] Holmström (1982 reprinted in 1999) model will be presented in the following Section. His reasoning will be somewhat adjusted to make it easier for the non-technical reader to appreciate the argument. Minor errors of the article are corrected.

32. Interpreting the level of incentives in the stationary state, it can be said that incentives will never be higher than the efficient level. They will always be efficient if the discount rate is zero $(\beta = 1)$. This was Fama's result. The result requires that there is some noise in the competence process (however small). $\mu^* < 1 \Rightarrow r > 0 \Rightarrow \sigma_\delta^2 > 0$. As soon as the discount rate is different from zero, incentives will be lower than the efficient level. Incentives will be closer to efficiency if the discount rate is low, updating of beliefs is fast and utility of effort increases slowly.

33. If precision of beliefs is initially lower than in the stationary state, speed of updating is high and therefore incentives are high. As they approach the stationary state over time precision increases, speed of updating decreases and incentives become lower. The opposite holds true if the precision of beliefs is initially higher than in the stationary state. In this case, incentives are low in the beginning and become higher over time. Therefore, the system is stable.

5.4.2 The Basic Model

It is assumed in the model of career concerns that the agent's output in each period y_t depends on his effort a_t, his productive capability η and a sequence of unrelated shocks ε_t representing the external factor:

$$y_t = \eta + a_t + \varepsilon_t \quad t = 1, 2, \ldots \tag{12.28}$$

where ε_t is normally distributed with 0 mean and a variance of σ_ε^2.

$$\varepsilon_t \sim N\left(0, \sigma_\varepsilon^2\right) \tag{12.29}$$

It is further assumed that both the agent and the principal do not know the agent's productive capability. They do, however, share the same prior beliefs. These beliefs are represented by an initial assessment m_1 of the agent's capabilities and the assumed precision of these beliefs h_ε (which equals the inverse of the variance $h_\varepsilon = 1/\sigma_\varepsilon^2$). As time proceeds, these beliefs are updated on the basis of the agent's performance track record. In the models of signaling and screening it is assumed that the agents have private information on their own capability. In these cases it will be explored if it is possible to extract information from the agents. In the model of career concerns, however, it can be seen that information is assumed to be imperfect but symmetric: The agent and the market monitor the same normal learning process.

The focus here will be to show that, in the described setting, career concerns will create incentives in the absence of explicit incentive contracts. This is done by creating an indirect link between current effort and future compensation. The objective of this model set up by Holmström is to formalize the well-known argument of Fama, who went so far as to claim that career concerns will make explicit incentive contracts redundant by providing efficient incentives costlessly. It is therefore central to understand why the agent should believe that his current effort would positively effect his future compensation.

First, the agent's problem is considered. His pay-off in any period t equals his compensation c_t minus his disutility of effort $g_t(a_t)$, which is assumed to be an increasing and convex function in effort.

$$u_t = c_t - g_t(a_t) \tag{12.30}$$

where

$$g_t(a_t) > 0, g_t'(\cdot) > 0, g_t''(\cdot) > 0 \tag{12.31}$$

The agent is not only concerned about his current pay-off, but tries to choose effort in order to maximize the present value of current and future pay-offs. It is obvious that this present value does not only depend on the current choice of effort, but also on all choices of effort in the future; but future decisions cannot be made today, because the information on which they are based is future information and therefore not currently available. Therefore, the agent's problem is to solve for the optimal decision rule which prescribes in every period t which decision a_t will be taken contingent on the basis of the information y_{t-1}, which will then be available. This will automatically produce the optimal current choice of effort by setting in current information:

$$a_t = a_t(y_{t-1}) \tag{12.32}$$

The fact that future information is not available today also implies that the agent is faced with a decision under uncertainty. It is assumed that the agent is risk-neutral and therefore maximizing expected present value. The optimal decision rule is therefore the solution to the following maximization problem:

$$a^*(\cdot) \in \arg\max_{a'(\cdot)} \sum_{t=1}^{\infty} \beta^{t-1} \left[Ec_t - Eg_t\left(a_t'\left(y_{t-1}\right)\right)\right] \tag{12.33}$$

where β is the discount factor and $a^*(\cdot)$ is a vector representing the optimal decision rule.

It will now be analysed, what determines compensation. It is assumed that the agent faces a competitive risk-neutral market. This implies that his compensation equals expected marginal output[386]:

$$c_t = E(y_t) \tag{12.34}$$

It follows from the production function (12.28) that the market determines compensation by adding expected capability and expected choice of effort.

$$c_t = E_t(\eta) + E(a_t) \tag{12.35}$$

It is obvious from the production function that effort is a substitute for capability. Therefore, the whole game played by the agent is to choose effort in order to bias the learning process of the market in his favour. But this is anticipated by the market. One might think that, because his action cannot be observed, asymmetric information will develop over time, but this is not the case[387]: His maximizing behaviour makes him perfectly predictable if his utility function is assumed to be common knowledge, in line with the usual assumptions of agency theory. His is trapped. He cannot fool the market, but if he did not show maximizing behaviour he would bias the learning process against him[388]. Therefore, expected effort choice in (12.35) equals the agent's optimal decision rule:

$$E(a_t) = a_t^*(y_{t-1}) \tag{12.36}$$

---

[386] Note that the assumption of competitive markets is a short-cut for saying that the agent faces a number of principals and that there is competition among these principals, driving their profits down to zero. This assumption is not as strong as it seems. Indeed, the market model could be replaced by a bargaining model, which would make the argument more complex but would not change its insights. So, the zero-profit hypothesis is just a way of holding one party's utility constant while maximizing the utility of the other party, which insures Pareto optimality. This is in the same spirit as setting agents' utility to their reservation level as was done in other instances.

[387] see Gibbons (2001)

[388] Holmström (1999) calls this situation a "rat race".

It was also mentioned that the market assesses capability on the basis of the agent's performance track record. So, assessment m_t in period t is a function of the assessment at the beginning of the last period $t-1$, updated by the observed outcome at the end of the last period y_{t-1}. As

$$y_{t-1} = \eta + a_{t-1} + \varepsilon_{t-1} \tag{12.37}$$

and a_{t-1} can perfectly be anticipated ($a_{t-1} = a^{*}_{t-1}$), (12.37) can be written as

$$z_{t-1} = y_{t-1} - a_{t-1} = \eta + \varepsilon_{t-1} \tag{12.38}$$

where z_t is a sequence of the agent's capability disturbed by an error term. Updating the market's beliefs on the agent's capability then occurs by calculating the weighted average of the initial belief and the observation. The weights are the precision of the initial belief h_{t-1} and the precision of the observation h_ε, respectively.

$$E_t(\eta) = m_t = \frac{h_{t-1}m_{t-1} + h_\varepsilon z_{t-1}}{h_{t-1} + h_\varepsilon} = \frac{h_1 m_1 + h_\varepsilon \sum_{s=1}^{t-1} z_s}{h_1 (1-t) h_\varepsilon} \tag{12.39}$$

The market's assessment of the agent's capability becomes ever more precise as the learning process continues (precision is increasing in t):

$$h_t = h_{t-1} + h_\varepsilon = h_1 + (t-1)h_\varepsilon \tag{12.40}$$

As the agent's maximization problem for finding the optimal decision rule depends on compensation (see (12.33)) but compensation in turn depends on the optimal decision rule (see (12.35) and (12.36)), there is an interdependence between the two decision problems, which means that they have to be solved simultaneously. Rewriting (12.33) and inserting (12.39) and (12.36) into (12.35), this simultaneous decision problem can be stated as:

$$a^{*}(\cdot) \subset \underset{a'(\cdot)}{\arg\max} \sum_{t=1}^{\infty} \beta^{t-1} \left[Ec_t - Eg_t\left(a_t'(y_{t-1})\right) \right] \tag{12.33}$$

And:

$$c_t = \frac{h_1 m_1 + h_\varepsilon \sum_{s=1}^{t-1} z_s}{h_t} + a_t^*(y_{t-1}) \qquad (12.35)'$$

This is solved by taking expectation of (12.35)'[389]

$$Ec_t = \frac{h_1 m_1}{h_t} + \frac{h_\varepsilon}{h_t} \sum_{s=1}^{t-1} \left[m_1 + a_s - Ea_s^*(y_{s-1}) \right] + Ea_t^*(y_{t-1}) \qquad (12.35)''$$

and inserting the resulting (12.35)'' into (12.33). Then, the first order conditions γ_t , $t = 1,2,...$ can be written as[390]:

$$\gamma_t \equiv \sum_{s=t+1}^{\infty} \beta^{s-t} \frac{h_\varepsilon}{h_s} = g'(a_t). \qquad (12.41)$$

Proposition 31: It can be seen that incentives are high if the discount rate is low[391], if the precision of the production technology is high[392] and if the disutility of effort does not increase too fast.

Efficient incentives are characterized by a situation where marginal product equals marginal cost:

$$g'(a) = 1 \qquad (12.42)$$

In the model described so far, equilibrium will be very inefficient: In the long run ($t \to \infty$) it can be seen that there will be no incentives from career concerns ($\gamma_t \to 0$) as the assessment will become indefinitely precise ($h_t \to \infty$). This is an intuitive result: The agent will only have incentives to exert effort from career concerns, as long as his capability is not fully known.

---

389 See Mathematical Appendix at the end of this Paragraph.

390 See Mathematical Appendix at the end of this Paragraph.

391 $r \downarrow \to \beta \uparrow \to g'(a) \uparrow \to a \uparrow$

392 $h_\varepsilon \uparrow \to g'(a) \uparrow \to a \uparrow$

Mathematical Appendix:

Footnote 389:

$$\begin{aligned} Ec_t &= E\frac{h_1 m_1}{h_t} + E\left(\frac{h_\varepsilon}{h_t}\sum_{s=1}^{t-1} z_s\right) + Ea_t^*(y_{t-1}) \\ &= \frac{h_1 m_1}{h_t} + \frac{h_\varepsilon}{h_t}\sum_{s=1}^{t-1} Ez_s + Ea_t^*(y_{t-1}) \end{aligned} \qquad (\alpha)$$

z_s can be written as:

$$z_s = y_s - a_s = \eta + \varepsilon_s - a_s + a_s = \eta + a_s + \varepsilon_s - a_s \qquad (\beta)$$

Inserting (β) into (α) gives:

$$Ec_t = \frac{h_1 m_1}{h_t} + \frac{h_\varepsilon}{h_t}\sum_{s=1}^{t-1}\left[m_1 + a_s - Ea_s^*(y_{s-1})\right] + Ea_t^*(y_{t-1})$$

Footnote 390:

$$\frac{\partial}{\partial a_t}\sum_{s=t}^{\infty}\beta^{s-t}\left[\frac{h_1 m_1}{h_s} + \frac{h_\varepsilon}{h_s}\sum_{i=1}^{s-1}\left[m_1 + a_i - Ea_i^*(y_{i-1})\right] + Ea_s^*(y_{s-1}) - Eg_s\left(a_s^*(y_{s-1})\right)\right]$$

$$\sum_{s=t}^{\infty}\beta^{s-t}\left[\frac{h_1 m_1}{h_s}\right] + \sum_{s=t}^{\infty}\beta^{s-t}\frac{h_\varepsilon}{h_s}\sum_{i=1}^{s-1}\left(m_1 + a_i - Ea_i^*(y_{i-1})\right)$$

$$+\sum_{s=t}^{\infty}\beta^{s-t}Ea_s^*(y_{s-1}) - \sum_{s=t}^{\infty}\beta^{s-t}Eg_s\left(a_s^*(y_{s-1})\right)$$

$$= 0 + \sum_{s=t+1}^{\infty}\beta^{s-t}\frac{h_\varepsilon}{h_s}\cdot 1 + 0 - g'(a_t) = \sum_{s=t+1}^{\infty}\beta^{s-t}\frac{h_\varepsilon}{h_s} - g'(a_t) = 0$$

5.4.3 Extension: Adding Innovation

The situation changes if a plausible assumption is added to the basic model. This is by assuming that competence is not invariant over time but is modelled as an autoregressive process. More specifically, it is assumed that this period's capability equals last period's capability plus a stochastic shock:

$$\eta_t = \eta_{t-1} + \delta_{t-1} \tag{12.43}$$

where the sequence of stochastic shocks is driftless with variance σ_δ^2:

$$\delta_{t-1} \sim N\left(0, \sigma_\delta^2\right) \tag{12.44}$$

The shocks can be interpreted as reflecting innovation. Innovation changes job characteristics. Therefore, someone who was well qualified to do the job in the past is not necessarily well qualified to do the job now or in the future.

Having motivated the noise term in the competence process, it will now be analysed which effects this assumption has on incentives. In fact, beliefs are still updated by calculating the weighted average of last period's initial beliefs and last period's observation, with the precision of the initial beliefs and the precision of the observation as weights, respectively:

$$m_t = \mu_{t-1} m_{t-1} + \left(1 - \mu_{t-1}\right) z_{t-1} \tag{12.45}$$

where

$$\mu_{t-1} = \frac{h_{t-1}}{h_{t-1} + h_\varepsilon} \tag{12.46}$$

What changes is the way the precision of the belief is assessed. By updating the initial belief it will be made more precise.

$$\hat{h} = h_{t-1} + h_\varepsilon \tag{12.47}$$

But the belief refers to last period's capability, which is irrelevant because last period's decisions have already been made before updating occurs. What is interesting is the current period's assessed capability. Contrary to the basic model, it is now assumed that last period's capability does not fully determine present capability. It is still the best estimate, which is why beliefs are updated in the same way. Yet, the precision of the present belief about capability will be lower than $\hat{h}$ because innovation adds uncertainty of whether someone who was capable in the past will also be capable at present and in the future.

$$\frac{1}{h_t}=\frac{1}{h_{t-1}+h_\varepsilon}+\frac{1}{h_\delta}=\frac{h_\delta+h_{t-1}+h_\varepsilon}{(h_{t-1}+h_\varepsilon)h_\delta} \tag{12.48}$$

What happens is that first precision is increased by making another observation and then decreased by adding the noise $(\sigma_\delta^2=1/h_\delta)$ of the competence process. Obviously, one can try to solve for a stationary state which is defined as the state where decrease of noise due to learning is exactly offset by the increase of noise due to innovation. It will later be shown that the stationary state actually is a stable equilibrium.

For technical reasons, the stationary state is calculated in terms of μs, which are tied to hs by expression (12.46). It can be shown that[393]:

$$\mu_t=\frac{1}{2+r-\mu_{t-1}} \tag{12.49}$$

In the stationary state the precision does not change anymore from one period to the other:

$$h^*=h_t=h_{t-1}\Rightarrow\mu^*=\mu_t=\mu_{t-1} \tag{12.50}$$

Inserting (12.50) into (12.49) gives:

$$\mu^*=\frac{1}{2+r-\mu^*}\Leftrightarrow-\mu^{*2}+(2+r)\mu^*-1=0 \tag{12.51}$$

Solving the quadratic equation gives:

$$\mu_{1/2}^*=1+\frac{1}{2}r\pm\sqrt{\frac{1}{4}r^2+r} \tag{12.52}$$

From (12.45) follows that $\mu^*<1$. Therefore:

$$\mu^*=1+\frac{1}{2}r-\sqrt{\frac{1}{4}r^2+r} \tag{12.53}$$

---

[393] See Mathematical Appendix at the end of this Paragraph.

Taking account of the modified learning process:

$$m_t = m_1 \prod_{i=1}^{t-1} \mu_i + \sum_{s=1}^{t-1} z_s \left[\prod_{i=s+1}^{t-1} \mu_i \right] (1-\mu_s) \tag{12.54}$$

the market's compensation rule can once again be inserted into the agent's maximization problem. The first order conditions γ_t can be written as[394]:

$$\gamma_t \equiv (1-\mu_t) \sum_{s=t+1}^{\infty} \beta^{s-1} \prod_{i=t+1}^{s-1} \mu_i = g'(a_t) \tag{12.55}$$

In the stationary state, first-order conditions can be further simplified[395]:

$$\gamma_t \equiv \frac{(1-\mu^*)\beta}{1-\beta\mu^*} = g'(a_t) \tag{12.56}$$

Proposition 32: Interpreting the level of incentives in the stationary state, it can be said, that incentives will never be higher than the efficient level:

$$\frac{\beta(1-\mu^*)}{1-\mu^*\beta} = g'(a^*) \leq 1 \tag{12.57}$$

They will always be efficient if the discount rate is zero $(\beta = 1)$. ***This was Fama's result. The result requires that there is some noise in the competence process (however small).*** $\mu^* < 1 \Rightarrow r > 0 \Rightarrow \sigma_\delta^2 > 0$.

$$\frac{1-\mu^*}{1-\mu^*} = 1 \tag{12.58}$$

As soon as the discount rate is different from zero, incentives will be lower than the efficient level. Incentives will be closer to efficiency if the discount rate is low, updating of beliefs is fast and utility of effort increases slowly.

---

[394] See Mathematical Appendix at the end of this Paragraph.

[395] See Mathematical Appendix at the end of this Paragraph.

Updating is a very intuitive concept. It is the weight $(1-\mu^*)$ which is given to the most recent observation. Updating will be fast if μ^* is low, which happens if the precision of the production process is high relative to the precision of the competence process, or equivalently if the competence process is very disturbed relative to the production process. These results are recorded in *Exhibit 10.*

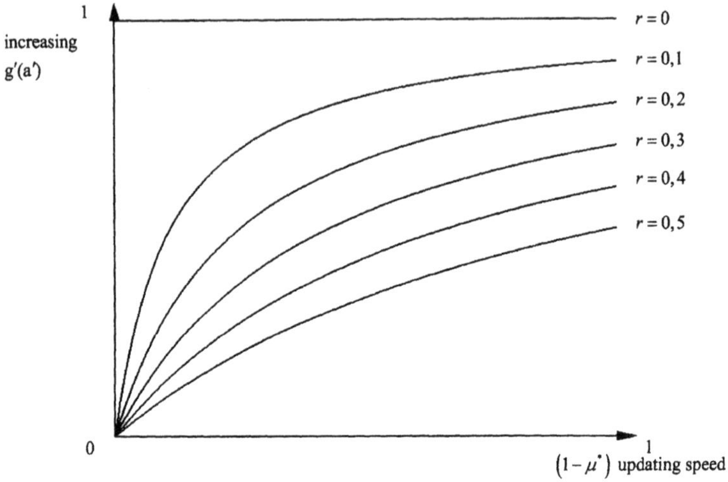

Exhibit 10: Career Concerns: Incentives in Equilibrium

The level of incentives is shown as a function of the speed of updating for different discount rates[396]. The surprising result is that Fama's prediction of efficient incentives becomes true for zero discount rate even at an infinitesimally small updating speed (if only a small amount of noise is added to the competence process), as was mentioned before.

---

[396] In this Exhibit, r represents the discount rate (not to be confused with the r in the text which refers to relative precision of the output process compared to the competence process).

Mathematical Appendix:

Footnote 393:

$$\mu_t = \frac{h_t}{h_t + h_\varepsilon} = \left(1 + \frac{h_\varepsilon}{h_t}\right)^{-1} \tag{α}$$

Inserting (12.48) into (α) gives:

$$\mu_t = \left(1 + \frac{h_\varepsilon\left(h_\delta + h_{t-1} + h_\varepsilon\right)}{\left(h_{t-1} + h_\varepsilon\right)h_\delta}\right)^{-1} = \left[1 + \frac{h_\varepsilon}{h_\delta}\left(\frac{h_\delta}{h_{t-1} + h_\varepsilon} + 1\right)\right]^{-1}$$

$$= \left[1 + \frac{h_\varepsilon}{h_\delta}\left(\left(\frac{h_\varepsilon}{h_\delta} + \frac{h_{t-1}}{h_\delta}\right)^{-1} + 1\right)\right]^{-1} \tag{β}$$

Solving (12.46) for h_{t-1} gives:

$$h_{t-1} = \frac{h_\varepsilon \mu_{t-1}}{1 - \mu_{t-1}} \tag{γ}$$

Inserting (γ) into (β) gives:

$$\mu_t = \left\{1 + \frac{h_\varepsilon}{h_\delta}\left[\left(\frac{h_\varepsilon}{h_\delta} + \frac{h_\varepsilon}{h_\delta}\frac{\mu_{t-1}}{1 - \mu_{t-1}}\right)^{-1} + 1\right]\right\}^{-1}$$

Setting $r = h_\varepsilon / h_\delta$ gives:

$$\mu_t = \left\{1 + r\left[r^{-1}\left(1 + \frac{\mu_{t-1}}{1 - \mu_{t-1}}\right)^{-1} + 1\right]\right\}^{-1} = \left\{1 + 1 - \mu_{t-1} + r\right\}^{-1}$$

$$= \frac{1}{2 + r - \mu_{t-1}}$$

Footnote 394:

$$Ec_t = m_1 \prod_{i=1}^{t-1} \mu_i + \sum_{s=1}^{t-1} E(z_s) \prod_{i=s+1}^{t-1} \mu_i (1-\mu_s) + Ea_t^*(\mu_{t-1})$$

Setting $z_s = \eta + a_s + \varepsilon_s - a_s$, it can be written:

$$Ec_t = m_1 \prod_{i=1}^{t-1} \mu_i + \sum_{s=1}^{t-1} \left\{ \left(m_1 + a_s - Ea_s^*(y_{s-1})\right) \left[\prod_{i=s+1}^{t-1} \mu_i \right] (1-\mu_s) \right\} + Ea_t^*(y_{t-1})$$

Inserting in the agent's maximisation problem and taking the derivative gives:

$$\frac{\partial}{\partial a_t} \sum_{s=t}^{\infty} \beta^{s-t} \left[Ec_s - Eg_s\left(a_s(y_{s-1})\right) \right]$$

$$= \left\{ \frac{\partial}{\partial a_t} \sum_{s=t}^{\infty} \beta^{s-t} m_1 \prod_{i=1}^{s-1} \mu_i \right\} + \left\{ \frac{\partial}{\partial a_t} \sum_{s=t}^{\infty} \beta^{s-t} \sum_{i=1}^{s-1} \left\{ \left(m_1 + a_i - Ea_i^*\right) \left[\prod_{j=1}^{s-1} \mu_j \right] (1-\mu_i) \right\} \right\}$$
$$+ \left\{ \frac{\partial}{\partial a_t} \sum_{s=t}^{\infty} \beta^{s-t} Ea_s^* \right\} - \left\{ \frac{\partial}{\partial a_t} \sum_{s=t}^{\infty} \beta^{s-t} Eg(a_s) \right\}$$

$$= 0 + \sum_{s=t+1}^{\infty} \beta^{s-1} \cdot 1 \cdot \prod_{j=t+1}^{s-1} \mu_j (1-\mu_t) + 0 - g'(a_t)$$

Therefore, the first order condition γ_t can be written as:

$$\gamma_t \equiv (1-\mu_t) \sum_{s=t+1}^{\infty} \beta^{s-1} \prod_{i=t+1}^{s-1} \mu_i = g'(a_t)$$

(Readers comparing this result with the original Holmström article will note that there is a typing error in the original.)

Footnote 395:

Applying the formula of the sum of infinite geometric sequences to the right hand side gives:

$$\gamma_t \equiv (1-\mu^*)\sum_{t=1}^{\infty}\beta^t \mu^{*t-1} = g'(a_t)$$

$$\gamma_t \equiv (1-\mu^*)\frac{1}{\mu^*}\left[\frac{1}{1-\beta\mu^*}-1\right] = g'(a_t) = (1-\mu^*)\frac{1}{\mu^*}\left(\frac{\beta\mu^*}{1-\beta\mu^*}\right) = g'(a_t)$$

$$\gamma_t \equiv \frac{(1-\mu^*)\beta}{1-\beta\mu^*} = g'(a_t)$$

The trick is that, in the stationary state, μ_i's with $i \geq \bar{t}$ equal μ^*. Also note the convention that

$$\prod_{s}^{s-1}\mu_i = 1.$$

5.4.4 Disequilibrium – Transient Effects

It is important to understand what happens before the stationary state is reached. This will be particularly relevant in situations where updating is slow and periods are very long. In such a situation, not many "learning loops" are possible in a given span of time, the observed signal is bad and competence is very stable over time. So, the market tends to stick with its prior beliefs. Here, the stationary state might never be reached in the considered period and disequilibrium might be the only relevant state.

The dynamics of incentives are studied by doing comparative statics in the first order conditions (12.55) of the agent's maximization problem. It can be seen that incentives increase in all periods if updating speed increases (μ_t decreases)[397]. The weight μ_t is an increasing function of h_t as can be seen in (12.46). Therefore, as precision of beliefs with respect to capability (h_t) increases, updating becomes slower and incentives decrease.

---

[397] see Holmström (1999), p. 174 for the formal proof by induction

As μ_t is an increasing function of μ_{t-1} as can be seen in (12.49), and there is only one stationary state in the relevant interval $(0,1)$, it can be seen from *Exhibit 11*[398] that if last period's speed of updating was higher than in the stationary state ($\mu_{t-t} < \mu^*$) – which is equivalent to saying that the precision of last period's belief was lower than the precision of beliefs in the stationary state ($h_{t-1} < h^*$), the speed of updating will decrease ($\mu_t > \mu_{t-1}$) or the precision of beliefs will increase ($h_t > h_{t-1}$). This means that the sequence μ_t will be approaching μ^* from below.

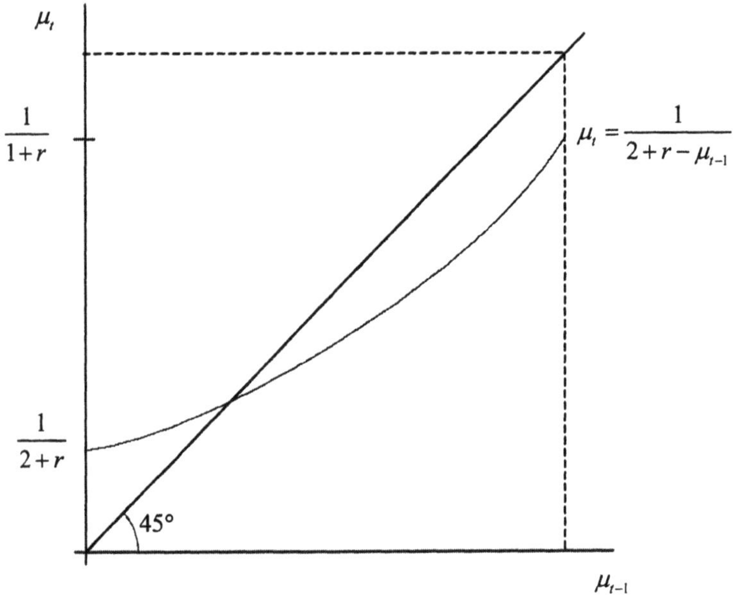

Exhibit 11: Career Concerns: Incentives in Disequilibrium

It can therefore be said that

Proposition 33: If precision of beliefs is initially lower than in the stationary state, speed of updating is high and therefore incentives are high. As they approach the stationary state over time precision increases, speed of updating decreases and incentives become lower. The opposite holds true if the precision of beliefs is initially higher than in the stationary state. In this case,

---

[398] Taken with small modification from Holmström (1999), p. 175

incentives are low in the beginning and become higher over time. Therefore, the system is stable.

5.4.5 Discussion

Holmström's formalization of Fama's argument shows that, in equilibrium, career concerns will provide efficient incentives only under very special conditions. The most notable assumption is a zero-discount rate. There also has to be some change of job characteristics due to innovation in order to prevent the market from eventually fully learning the agent's capability.

If the discount rate is not zero, incentives will never be efficient in equilibrium. They will, however, be close to efficiency if the discount rate is low, job characteristics change considerably due to innovation, and the external factor in the output process is unimportant. In absolute terms, incentives will also be higher if the disutility of effort rises only slowly. A useful and intuitive concept in this context is the speed of updating. In fact, if the noise of the production function is low relative to the noise of the competence process, the speed of updating will be high, which in turn will make incentive increase since the agent knows that higher effort will have an impact. If, however, talent will be expected to last forever, once it has been proven and potential signals to the contrary are very unreliable, one will stick to the prior belief.

Therefore, if the discount rate is low and updating fast, there will be fairly high incentives to perform in equilibrium. The intuitive idea is that reputation is not worth so much, or high reputation has to be reproven very often. In this situation, career concerns solve the shirking problem. Conversely, if the discount rate is high (the agent does not care about the future) and updating is slow, there will be low incentives in the steady state.

In some situations, incentives in disequilibrium will be very important. This is especially true in cases where updating is slow and the frequency of observation is low (due to a long production process). Incentives will be initially high if the precision of the initial belief is thought to be higher in later periods. Incentives will be initially low if the precision of the initial belief is thought to be lower in later periods. The first case will be true in most cases. In the beginning, not much is known about the agent. Therefore, beliefs will be relatively imprecise.

In a situation where the noise of the production function is high relative to noise of the competence process, which is equivalent to a situation where there is little change of job characteristics due to innovations, and observation of output is only a very bad signal due to an important external factor, it was said that updating will be slow and incentives will be much too low in equilibrium. If there is low initial precision it was also said that incentives will be much too high in the beginning. This situation will persist for quite some time as the speed of updating is low. Therefore, an agent working in an industry where job characteristics are not expected to change much and the external factor is very important, as might be expected for many service industries, will get very inefficient incentives from career concerns.

V Conclusions

1.1 Results

It was shown in Section (IV2.1) that, if effort is not contractible, compensation shall be made contingent on output. It was also shown that, in this case, welfare levels can never be higher than in the case of observable effort. Barring the unrealistic cases of a deterministic production function and risk neutrality of both the principal and the agent, the optimal compensation scheme leads to a welfare loss due to imperfect risk sharing.

Section (IV2.2) derives a closed-form solution which negatively links the use of variable fee contracts to the agent's level of risk aversion, the level of project risk and the convexity of the disutility function. The weakness of this model is its lack of generality and its unrealistic assumptions as e.g. the constant absolute risk averseness of the agent's preferences. Especially the linear sharing rule seems to be completely arbitrary.

So far, it has been argued that variable fees may provide useful incentives in situations of hidden action, but also create imperfect risk sharing. Quite apart from any other consideration, Section (IV2.3) looks closer at the **mechanics of risk sharing:** In the traditional agency models, the principal is always assumed to be risk-neutral, while the agent is assumed to be risk-averse or risk-neutral. This need not be the case. The assumption that the principal is risk-neutral is often justified by the argument that he is the economically more potent party to the contract. This is largely inspired by the traditional story behind principal-agency models referring to the relationship between a company and its employees. There are several arguments why the economically more potent party should be less risk-averse: First, it is often plausible to assume that as a person becomes wealthier his absolute level of risk aversion decreases. Second, if the company is held by an entrepreneur he might be the less risk-averse type of person in the first place. In addition, employees usually only work for one company, while the owner might hold many different companies. So, he is probably better diversified. This last point is especially true for publicly held companies. However,ut in the case of a client and his consultant, things can be different. The small consultant partnership is clearly more risk-averse than its multinational client, but this changes if the big international consultancy firm provides services to a small start-up company through its incubator branch. Clearly, in the setting analysed so far - the case where, say, the principal is risk-averse and the agent risk-neutral - does not appear to be problematic as optimal incentive provision and optimal risk sharing are compatible. But what if there is a bilateral moral hazard problem? To answer this and other questions, one has to look at risk sharing in its own right. Two separate sources of value creation by risk sharing are explored: **differences in risk attitudes** which might arise from predisposition or different levels of wealth, and **differences in diversification**. The result of this Section highlights the parties' level of risk tolerance (both absolute and relative to each other), the specific quality of the risk involved as determined by its correlation with existing risk exposure and the level of project risk as relevant factors of optimal risk sharing. If a risk-neutral party is involved it carries all the risk. The sharing rule is independent in each state of the probability assigned to that state. Finally, the risky part of each party's compensation is proportional to its own risk tolerance divided by the overall risk tolerance of society, if the parties' preferences over lotteries exhibit constant risk aversion (which can be assumed locally).

In Section (IV2.4), a control theory model is set up to determine the optimal sharing rule. It is possible to reprove some of the results of earlier sections. If effort is contractible, flat fee contracts will be used. If it is not contractible it will depend on output. However, contrary to earlier results, it is also possible to shed some light on the mechanics of the optimal sharing rule. Compensation depends on output through the likelihood ratio. There are two implications: The optimal sharing rule can be understood quite intuitively as rewarding the agent if the signal makes it likely that high effort was chosen, but it also explains why little general constraints can be derived for the shape of the optimal sharing rule: It is very sensitive to specifications of utility functions and distributional assumptions. Although the optimal contract can only be derived to be linear under awkwardly improbable assumptions, there are a number of reasons explaining the practical prominence of such contracts. First, there is the transaction cost argument. Setting up complex contracts is just too expensive. Second, linear contracts are argued to be relatively robust for a large number of settings. But also non-distributional assumptions like the number of different options available to the agent affects the optimal incentive scheme. So, paradoxically, there are reasons to believe that adding complexity makes contracts simpler. It is also shown that information is only valuable if it affects posterior assessment of the effort level chosen. It must therefore be related to effort choice, but it must also be impossible to perfectly infer the information - to the extent that it is relevant to this assessment - from information of variables already included into the contract.

A common assumption is that there is a **comparative cost advantage** of output monitoring compared to input monitoring. Why should this be the case? In order to implement input monitoring, the principal has to watch the agent while performing the required task. This causes **opportunity costs** to the principal. Still worse, if the principal does not know the production function of the agent he may well watch the agent while performing a task but will be **unable to interpret his actions** as to whether they are instrumental in achieving the required output.

These costs are amplified by the fact that usually the very motivation to hire an agent in the first place was that the principal either did not want or could not perform the task himself. So, either the principal has something else to do, which means that his opportunity costs are high, or the performance of the task requires specialized knowledge that the principal does not possess. The latter case does make it difficult for the principal to monitor the agent effectively. Alternatively, the principal could hire **other qualified agents** to do the monitoring for him, but then it may be difficult to prevent these monitoring agents from colluding with the operative agents. For all these reasons, input monitoring is likely to be very costly in many circumstances. On the other hand, **output monitoring should be very easy**. One only has to look to which extent the required result was achieved providing that it can be properly defined. So, if a client hires a consultant to perform a cost cutting project, it will be much easier for the client to evaluate how much cost was reduced than to interpret the wide variety of single measures the consultant takes to achieve his goal. Having clearly established the intuition for comparative cost advantage of output monitoring compared to input monitoring in a wide variety of situations, it may come as a surprise that **input monitoring can theoretically infinitely approximate first best**. This is because the agent, in his decision whether to cheat or not, will weigh the benefits of cheating (in the case of shirking reduced disutility of effort) against the expected value of punishment. Therefore, if **harsh enough punishments are announced**, the probability of detection and therefore the number and thoroughness of inspection can be infinitely reduced. In this case, there seems **no rationale for output monitoring**. If it is not cheaper, it will only provide an additional drawback: imperfect risk sharing. The traditional argument is that **input monitoring always establishes the truth** while output monitoring is prone to error. This is a crucial point, because the **driving force behind imperfect risk sharing** in output monitoring is the possibility of error in judgement and the subsequent punishment of the innocent. If it can be shown that output monitoring can achieve perfect accuracy or input monitoring is prone to error as well, this distinction breaks down. In fact, both can be shown to be plausible assumptions in some circumstances: Output **monitoring will be perfectly accurate** in the case of deterministic production functions but also if there is **shifting support**[399]. Indeed the argument of Mirrlees on step-functions is in the same spirit. On the other hand, it seems implausible to assume that input monitoring will be able to prove cheating at 100%. There will always be judgement, inferences, circumstantial evidence. Whatever the process, there is a chance of error. Therefore, the above assumption needs to be relaxed to allow for **error in input monitoring**. These arguments appear construed, and in fact they are. In general, input monitoring will be more costly and output

---

[399] see next Section

monitoring more prone to error. Ignoring these arguments therefore seems to be a justified abstraction, but there still is some merit to taking them seriously. In brief, they say that regardless of whether one is looking at input monitoring or at output monitoring there are two relevant issues: **Error in judgement** and **cost of monitoring,** and that under some circumstances both schemes fare equally well or bad on these two dimensions. By acknowledging that there generally is a distinction between input monitoring and output monitoring, one is actually saying that these circumstances will rarely be present. Understanding why this is the case helps to identify other relevant situational variables which influence the problem of optimal contracting.

Chapter (IV3) discusses the role of the **bankruptcy constraints** and the **role of error** in the monitoring process. Section (IV3.1) shows that input monitoring can approximate first best even if it comes at a cost if there are no bankruptcy constraints and no possibility of error in judgement. If there is a bankruptcy constraint there will be welfare loss, because of direct monitoring cost and possibly efficiency wages or complete uncontractability (no trade). The phenomenon of efficiency wages can be understood by realizing that, for purposes of incentive, provision differentials in agent pay utility, and not absolute pay levels, are relevant. Therefore, in the absence of error in judgement, increasing agent risk averseness even helps to set up cheap incentive schemes. Yet, if error in judgement is permitted, problems of imperfect risk-sharing arise, requiring the simultaneous minimization of the cost arising from investment in the monitoring technology, the frequency of inspections and the risk-premium.

Just as input monitoring can have a problem of imperfect risk sharing due to pitfalls in the monitoring process, there are **situations where output monitoring is perfectly accurate** and can achieve first best beyond the obvious case of a deterministic production function. This will be the case for shifting support schemes, but Section (IV3.2) shows that such schemes are often unrealistic because of bankruptcy constraints (legal, moral, economic) and the problem of fine tuning. Another problem is **moral hazard with respect to risk** which arises in output monitoring schemes in the presence of bankruptcy constraints which make incentive schemes de facto asymmetrical, limiting the downside. The agent will have the incentive to choose very risky projects even if they have a lower expected value than alternative projects (this can be thought of as a call option).

Section (IV4.1) mentions **direct transaction costs** which arise for input monitoring and for output monitoring, though it will often be plausible that they are **lower for output monitoring**. However, there are also **indirect transaction costs** which arise from provisions which designed to lower direct transaction costs. The goal is to **rationalize monitoring** or to **directly influence the agent's**

disutility function. This leads to inefficiencies because production technology is prescribed from top to bottom in a way that is known to be inefficient. In addition, innovation from bottom to top is stifled. This is a distortive effect.

Section (IV4.2) deals with distortion. **Distortion** arises if there is tension between what the principal wants and what the agent is rewarded for. Often it is not possible to eliminate this tension. What the principal wants just might not be contractible. As was shown in this subsection, distortion can be divided into two components: scaling and alignment. Scaling refers to the relative sensitivity of the two measures to changes in the drivers and alignment to the similarity of driver patterns. If a university rewards a scientist (by promotion, or resources) by the number of published articles during a certain period of time (driver), there will be a problem of **alignment** if the university cares about both quantity and quality. Indeed, the researcher would have the incentive to publish many of articles in low quality journals. If no ranking of journals to account for quality is available, rewards should not depend too much on the number of published articles. Now, considering different departments it could be that a typical researcher in, say, marketing has 5 times as many publications than a typical researcher in, say, mathematics. If the basis for the bonus is the number of published articles, a **scaling** argument suggests the bonus rate for marketing researchers to be one-fifth of the bonus rate for mathematicians. It is obvious that there is a conflict with the risk-incentive trade-off. This model suggests that the bonus rate should be high if the observed variable is relatively undisturbed[400]. This will be the case for parameters close to the agent. These, however, will be the most distorted, suggesting that the bonus rate should be low. This is consistent with the observation that variable compensation is used more often for top managers than for middle managers. For top managers, undistorted incentives (the share price) happen to correspond with their direct responsibility for the whole company. For middle managers, however, incentives are either distorted if they depend on the individual performance of the department (failing to take into account that it is important to cooperate among departments for the benefit of the company as a whole), or too disturbed, as the share price depends on many factors beyond the reach of the middle manager.

The basic problem of contracting is to find the best contract parameters or the best mix of contract parameters. **Multi-period models do not solve the contracting problem costlessly** as is sometimes claimed, but rather add predictions as to which contract parameters should enter the contract given the situational setting. It could well be that parties have to decide whether they want

---

[400] see Proposition 4

to contract on an input or an output parameter. They predict that using the input variable will lead to considerable monitoring costs, distortion and enforcement problems. They will therefore consider output contracting, but as the agent is very risk-averse they will abandon this alternative and ultimately decide to contract on the input variable. In multi-period settings this might change, as is discussed in Section (IV5.2), because the **law of large numbers** filters out uncertainty, reducing the problem of imperfect risk sharing. Therefore, multi-period contracting could become an attractive alternative. The model also stipulates situational conditions where this will work. First of all, there has to be a **possibility to conclude long-term contracts**. Therefore, the business relationship must be such that similar projects will repeatedly arise. In this case, long-term contracts will still be less flexible than a sequence of short-term contracts. Therefore, the question is how important flexibility is or how predictable the future will be. Moreover, it will be more expensive to write long-term contracts compared to short-term contracts. Therefore, increased transaction cost becomes an issue. Finally, parties will value long-term contracts only if there are **saving and borrowing constraints** for the agent outside the primary principal-agent relationship. This might plausibly be the case for informational reasons. Therefore, if time is built into an explicit long-term contract it is possible to reduce the cost of incentives by reducing imperfect risk sharing of output-based contracts.

It has already been argued that contractibility presupposes the knowledge of the production function, observability and verifiability. An especially interesting case is discussed in Section (IV5.3) where parties can observe a performance measure that will not be verifiable by a third party such as a court. There are certain situations where a self-enforcing mechanism, also referred to as an implicit contract, exists, sustaining a contract based on such **subjective performance measures**. The fundamental reasoning for these mechanisms is that if one of the parties makes a promise, it must be able to commit to this promise. Otherwise, the promise is worthless and cannot create incentives. In other words, it must be clear that at the moment when the party will have to make good on its promise it must be in its interest to do so. Otherwise, it can hold up the other party. Thus, the centre of interest is the decision rule of the party. Consider, for instance, a situation where effort is observable but cannot be objectively verified. The principal cannot commit to paying a bonus contingent on effort because it will always be in his interest to renege later. So, maybe he commits on something else that constrains his future action space in such a way that it will be in his interest to make good on his promise. The **tournament mechanism** is a case in point. The principal facing many agents commits on the total amount of bonuses paid out. By taking away the option of saving money by reneging, he can also credibly commit to paying the bonus as promised if only an infinitesimal preference for honesty is assumed. Also, long-term relationships are actually able to create circumstances in which parties find it easier to commit. The basic intuition is simple: If one party has experienced that the other party acted opportunistically, it will stop doing business with this party. However, if the other party values the ongoing trade relationship, it will, anticipating this decision, not let its business partner down in the first place. It was therefore argued that long-term relationships can in some circumstances support contracts that may otherwise not be feasible by **reputation effects** created between the parties. This is the case in a situation where one would like to contract on an input parameter but effort is not contractible as it cannot be objectively verified. Or, alternatively, one would like to contract on an output parameter but the principal cannot commit on promised bonus because it is not verifiable. In these situations a reputation effect can sustain these contracts if the trade relationship is valuable and likely to increase in value, the time horizon of the parties will not be short-term (low discount rate), the expected probability of the relationship ending is low, and the bargaining power of the agent is not too low. Moreover, the project's visibility and the parties' entrenchment in business circles also will play a role.

In Section (IV5.4) a situation is considered where the input parameter is not observable, but one can act as if it were contractible because of an implicit contract. This is because the agent's "**career**" will depend on his performance track record. The market monitors past performance and only agents who achieve high performance levels will be promoted. So, they will exert effort in order to positively affect their career chances. In such a case one would not be forced to change to output contracting, which might be very expensive. If the discount rate is not zero, incentives will never be efficient in equilibrium. They will, however, be close to efficiency if the discount rate is low, job characteristics change considerably due to innovation, and the external factor in the output process is unimportant. In absolute terms, incentives will be also higher if the disutility of effort only rises slowly. A useful and intuitive concept in this context is the **speed of updating**. In fact, if the noise of the production function is low relative to the noise of the competence process, the speed of updating will be high, which in turn will make incentive increase, because the agent knows that higher effort will have an impact. If, however, talent will be expected to last forever, once it has been proven and potential signals to the contrary are very unreliable, one will stick to the prior belief. Therefore, if the discount rate is low and updating fast, there will be fairly high incentives to perform in equilibrium. The intuitive idea is that reputation is not worth so much, or high reputation has to be reproved very often. In this situation, career concerns solve the shirking problem. Conversely, if the discount rate is high (the agent does not care about the future) and updating is slow, there will be low incentives in the steady state. In some situations, **incentives in disequilibrium** will be very important. This is especially true in cases where updating is slow and the frequency of observation is low (due to a long production process). Incentives will be initially high if the precision of the initial belief is thought to be higher in later periods. Incentives will initially be low if the precision of the initial belief is thought to be lower in later periods. The first case will be true in most cases. In the beginning, not much is known about the agent. Therefore, beliefs will be relatively imprecise. In a situation where noise of the production function is high relative to the noise of the competence process, which is equivalent to a situation where there is little change of job characteristics due to innovations, and observation of output is only a very bad signal due to an important external factor, it was said that updating will be slow and incentives will be much too low in equilibrium. If there is low initial precision it was also said that incentives will be much too high in the beginning. This situation will persist for quite some time as the speed of updating is low. Therefore, an agent working in an industry where job characteristics are not expected to change much and the external factor is very important, as might be expected for many service industries, will get very inefficient incentives from career concerns. Situations relevant for the viability of such an implicit contract will therefore be the agent's time horizon, the role of the external factor in the production process, the amount of innovation in the relevant industry, the duration of projects, the precision of initial beliefs concerning the talent of the agent, the market's capability to monitor the agent's track record. The thesis that time can solve incentive problems costlessly cannot be generally upheld. It was shown that this will only be the case under very unrealistic circumstances like zero discount rate and infinite repetition. Yet, the important insight from Chapter (IV5) is that the conclusions from the one-period models are not necessarily valid in the multi-period settings. The optimal contract in the one-shot relationship will be different from the optimal contract in multi-period relationships.

1.2 Checklist

Given the complexity of contract theoretic models, it would be tempting to develop tools which allow the practitioner to apply the insights of contract theory without bothering too much about the underlying models. There are, however, two obstacles to such an approach that were already mentioned. First, no recipe or scorecard to solve for the optimal contract can be given as the final step of application requires qualitative judgement close to the specific problem. Second, even if it is possible to give a checklist of factors which are relevant to the contracting problem, it is probably difficult to apply the checklist without having understood at least the general thrust of the models they are derived from. In the following, such a checklist of all the identified relevant factors shall nevertheless be given.

1. **Production technology and monitoring technology:** The production and monitoring technologies determine the quality of the signal that can be used in output monitoring and input monitoring, respectively. It can be deterministic or stochastic (relevant for error in judgement but also for implicit contract based on learning process). If it is stochastic, it can be more or less so (project risk may be higher or lower). Furthermore, the production technology can be known or unknown to the parties. Besides output there may be other signals of effort. If there are many available signals it is important to understand how these signals depend on each other in order to decide which mix of signals should enter the optimal contract (there is no use to incur the cost to monitor signals which contain no additional information).

2. **Inefficiency of prescribed production technology:** The principal might prescribe a production technology which is easy to monitor but inefficient (the prescription itself stifles innovation from bottom to top).

3. **Direct monitoring cost:** Effort may be readily contractible at low cost. In other situations, it can only be contracted if a very high-cost input monitoring scheme is put in place. Not only input monitoring but also output monitoring may cause such extra transaction costs, though they will usually be lower: Required output has to be defined and provisions have to be made to record output thus defined, sometimes resulting in extra accounting expenses. Monitoring cost will depend on **legal and technological possibilities**.

4. Definition of what is wanted and of what is measured and the divergence between the two: If there is a divergence this may lead to distortion.

5. **Quality of the courts or other third party enforcement facilities:** The quality of the courts can be thought of as the extent of potential contract parameters, which the court can verify, and the cost of doing so.

6. **Risk attitudes of the agent and the principal**: Both can be risk-neutral and risk-averse. If both are risk-averse, it is relevant to know the relative strength of risk averseness of one party compared to the other, but also the combined absolute level of risk averseness of both parties.

7. **Properties of the two parties' portfolios with respect to the project**: In particular, the relative strength of diversification effects within the respective portfolios if the project is added.

8. The shape of the function specifying disutility of labour and the possibilities to influence it.

9. **The assumptions about the projects outcome:** The shape of the optimal incentive scheme depends on the distributional assumptions. For some projects a normal distribution or a lognormal distribution will be adequate. For others, there will be e.g. just two outcomes. Still others will have a bimodal distribution (if either very high or very low outcome is likely). Generally speaking, any distribution of outcome can be imagined depending on the specific circumstances.

10. **The precision of assumptions made**: Some schemes may require very accurate information with respect to parties' risk preferences and the distribution of the project's outcome (e.g. step function schemes).

11. **The action space of the parties:** The question is whether all relevant actions available to the parties are captured in the model. If e.g. parties can observe their performance in the process of performance, the issue of path-dependency of incentives arises.

12. **The bankruptcy constraint:** The amount of loss that a party can absorb, which may be limited by legal, economic and moral constraints.

13. **The scope of cheating:** The absolute extent of the benefit that the agent can appropriate by using his informational advantage.

14. **Time horizon:** How long will the relationship last? Is there a definite ending? What is the probability of the relationship after each trade ending?

15. **The presence of borrowing constraints:** If there is a sequence of separable projects, imperfect risk-sharing can be solved by borrowing or by dissaving if outcome is low, and saving if outcome is high.

16. **Potential gains of trade:** The utility that can be created if the trade can take place.

17. **The patience of the parties:** Extent to which parties value present payments over future payments.

18. **Expected growth rate of the value of the relationship over time**: Is the relationship of the two parties expected to bring ever more utility to the parties each time it is repeated?

19. **The relative bargaining power of the parties**: How are gains of trade divided between the two parties?

20. **Innovation:** The extent to which job characteristics change and therefore the extent to which it is possible to infer from past to present and future talent. Innovation will arguably be lower for a lawyer than for a software developer.

21. **Precision of prior beliefs about capability:** The extent to which a party considers its prior assessment to be precise as opposed to ambiguous.

1.3 Outlook

Traditionally, economists specializing in contract theory advise government regulation authorities or appear as expert witnesses in competition lawsuits if they have a practical interest at all. This is surely a very important field of application. The objective to help individuals, companies and lawyers to design better contracts and organizations in the course of their business is relatively less prominent.

There is a reason for that. It was already discussed that it is questionable whether contract theory can actually provide any added value in this field. It could be argued that most of what it has to say is already known by lawyers and practitioners of other fields. The underlying argument is that contracts and institutions are the product of evolution and that they survived because they proved to be successful in the past. Especially in very stable settings, it is difficult to imagine that something which was used and tested in a myriad of situations for decades or even centuries (like basic contract types of civil law) should be fundamentally flawed. Claiming such a thing would indeed be an example of the most naïve form of rationalist hubris.

Still, it was argued that there is some scope for rational construction. The analytical approach provides the notions necessary to analyse complex phenomena. It helps to understand that what drives the success of established institutions, to classify and describe institutional phenomena and to teach and communicate about what happens in institutions; but beyond that it would not have much practical relevance in improving existing contracts. It may, however, be speculated that this argument does not apply in situations which are relatively new. Explicit knowledge is unimportant for doing routine business, but as soon as a new situation arises there is an advantage of turning implicit knowledge into explicit knowledge. This facilitates thinking about these new challenges and making use of past experience by means of recombination[401].

Moreover, even if some features of the underlying problem of contracting like information asymmetry and uncertainty will always be the same, the pace of institutional change has arguably increased at a time of rapid technological innovation and an increasingly deregulated and globalized economy. Deregulation allows for new kinds of labour contracts, financial innovation and increased global competition increasing the action space of individual agents. The revolution in communication technology led to innovations in transactions (peer-to-peer online auctions, e-commerce). Global competition leads to an increased need for flexible and unorthodox transnational company alliances, but also cultural change affects contracting: The decline of moral institutions[402], but also the break-up of cosy national clubs where a renegade agent could easily be punished by social sanctioning changes the way contracts can be enforced.

On a fundamental level, it could be questioned if adaptation to change should not be left to decentralized spontaneous order. In a provocative way one could ask if the rationalist who was ousted as the great central planner should have a comeback as an advisor of individual agents. In other words, even if evolution did not have a chance, it may still be better to proceed by trial-and-error than by trying to save time by taking a short-cut using analytical models. This is not the view of the author. Still, it has to be acknowledged that economic contract theory still has to undergo much more of a market test. It is the ability of such theories to explain existing institutions and the extent to which it is possible to convince practitioners of the value and the additional insight provided by this approach which validates these modes much more than any econometric test. It is in this respect that contract theory still has a long way to go.

Of course, some examples were mentioned in the text. The predictions of contract theory seem to fit quite well with certain institutional phenomena. Yet, it is far from playing a role as a framework for setting up real world contracts. Economists routinely complain about the fact that lawyers apparently do not care about what economists have to say, but the experience of the author suggests otherwise. Lawyers and managers are very interested in the promise of contract

---

401 This is actually the method of analysis-synthesis.

402 If everybody believed in divine justice this would be a very elegant way to solve the problem of moral hazard. But it is hard to believe that this mechanism ever worked effectively. Historically, it seems that it worked to some extent to suppress the lower classes, but even at the time failed to convince the estate manager to be honest towards the absentee noble landowner.

theory but soon get frustrated when they see what they think is considerable analytical complication for relatively meagre results. This is partly to blame on the mathematical illiteracy of most lawyers, or conversely the unwillingness of economists to "translate" their findings into common language, but there are still other problems: As was already mentioned in the introduction, there is the obsession of many economists with modeling single effects rather than dealing with concrete problems. Some effects are certainly more important than others, but in order to decide which effect is important and what can safely be ignored, one must see the whole picture. While there may be some importance in modeling small effects, there is certainly an imbalance between modeling such effects and summarizing, describing and applying them. It was also argued in the methodological part that analytical models can very fruitfully be used to derive qualitative results but that casuistic work should be used for the applications, leaving out the intractible middle ground; but the wrong conclusion for an economist would be to stop when analysis ends and informed judgement begins. This could be justified by citing separation of labour, saying that the development of applications can be done by others. The truth is, however, that nobody is waiting on the other side of this unilaterally defined interface. The fact that applications require judgement and are no longer analytically tractable or can be accessed by econometrics does not mean that they are any less "scientific". Indeed, they are a very important part of the argument.

The following research programme is therefore proposed: First the analytical contract theoretical models should be summarized and systematically arranged. This should be done in a way that makes it possible for readers to treat these models largely as black box models. Then, much of casuistic work should be done in order to apply the models, mindful of the act that this application is nothing mechanical but rather an integral part of problem solving. Such casuistic work would not only display best practice of problem solving and be a good way of communication and teaching, but also enrich the model by helping to understand phenomena which evolved over time. In addition, translation into specific contexts allows submitting contract theory to a market test which is arguably the best empirical corroboration available for contract theory. A particularly interesting avenue for future research would be not just to analyse codified civil law but also model-contract collections of law firms and organizational solutions within companies.

References

Akerlof, G. A.; (1970): The Market for "Lemons": Quality, Uncertainty and the Market Mechanism; Quarterly Journal of Economics, Vol. 84, Issue 3, (Aug. 1970): 488-500 http://mitpress.mit.edu/journals/pdf/lemons_low.pdf

Albert, H. (1968): Traktat über kritische Vernunft; 3rd extended ed.; Verlag Mohr Siebeck, Tübingen, 1975 (English translation: Treatise on Critical Reason, Princeton University Press, Princeton 1985.)

Alchian, A. (1950); Uncertainty, evolution and economic theory; Journal of Political Economy 58 (June), 1950

Allen, F; (1985): Repeated Principal-Agent Relationships with Lending and Borrowing; Economic Letters 17: 27-31

Arrow, K. J.; (1985); The Economics of Agency, in: Pratt, Zeckhauser (ed.), Principals and Agents: The Structure of Business, Harvard Business School Press, Boston 1995, pp. 37-51.

Arrow, K.J.; **Hahn**, F.H. (1971): General Competitive Analysis; San Francisco, 1971

Backhouse, R. E.;(1994): New Directions in Economic Methodology; in: New Directions in Economic Methodology ed. Backhouse, R. E.; Routledge, London, New York, 1994

Baker, G. (2000): Distortion and Risk in Optimal Incentive Contracts. Unpublished manuscript, Harvard Business School.

Becker, G. (1968): Crime and Punishment: An Economic Approach; Journal of Political Economy, March/April 1968, 76: 169-217

Bester, H.; (2001): Vorlesungsnotizen zur Industrieökonomie, http://www.wiwiss.fu-berlin.de/w3/w3bester/ FU-Berlin.

Bewley, T (2002): Knightian decision theory. Part 1.; DEF Decisions in Economics and Finance, Springer Italy, Milano, 2002

Blaug, M.; (1990): Economic Theories: True or False? Essays in the History and Methodology of Economics; Aldershot, Edward Elgar, 1990

Blaug, M.; (1994): Confessions of an Unrepentant Popperian; in : New Directions in Economic Methodology ed. Backhouse, R. E.; Routledge, London, New York, 1994

Boland, L.;(1994): Scientific Thinking without Scientific Method: Two Views of Popper; in: New Directions in Economic Methodology ed. Backhouse, R. E.; Routledge, London, New York, 1994

Brennan, G.; **Buchanan**, J.; (1985): The Reason of Rules; Cambridge: Cambridge University Press, 1985.

Buchanan, J.;(1989): Explorations in Constitutional Economics, College Station: Texas A&M Press, 1989

Bull, C. (1987): The Existence of Self-Enforcing Relational Contracts; Quarterly Journal of Economics 102: 147-59

Caldwell, B. J.; (1994): Proposals for the Recovery of Economic Practice; in: New Directions in Economic Methodology ed. Backhouse, R. E.; Routledge, London, New York, 1994

Camerer, C.; **Weber**, M.; (1992): Recent Developments in Modeling Preferences: Uncertainty and Ambiguity; Journal of Risk and Uncertainty, vol. 5, pp. 325-376

Casey, C.;(2000): Zur Modellierung von Unternehmenswerten und Aktienpreisen auf dem Kapitalmarkt: Die Mikrostruktur des Kapitalmarktes, Wiesbaden, 2000

Chalmers, A., F.; (1994); Wege der Wissenschaft - Einführung in die Wissenschaftstheorie; Bergeman/Prümper (Hrsg.); 3. Aufl.; Springer-Verlag, Berlin - Heidelberg, 1994

Clausewitz, C..; (1832): Vom Kriege; ed. Marwedel, U; Reclam, Stuttgart, (1995).

Clausewitz, C.; (1832): On War; translated by: Graham, J. J.; N. Trübner, London (1873) http://www.clausewitz.com/CWZHOME/On_War/ONWARTOC.html

Colander, D.;(1994): The Art of Economics by the Numbers; in: New Directions in Economic Methodology ed. Backhouse, R. E.; Routledge, London, New York, 1994

Comte, A. (1852): Catéchisme Positiviste, ed. Tremblay, J-M. : reproduction of the orignal version of 1852; http://www.uqac.uquebec.ca/zone30/Classiques_des_sciences_ sociales/index.html, (2002)

Connor, G.; (1995): The Three Types of Factor Models: A Comparison of Their explanatory Power.; Financial Analysts Journal, May/June 1995: 42-46

Copeland, T. E.; **Weston**, J. F. (1992): Financial Theory and Corporate Policy – 3rd ed.; Eddison-Wesley Publishing Company, Reading MA et al., 1992

Czayka, L (1991): Formale Logik und Wissenschaftsphilosophie: Einführung für Wirtschaftswissenschaftler; Oldenbourg, München, Wien, 1991

DeGroot, M. H.; (1970): Optimal Statistical Decisions; McGraw-Hill Book Company, New York, 1970

Drucker, P.;(1939): The End of Economic Man – The Origins of Totalitarianism; Transaction Publishers, New Brunswick (U.S.A) – London (U.K.), 1995

Ellsberg, D.;(1961): Risk, ambiguity, and the Savage axioms. Quarterly Journal of Economics 75: 643-69, 1961

Fama, E; (1980): Agency Problems and Theory of the Firm; Journal of Political Economy, 88, 288-307.

Feldstein, M. S. (1968): Mean-Variance Analysis in the Theory of Liquidity Preference and Portfolio Selection, Review of Economic Studies, Vol. 35, S. 5-12

Feltham, G.; **Xie**, J. (1994): Performance Measure Congruity and Diversity in Multi-Task Principal/Agent Relations *The Accounting Review*

Fisher, F.; (1989): Games Economists Play: A Noncooperative View; RAND Journal of Economics. Spring 1989. 20: 113-24- 3, 86n

Friedman, M.; (1966): The Methodology of Positive Economics; in: Essays In Positive Economics; Univ. of Chicago Press, Chicago, 1966 pp. 1-16, 30-43 http://dept.econ.yorku.ca/~avicohen/reading2.PDF

Fudenberg, D; **Tirole**, J.; (1990): Moral Hazard and Renegotiation in Agency Contracts, Econometrica, November 1990, 58: 1279-1320

Gibbons, R.;(2001): Incentives Between Firms (and Within); mimeo. http://econ-www.mit.edu/faculty/rgibbons/papers.htm , Forthcoming in Management Science

Gilboa, I.; **Schmeidler** (1989): Maximin expected utility with a unique prior: Journal of Mathematical Economics, 1989

Gjesdal, F.; (1982): Information and Incentives: The Agency Information Problem; Review of Economic Studies 49: 373-90

Granger, C.W.J.; (1988): Some recent developments in a concept of causality, Journal of Econometrics 39, 199-211.

Granger, C.W.J.;(1969): Investigating causal relations by econometric models and cross-spectral methods, Econometrica 37: pp.424-438.

Grossmann, S.; **Hart**, O.;(1983): An Analysis of the Principal Agent Problem; Econometrica 51, 1983, 7-46

Hart, O; **Holmström**, B; (1987): The Theory of Contracts, In: Advances in economic theory: fifth world congress. Econometric society monographs; no. 12; ed. Bewley, T. F.; 71-155

Hausman, D. M.; (1992): The Inexact and Separate Science of Economics; Cambridge University Press, Cambridge, 1992

Hausman, D. M.;(1988): An Appraisal of Popperian methodology; in: The Popperian Legacy in Economics, ed. de Marchi, N.; Cambridge University press, Cambridge,1988: pp.65-85

Hausman, D. M.;(1998): Rationality and Knavery; in: Leinfellner, W.; Köhler, E.; eds. Game Theory, Experience, Rationality; Foundations of Social Sciences; Economics and Ethics: In Honour of John C. Harsanyi; Dordrecht: Kluwer, 1998, pp. 67-79

Hayek, F.A.; (1967): The Theory of Complex Phenomena; in: Hayek, F.A., Studies in Philosophy, Economics and Politics, Chicago: University of Chicago Press.

Hirshleifer, J; **Riley**, J.G. (1992): The Analytics of Uncertainty and Information; Cambridge University Press, 1992

Holmström, B. (1999): Managerial Incentive Problems: A Dynamic Perspective (originally published in 1982); Review of Economic Studies (1999) 66, 169-182

Holmström, B., **Milgrom**, P.;(1991): Multitask Principal-Agent Analyses; Incentive Contracts, Asset Ownership, and Job Design; Journal of Law, Economics and Organization 7, 24-52

Holmström, B.; (1979): Moral Hazard and Observability, Bell Journal of Economics 10: 74-91

Holmström, B.; **Milgrom**; P.;(1987): Aggregation and Linearity in the Provision of Intertemporal Incentives, Econometrica 55: 303-328

Hume, D.; (1741): Of the Independency of Parliament; in: Essays Moral, Political, and Literary. Rpt. Oxford: Oxford University Press, 1963, pp. 40-47.

Hutchison, T. H.;(1994): Ends and Means in the Methodology of Economics; in: New Directions in Economic Methodology ed. Backhouse, R. E.; Routledge, London, New York, 1994

James, W. (1896): The Will to Believe; ed.: Burkhardt, F. et al; Harvard University Press, 1979.

Kant, I. (1783): Prolegomena zu einer jeden künftigen Metaphysik die als Wissenschaft wird auftreten können, Johann Friedrich Hartknoch, Riga, 1783; http://www.uni-potsdam.de/u/philosophie/texte/prolegom/!start.htm

Kerr, S. (1975): On the Folly of Rewarding A, while hoping for B; Academy of Management Journal 18; 769-783

Keynes, J. N.; (1891): The Scope and Method of Political Economy; Batoche Books, Kitchener,http://socserv2.socsci.mcmaster.ca/~econ/ugcm/3ll3/keynesjn/Scope.pdf, 1999

Kirtzner, I. M.; (1997): Entrepreneurial Discovery and the Competitive Market Process: An Austrian Approach.; Journal of Economic Literature Vol. XXXV, (March 1997), pp. 60-85

Knight, F. (1921): Risk, Uncertainty and Profit; Houghton Mifflin Co, Boston and New York, The Riverside Press: http://www.econlib.org/library/Knight/knRUP.html

Kreps, D. (1990): A Course in Microeconomic Theory; Pearson Education, Harlow, England

Kulp, S.; **Datar**, S.; **Lambert**, R.; (1999): Balancing Performance Measures.; Unpublished manuscript, Stanford University.

Lazear, E; **Rosen**, S; (1981): Rank-Order Tournaments as Optimal Labor Contracts; Journal of Political Economy 89: 841-864

Levin, J. (2003): Relational Incentive Contracts, mimeo. Forthcoming: American Economic Review.http://www.stanford.edu/~jdlevin/Papers/RIC.pdf

Lindenberg, S.; (2000): Contracting: A Matter of Both Trust and Mistrust; in: Wirtschaftswissenschaftliches Seminar Ottobeuren, Band 29: Ökonomische Analyse von Verträgen, eds: Franz, W.; Hesse, H.; Ramser, H. J.; Stadler, M.; J. B. V. Mohr (Paul Siebeck), Tübingen, 2000: pp. 25-53

Loistl, O./**Vetter**, O.;(1999): KapSyn. Computerprogramm zur Effizienzmessung von Börsenorganisationen Version 3.0, http://ifm.wu-wien.ac.at/Forschung, 1999

Mader, J; (1992a); Von Parmenides zu Hegel, Einführung in die Philosophie I; WUV - Universitätsverlag, Wien, 1992

Mader, J; (1992b); Von der Romantik zur Post-Moderne, Einführung in die Philosophie II; WUV-Universitätsverlag, Wien, 1992

Mäki, U.; (1994): Reorienting the Assumptions Issue; in: New Directions in Economic Methodology ed. Backhouse, R. E.; Routledge, London, New York, 1994

Mas-Colell, A.; **Whinston**, M. D.; **Green**, J. R.; (1995): Microeconomic Theory; Oxford University Press, New York, Oxford, 1995

Mayer, T.;(1993): Truth vs. Precision in Economics, Aldershot: Edward Elgar, 1993

Milgrom, P. (1981): Good News and Bad News: Representation Theorems and Applications; Bell Journal of Economics 12: 380-91

Mirowski, Ph.; (1994): What are the Questions?; in: New Directions in Economic Methodology ed. Backhouse, R. E.; Routledge, London, New York, 1994

Mirrlees, J.;(1974): Notes on Welfare Economics, Information and Uncertainty; In: Essays on Economic Behaviour under Uncertainty, ed. Balch, M; McFadden, D.; Wu, S; Amsterdam North Holland, 1974

Mirrlees, J.;(1976): The Optimal Structure of Authority and Incentives within an Organization Bell Journal of Economics, 7: 105-31

Mises, L.; (1949); Human Action: A Treatise on Economics, 4th ed.; copyright 1996 by Bettina B. Greaves; Irvington: Foundation for Economic Education, 1996 http://www.mises.org/humanaction.asp

N.N.; (2003): Punitive Damages: Rule by numbers; The Economist, April 10, 2003

Pascal, B.(1993); Pensées, Granier-Flammarion. Texte integrale, Paris, 1993

Plato (1993): Politeia; Rüdiger Buber ed.: Geschichte der Philosophie in Text und Darstellung. Antike.; Philipp Reclam jun., Stuttgart, 1993

Polinsky, A.; **Che**, Y. K.;(1991): Decoupling Liability: Optimal Incentives for Care and Litigation, Rand Journal of Economics, Winter 1991, 22: pp. 562-70

Popper, K. R. (1959): The logic of scientific discovery. Hutchinson, London

Prendergast, C.; (1993): The Provision of Incentives in Firms; Journal of Economic Literature 37, 7-63

Prendergast, C.;(2002): The Tenuous Trade-Off between Risk and Incentives; Journal of Political Economy, 2002 vol. 110 no. 5: 1071-1102

Radner, R; (1981): Monitoring Cooperative Agreements in a Repeated Principal-Agent Relationship; Econometrica 49: 1127-48

Raffée, H.; (1974): Grundprobleme der Betriebswirtschaftslehre, Göttingen 1974

Rasmusen, E.; (1994): Games and Information; 2nd ed. Reprinted; Blackwell, Cambridge MA – Oxford UK, 1995

Rogerson, W. (1995): The First Order Approach to Principal-Agent Problems.; Econometrica 53: 1357-68

Rosenberg, A.; (1992): Economics-Mathematical Politics or Science of Diminishing Returns.; Chicago: University of Chicago Press, 1992

Rothschild, M.; **Stiglitz,** J. E.; (1970): Increasing Risk: I. A Definition; Journal of Economic Theory, Vol. 2, No. 3, September 1970

Rousseau, J.-J. (1762): Vom Gesellschaftsvertrag oder Grundsätze des Staatsrechts; ed. Brockard, H.; Philipp Reclam Jun., Stuttgart, 1994

Ryshik, I.M.; **Gradstejn**, I.S.;(1965): Table of Integrals, Series, and Products, New York

Salanié, B. (1997): The Economics of Contracts: A Primer; MIT-Press, Cambridge, 1997

Sappington, D.;(1991): Incentives in Principal Agent Relationships; Journal of Economic Perspectives, 5, 1991, 45-66

Schneeweiß, H.; (1967); Entscheidungskriterien bei Risiko; Springer Verlag, Berlin u.a., 1967

Schülein, J. A.; **Reitze**, S (2002): Wissenschaftstheorie für Einsteiger; WUV-Univ.-Verl., Wien, 2002

Schumpeter, J.A.;(1916): Das Grundprinzip der Verteilungstheorie"; Archiv für Sozial-wissenschaft und Sozialpolitik 42, 1916/17, 1-88, cit. idem, "Aufsätze zur ökonomischen Theorie", Tübingen 1952, 321n.

Sen, A.; (1977): Rational Fools; Philosophy and Public Affairs 6,1977, pp. 317-44.

Simon, H. A.; (1947): Administrative Behavior; 2nd ed, The Free Press, New York, 1947

Smith, V.; (1991): Rational Choice: The Contrast Between Economics and Psychology.; Journal of Political Economy, Vol. 99 issue 4: 877-97

Spence, M; **Zeckhauser**, R.; (1971): Insurance, Information and Individual Action; American Economic Review, Papers and Proceedings, 61: 380-7

Stiglitz, J. E; (2000): The Contributions of the Economics of Information to Twentieth Century Economics, Quarterly Journal of Economics, Cambridge, Mass., November 2000, pp. 1441-1478

Summers, L.;(1991): The scientific illusion in empirical macroeconomics; Scandinavian Journal of Economics, 93 (2): 129-48

Tirole, J.; (2000): The Theory of Industrial Organization; MIT-Press, Cambridge MA, 2000

Varian, H. (1992): Microeconomic Analysis; W. W. Norton & Company, Inc., 3rd Ed. New York, London, 1992

Wilson, R. (1968): The Theory of Syndicates; Econometrica 36: 119-32

Forschungsergebnisse der Wirtschaftsuniversität Wien

Herausgeber: Wirtschaftsuniversität Wien –
vertreten durch a.o. Univ. Prof. Dr. Barbara Sporn

Band 1 Stefan Felder: Frequenzallokation in der Telekommunikation. Ökonomische Analyse der Vergabe von Frequenzen unter besonderer Berücksichtigung der UMTS-Auktionen. 2004.

Band 2 Thomas Haller: Marketing im liberalisierten Strommarkt. Kommunikation und Produktplanung im Privatkundenmarkt. 2005.

Band 3 Alexander Stremitzer: Agency Theory: Methodology, Analysis. A Structured Approach to Writing Contracts. 2005.

www.peterlang.de